PLAIN SPEAKING

PLAIN SPEAKING

N. Chandrababu Naidu

with

Sevanti Ninan

VIKING

VIKING

Penguin Books India (P) Ltd., 11 Community Centre, Panchsheel Park, New Delhi 110 017, India
Penguin Books Ltd., 27 Wrights Lane, London W8 5TZ, UK
Penguin Putnam Inc., 375 Hudson Street, New York, NY 10014, USA
Penguin Books Australia Ltd., Ringwood, Victoria, Australia
Penguin Books Canada Ltd., 10 Alcorn Avenue, Suite 300, Toronto, Ontario, M4V 3B2, Canada
Penguin Books (NZ) Ltd., Cnr Rosedale and Airborne Roads, Albany, Auckland, New Zealand

First published in Viking by Penguin Books India 2000

Copyright © N. Chandrababu Naidu 2000

10 9 8 7 6 5 4 3 2 1

Typeset in *Casablanca* by SÜRYA, New Delhi
Printed at Chaman Offset Printers, New Delhi

Dedicated to the poor of India who show great nobility and dignity in the face of constant adversity

CONTENTS

ACKNOWLEDGEMENTS

This book would not have been possible without the assistance, guidance and coordination provided by Randeep Sudan. Krishan Chopra at Penguin conceived the project and saw it through.

The authors are also indebted to the following for their time, ideas or help: P.K. Agarwal, Sanjaya Baru, S.V.B. Krishna Bhagavan, Amitabh Bhattacharya, Suresh Chanda, R. Chandrashekhar, Rachel Chatterjee, Tishya Chatterjee, CII Hyderabad, Anjana Das, Tarun Das, Ramesh Datla, Ajay Dua, Ratna and Sankar De, K.S. Gopal, Ramesh Gelli, S. Hariharan, Ashok Jha, Dhir Jhingran, Vinita Kaul, S. Vijay Kumar, N.J. Kurien, Sheila Bhide, Prof. C. Lakshmanna, Ed Lim, K.S. Madhavan, D.V. Manohar, Shalini Mishra, P.K. Mohanty, D.L. Naraina, Jayaprakash Narayan, A.K. Parida, J. Parthasarathy, Prabhakar, Prabhakar Reddy, Nandini Prasad, S.V. Prasad, Raymond Peter, Prof. R. Radhakrishna, C.S. Rama Lakshmi, Anita Ramachandran, Anand Ram, R. Ramachandriah, Dr Ranga Rao, D. Venkateshwar Rao, R.S. Pathak, Smarajit Ray, M. Sahoo, S.R. Sankaran, J. Satyanarayana, T.L. Shankar, R. Srinivasan, Suhasini, Sunil Sethi, Prof. F.D. Vakil, Uma Reddy Venkateshwarulu, T. Vijay Kumar, B.N. Yugandhar, and Vijay Lakshmi.

INTRODUCTION

Sevanti Ninan

In 1984, when a two-year-old regional party found itself occupying the position of the single largest opposition party in India's eighth Lok Sabha, it must have surprised even itself. It had several first-time politicians among its members of Parliament: teachers, lawyers and doctors from Andhra Pradesh, some of whom could not even speak the official language. They had, however, been instructed by their leadership to think of themselves as national rather than regional politicians. 'We were second to none in protecting the national interest,' recounts one of those MPs today. It was the heady start of a new era in national politics, though few may have recognized it as such at that time.

This general election came in the wake of Indira Gandhi's assassination. The Congress party, led by her son Rajiv Gandhi, had swept the polls riding on a massive sympathy vote. But the voters of Andhra Pradesh, usually unpredictable in their electoral behaviour, held out against the tide. In 1977, when Indira Gandhi had been rejected by most of the country following the period of the Emergency, Andhra had voted generously for her, returning forty-one Congress MPs out of a total of forty-two.

In 1984, however, they were endorsing a new party, the Telugu Desam, that had been swept into power in the state assembly the previous year. They were also casting a sympathy vote of another kind. Less than three months before she was

assassinated, Mrs Gandhi's party in the state had been
instrumental in dislodging the Telugu Desam government
by ganging up with a body of disaffected legislators. There
were massive public protests and the ruling party at the
Centre backed down and re-installed the government. The
net result was that when the parliamentary elections took
place at the end of the year, the voters decided to send the
Centre a message.

There have not been many dull moments in the eighteen-
year history of the Telugu Desam since it followed the lead
of the Dravida Munnetra Kazhagam in Tamil Nadu in setting
itself up as a regional party. The TDP owed its birth and
consolidation to the Delhi-centric nature of the Congress
party, which used to install chief ministers of state
governments by fiat from Delhi. It had a charismatic film
actor at the helm, and, like the DMK, it experimented with
sweeping welfare measures that endeared the party to the
poor.

Nandamuri Taraka Rama Rao, who founded the Telugu
Desam in March 1982 at the age of sixty-five, was a man with
an extraordinary profile. The son of a poor farmer of Krishna
district who had worked in his father's fields, he was to
become an enormously successful film actor, director and
producer, associated in one capacity or another with more
than 300 films by the time he came to take the plunge into
politics.

His many starring roles helped to pave the way for the
political reformer he wanted to become: he either played
mythological roles such as those of Krishna, Karna, Bhishma,
Sri Rama and Brahma Nayadu, or produced films in which he
played a poor man who conquered adversity. NTR was
literally a godsend to a state looking for an alternative after
some thirty years of Congress rule.

Many people came forward to bankroll the new party.
Intellectuals in Andhra University in Vijaywada and an

influential newspaper proprietor, Ramoji Rao, rallied around
to plan strategy for the Telugu Desam. Huge cutouts of the
actor in saffron garb sprang up with an exhortation in Telugu
to arise and join, because the Telugu Desam (literally, land
of the Telugus) was calling. 'Telugu Desam pilustondi, ra
kadalli ra.'

Regional pride and the disenchantment with the Congress
style of functioning were the two most compelling locomotives
driving the emergence of the Telugu Desam in March 1982.
NTR tried to ally with other non-Congress parties in the
state for the 1982 assembly elections, but since they wanted
more seats to contest than he was willing to part with, the
seat-sharing attempts did not materialize; nevertheless the
new party swept the state.

Its ideology at the time of its birth and flowering was not
identifiably that of left, right or centre as much as one of
safeguarding regional interests. And that remains the case in
the year 2000 when, with one seat less in the 13th Lok Sabha
than it had then, the Telugu Desam has assumed the lead in
making regional parties indispensable to coalition
governments. It is the second largest party in the ruling
National Democratic Alliance which came to power in October
1999.

In 1984 it had a seat adjustment with the Bharatiya Janata
Party for the elections, as it did in the elections leading to
the formation of the 13th Lok Sabha in 1999. It had wrested
thirty seats in that House, it won twenty-nine in this one.
Essentially, on both occasions, the same key person was
behind the shrewd political calculations that helped to convert
vote share into seats. Strategy is N. Chandrababu Naidu's
middle name.

While ideology is not a moving force for the Telugu
Desam, what does count is the conviction spawned by a man
called C.N. Annadurai who founded south India's first regional
party, the DMK, in Tamil Nadu. It is the belief that the

centralizing tendency of the Indian state must be resisted, and autonomy progressively restored to the states.

Having said that, there was a significant difference between the DMK and the Telugu Desam. There was no element of separatism in the agenda of the latter. Right from the start N.T. Rama Rao made it clear that while seeking more autonomy for Andhra Pradesh in matters of governance, his party stood for national unity and integration. 'We owe allegiance to the Centre and wish to strengthen it so that it can fulfil its responsibilities,' he told a newspaper in January 1983.

When he founded his party in 1982, NTR was seizing upon a growing disaffection in his state, similar to that which had given birth to the DMK in Tamil Nadu. A disenchantment with a ruling party which invariably saw chief ministers change in a five-year elected period, and where the regional leadership was always decided in Delhi. Said the new party's manifesto: 'The 35 years [of] Congress misrule has created such a mess that Telugus have to hang their heads in shame . . . the enthronement of four and dethronement of three chief ministers within a span of five years is an indication of the sorry state of affairs . . .'

To understand the phenomenon of the Telugu Desam, one has to examine the political history of Andhra Pradesh, where the Congress party ruled unchallenged for thirty years. It began winning Lok Sabha elections there from 1952 when Hyderabad state and Andhra State were still separate entities. The Congress government at the Centre was responsible for conceding the demand for the formation of 'Vishalandhra', which would be a larger state established on a linguistic basis.

Andhra Pradesh was formed in November 1956 by merging Telengana—the region of nine Telugu-speaking districts of Hyderabad state—with the eleven districts of Andhra State. The former was essentially the domain of the Nizam until it became part of the Indian Union; the latter had been carved out of the Telugu-speaking districts of the Madras Presidency in 1953. When the first vidhan sabha elections were held in Andhra Pradesh in 1957, the Congress won 187 out of 301 seats and slipped with some ease into a position of supremacy which it would retain for the next twenty-five years.

For the first ten to fifteen years after Independence, this part of the country had a sizeable and credible communist presence which evolved, post-1956, into an electoral opposition. The communists had come into existence to fight the rule of the Nizam of Hyderabad. But by the time they came into electoral politics the communists and socialists who formed the left had splintered into smaller parties that were thereafter never big enough or united enough to dislodge the Congress from power. Not just because they had splintered but also because the Congress party in Andhra Pradesh effectively hijacked their agenda on two emotive issues: the demand for the linguistic formation of a single state, and on agrarian reform.

The first was conceded with the formation of Andhra Pradesh, the second was diffused through different agrarian reform measures introduced by the Congress. The fact that the Soviet Union endorsed the Congress government's formal commitment to creating a 'socialist pattern of society' didn't help the left either. They were losing their bandwagon.

In the 1962 vidhan sabha elections in Andhra Pradesh the Communist Party of India (CPI) won fifty-one seats. The next time around it won eleven, and continued its downward trend till an electoral alliance with the TDP for the 1985 assembly elections revived its fortunes somewhat. The CPM had its best showing in the Andhra assembly elections in 1985, thanks to the electoral adjustment with the TDP.

With the left not posing much of a challenge, the Congress had practically no political opposition in the state, which continued to return the party from here even when it was routed elsewhere. In 1977, when it suffered its post-Emergency debacle, Andhra Pradesh sent forty-one members to the Lok Sabha. It was at this time that Chandrababu Naidu abandoned studies for his Ph.D. and entered the Congress party, winning a party ticket for the 1978 assembly elections.

Popular disenchantment with the Congress never found expression at the hustings simply because there was no real alternative. But in the early 1980s one was emerging. N.T. Rama Rao, who had a vast fan-following, forged an unusual combination of personal charisma, sound populist instincts, able lieutenants and shrewd advisers. The party he founded opened a colourful new chapter in the history of this Congress-dominated state.

Meanwhile, a much younger man was making his way through the Congress party. Like NTR, Chandrababu Naidu was not from a wealthy family: he was the son of a medium farmer from Chittoor. But he never lacked for money. In college he always had enough to spend on his fellow students, which, as he said later, helped him become a leader. When he went to Tirupati to study at Sri Venkateshwara University his friends discovered his talent for organization.

When a cyclone devastated coastal Andhra Pradesh in 1977 he left his studies to plunge into relief work, first surveying the damaged villages, then collecting relief material and going back to distribute it. Twenty-two years later, when Orissa was devastated by a killer cyclone and Naidu as a neighbouring chief minister rushed across men and material to help, it was a replay of his first plunge into public service.

On the campus his academic mentor was an economics professor, D.L. Naraina. Eventually, through Naraina, Naidu also got to know Rajgopal Naidu, the Congress member of Parliament from Chitoor. He completed an M.A. in economics, and when no lecturer's job was forthcoming, Naraina suggested he enrol for a Ph.D. in economics under his guidance.

The subject chosen with help from his guide was the economic policies of N.G. Ranga. Parliamentarians do not necessarily have economic convictions worth writing about, let alone doing a Ph.D. on. But N.G. Ranga was a brilliant and unusual politician. He was a Kamma who had been to Oxford, and had been influenced by the peasant movements in Europe.

Ranga's thrust was on the rural economy. He carried out village studies on artisans, toddy tappers, weavers and small farmers. He was in his early thirties. He would found his own party, the Krishikar Lok Party. By the time Naidu came to meet him, however, he was a Congress parliamentarian.

Being a student leader Naidu secured a Congress ticket from Chandragiri constituency in the 1978 assembly elections. There were no other takers from that party for the seat. He was then twenty-eight years old. Then and much later as chief minister, he would prove adept at getting students to work for him. They campaigned for him and he won. Several others of his age joined the party around that time from the same university and he became their informal leader. In two short years, with a following to show, he would become a minister in T.N. Anjiah's cabinet. When the party high command in Delhi changed chief ministers, he once again became a minister in the next cabinet.

There was, however, a revealing incident around this time. Naidu supported someone other than the party's official candidate in a local election and was expelled for anti-party activities by the state unit. He went to Delhi, pleaded his case before Indira Gandhi, and had himself reinstated. This was not a man who would give in easily in a political tussle.

As a young minister Naidu came to meet N.T. Rama Rao, then a wealthy and hugely successful actor. They had discussions on politics, and the actor got to know the young politician. NTR had four daughters, and before long decided

to send a proposal for one of them, Bhuvaneshwari, to
Naidu's family. Eventually Chandrababu became his son-in-
law.

Shortly thereafter NTR floated the Telugu Desam, but
Naidu did not immediately join the party. He did not think
it would succeed at the hustings. He contested the 1983
vidhan sabha elections—which swept his father-in-law
spectacularly into power—on a Congress ticket, and lost to
the TDP candidate in the constituency where he was a
sitting MLA. When he lost the elections he decided to retire
from politics and go into business. He says today that he
thought one politician in the family was sufficient. But his
father-in-law persuaded him to join the party.

As they tell you about this party in Andhra Pradesh,
NTR founded it and Chandrababu Naidu built it. NTR was
an actor with genuine feeling for the poor and a strong
instinct for political populism. Naidu's instinct was for being
an outstanding back-room organizer. Significantly, in both
1984 and 1985 he chose not to contest either the Lok Sabha
or vidhan sabha elections, concentrating on setting up the
party.

NTR did not know as much about the party MLAs as
Naidu did, and he also had their names on his computer. In
1985, when Rajiv Gandhi was being hailed as the country's
first computer-savvy politician, Chandrababu Naidu was
already using computers to build a database on his party's
MLAs.

More interestingly, he experimented with training
politicians, as N.G. Ranga had done some decades ago.
However, he says he did not borrow the idea from Ranga but
from what he knew of private sector HRD programmes. He
and NTR discussed the idea and thought it would benefit
their people who were new to politics. In 1986 he started
training programmes for party workers at an institution set up
in Gandhipet, near Hyderabad, and rather grandly designated

it the National Institute of Political Consciousness. The institute ran nine-month courses and produced two batches of thirty students each. Some of them ended up becoming personal assistants to TDP ministers. In 1988 the experiment was discontinued. In the late 1990s, as chief minister, Naidu would preside over the launching of another training institute for politicians of his own party.

Any potted history of the Telugu Desam must take into account the shrewd crafting of a new political base that would be strong enough to present viable competition to the Congress party's entrenched support base in Andhra Pradesh. NTR's public life had begun a couple of decades ago with a dramatic ability to stir up people for a cause. When there was a national crisis such as the Indo-China war of 1962 or the Indo-Pak conflict of 1965, he was able to mobilize contributions from the public. His appeal cut across community and caste lines. He also did major fund-raising at the time of the Anantpur drought.

Those who worked with him during his first tenure as chief minister point out that the state government's welfare schemes did not have caste as a basis—they were primarily for those below the poverty line, backward or scheduled castes and tribes. He was also mindful of the needs of artisans who were beginning to swell the ranks of landless labour.

NTR borrowed the ideas of rice at Rs 2 a kg and the midday meal scheme for schoolchildren from the DMK in Tamil Nadu, and wooed the poor, the backward castes and rural women. He also promised highly subsidized housing and sought women's support with legislative measures to give them equal inheritance rights.

The 1983 assembly elections saw the Congress reduced to 60 seats from the 175 it had won in the previous elections in 1978, and the Telugu Desam swept in with 202.

When he became chief minister NTR followed through

quickly with the welfare measures he had promised during
his election campaign. His older son-in-law, D. Venkateshwar
Rao, recalls how he took a piece of paper and drew upon it
for the benefit of his officials a sketch of the kind of houses
he wanted built for the poor: concrete, with pucca roofs and
two rooms.

He knew something about construction, having built
theatres, studios and houses in his lifetime. He knew what it
would cost, and he told his bureaucracy that it had to be
done because he had made an election promise to build one
lakh houses a year for the poor. Ultimately, over a decade
and a half Andhra Pradesh built so many houses that more
than 50 per cent of the subsidized houses built for the
homeless in the entire country are in this state.

He put the scheme of two-rupees rice into operation and
initiated administrative reforms that struck at the support
base of the Congress by abolishing the patels and patwaris—
village officers who had powers to maintain law and order
and to collect land revenue. He decentralized administration
by introducing mandals as an administrative unit. These
were smaller than the existing talukas, and brought the
government closer to the people. Both measures helped to
consolidate the TDP's new-found mass base.

He legislated property rights for women and gave them
9 per cent reservation in local bodies. Recognizing the
importance of the backward classes as the mainstay of the
party, he gave them 20 per cent reservation in zilla parishads.

He also brought into the government a highly original
style of personal functioning, choosing to begin his working
day at one or two a.m., and summoning his bureaucrats for
meetings at that hour. He would have people read out
everything to him, including the morning newspapers, because
he preferred not to read. He would tell his associates that he
had preserved the gleam in his eye as an actor because he
did not read so much.

But he had a phenomenal memory: as an actor he would do multiple roles in multiple films at the same time, on one occasion playng eight roles in two different films and remembering not just his own dialogues for all the parts but also those of his co-stars. He transferred this ability to politics. If he had to speak at a meeting he would have somebody prepare a brief, listen carefully while it was read out to him, and then go and deliver his speech without missing any salient point.

Chandrababu, meanwhile, was to prove himself as a man who could take command in a crisis and outmanoeuvre the opposition when required. The first crisis came within a year and a half of the Telugu Desam assuming office in Andhra Pradesh, when he was general secretary of the party. In 1984, when N.T. Rama Rao was abroad undergoing surgery, his finance minister, Nadendla Bhaskar Rao, who had joined him from the Congress, initiated a revolt and struck a deal with the Congress that they would support him from outside in forming a government. The governor of the state declared that NTR had lost his majority in the assembly and swore in Bhaskar Rao as chief minister.

The TDP was not inclined to take such a state of affairs lying down, and a memorable drama ensued. While NTR flew to Delhi to protest to the President, Naidu and others packed the legislators who were with them into second-class compartments and took them to Delhi by train to prove to the President that injustice had been done. Then Naidu masterminded the plan to take them to Bangalore and keep them there till the crisis had blown over so that the state Congress could not poach upon them. Meanwhile, suitably dramatic demonstrations in Hyderabad drove the point home. In response to public outrage, the government of NTR was quickly reinstated.

The whole drama led N.T. Rama Rao to publicly express gratitude to his son-in-law. 'Chandrababu Naidu is an astute politician. But for his struggle the Telugu Desam would not have been reborn. I will never forget his services.' He then shrewdly decided to dissolve the assembly and seek a fresh mandate early in 1985. Seat adjustments were entered into with non-Congress parties including the left. The TDP and its allies fared handsomely.

Despite the majority and the welfare measures initiated, Rama Rao and his TDP lost in the next assembly elections in 1989. Sycophancy and infighting in the party took their toll of NTR's popularity. Naidu for his part felt that NTR had concentrated on welfare measures but not enough on development. He says today that he did not balance the two.

NTR had a strong empathy with people. When he went out to begin campaigning he was able to judge from the first few meetings that he was likely to lose this election. But Chandrababu Naidu contested this time on a TDP ticket and won. While occupying the opposition benches in the legislature one day NTR was insulted on the floor of the House by an opposition member. He took such deep offence at this that he swore that he would not enter the legislature again except as chief minister. He stuck to his promise.

For all practical purposes thereafter, his younger son-in-law, Chandrababu Naidu, functioned as leader of the opposition. He saw opportunity in this role and exploited it. He likes to say today that people are watching the opposition and its conduct so it is a role that must be taken seriously. In the interregnum the Congress party had raised the price of subsidized rice and gone back to its internal warfare.

In the next elections the TDP came back to power with an even bigger majority than in 1985 on two major planks: prohibition, which was a major demand of rural women, and a reversion of the price of subsidized rice to Rs 2 a kg.

Meanwhile, when NTR was out of power and not attending the assembly proceedings, Lakshmi Parvati entered his life. She was a harikatha artist and had come into contact with the grand old man while performing in TDP campaigns. She offered to write his biography and began spending time with him in Ramakrishna Studios, the film studio that he owned. At a film function at Tirupati he announced his intention of marrying Lakshmi Parvati. His family disapproved, but he went ahead with his decision.

By the time the next elections came around she was sufficiently involved in his political decision making to influence the choice of TDP candidates in the first list that was announced. NTR's sons and sons-in-law protested. When confronted, their father backed down and kept her out of being involved in the selection of the second list. However, once NTR was re-elected and became chief minister for the third time, Lakshmi Parvati began playing a role in day-to-day governance, with some officials even reporting to her. NTR's son Harikrishna also began to agitate against her involvement in governance, and went public on the issue.

As bureaucrats, members of Parliament and NTR's family members tell it, some seven or eight months into the new government's tenure, those around NTR began to get the sense that he was planning to make Lakshmi Parvati the deputy chief minister. At that point the Lok Sabha elections were less than a year away and the party feared that the opposition would make capital out of such a move, if it were to take place.

To deflect that eventuality a delegation of four party stalwarts was sent to the chief minister to explain that her interference was not liked by the party cadre and leaders and to suggest to him that he keep her out of affairs of state. NTR did not take kindly to that suggestion. This was in August 1995. The party decided upon a change of leadership with the support of key members of NTR's family, including his son Balakrishna, who was an actor, and his other son-in-law, D. Venkateshwar Rao.

A preliminary gathering of legislators was held in Naidu's

chamber. Much dramatic shepherding of MLAs followed, with a majority of them gathering in the Viceroy hotel in Secunderabad to elect Chandrababu Naidu as their next leader. NTR tried, unsuccessfully, to seek dissolution of the legislative assembly.

Naidu was sworn in as chief minister and NTR went to the people to protest his removal as party leader. But, unlike the 1984 coup by Nadendla Bhaskar Rao, this one evoked little popular sympathy for the ageing actor, though some of the MLAs who had backed Naidu, including his other son-in-law, did return to NTR. A few months later he died, and the advent of the 1996 Lok Sabha elections saw a battle for NTR's formidable political legacy between Lakshmi Parvati and Chandrababu Naidu. It became primarily a contest between histrionics and calculated political savvy.

The party split into two factions, the TDP Naidu, known as TDPN, and the TDP Lakshmi Parvati, known as TDPLP. The Election Commission asked both factions to submit lists of their total supporters, and after verifying that the Naidu faction had the majority, allotted it NTR's election symbol, the bicycle. Lakshmi Parvati, however, made wonderful dramatic use of this setback. She told people to vote for her new symbol, the lion, because the bicycle had been stolen by thieves. She summoned her histrionic skills from her harikatha background and took to the streets, campaigning as NTR's widow.

Considerable election-time drama ensued. Both claimants of NTR's legacy freely used his tape-recorded speeches, albeit selectively. Lakshmi Parvati played those bits in which NTR called Naidu and the MLAs who supported him traitors. Naidu played those bits in which NTR had acknowledged his debt of gratitude to him in the aftermath of the 1984 coup. He also used the private satellite channels to reach the electorate in villages, apart from working overtime to ensure that his government was delivering. He used

NTR's portraits and speeches to whip up voter enthusiasm.

Lakshmi Parvati travelled across the state in a campaign vehicle similar to the 'Chaitanya ratham' used by NTR in the 1994 elections. She had hugely successful election meetings. She allied with the Janata Dal and the Bahujan Samaj Party. But she did not have a sufficiently able strategist in her camp to help her convert sympathy into votes.

Her faction of the TDP garnered about 10 per cent of the popular vote but won no seats.

The 1996 Lok Sabha elections were the turning point for the TDP's emergence as a national player. It won sixteen Lok Sabha seats and Naidu became a key player in the Third Front not just because of the seats he brought to the table but also because his organizing skills came into play. He made it clear that he was not a prime ministerial candidate and then camped in Delhi, visibly central to the process of working out a consensus. He would listen to all sides, consult everybody, and then push for a decision.

In 1998 the TDP won fewer Lok Sabha seats but became even more crucial to government formation because no coalition grouping could summon the requisite number of seats. Its historical anti-Congressism led it to offer issue-based support to the BJP-led front. In 1999, when the government at the Centre fell and yet another Lok Sabha election was held, it won enough seats in Parliament to become the second biggest partner in the ruling coalition of the National Democratic Alliance.

Between 1982, when one charismatic and colourful figure launched the Telugu Desam Party, and 1999, when a very different kind of politician led it to become a significant national player, much had changed, both within the party and in the political landscape outside it. Single-party rule at the Centre was becoming a thing of the past. Political grandstanding was also becoming a thing of the past.

Governance had been an issue even in 1982 in Andhra

Pradesh: NTR swept into power despite having no political experience because the experienced politicians running the state were perceived to have made a mess of it. But the governance of Andhra Pradesh, or for that matter any other state, had not become a national issue. Today the focus of governance in India has shifted to the states much more than before, and that is where media attention is focussed, as much as it is on the Central government.

In a liberalized economy states have become individual players, attracting both investment and attention on the basis of their performance. And in a country where the era of coalition politics has dawned, players at the state level have come to count much more than before.

Some reference points of good politics have also changed from NTR to Chandrababu Naidu, from one farmer's son to another. Rice at two rupees was good politics in 1982. It is unaffordable in 2000. Prohibition was good politics in 1994. It is considered unsustainable in 2000, even though women suffer from its lifting, because of the increase in crime on account of liquor smuggling, brewing of illicit liquor and other activities that defeat the purpose of prohibition. Risking bankruptcy to endear oneself to the common man was good politics then, but stressing on governance is better politics today.

Some reference points of good governance have changed. In NTR's time nobody in Andhra Pradesh had begun to talk of 'benchmarking' themselves against 'global standards'. Or of having a vision for the next twenty years. In those days chief ministers had not learnt to go out and hustle for investment in their states. Today a chief minister who does not hustle in the market place loses projects that could create much needed employment in his state.

In 1982 technology was not considered central to progress. Today it is, with state governments from Goa to Madhya Pradesh falling over each other to announce their information technology policies.

But some reference points remain the same for the Telugu Desam from 1982 to 2000. Anti-Congressism is one of them, and exercising regional clout with a sense of national responsibility is another.

I

THE POLITICS OF GOVERNANCE

1

GOING FORWARD

To be poised at the beginning of a new millennium with the mandate to make a difference to the lives of some seventy-five million people is an exhilarating prospect. When I fought to be re-elected as chief minister of Andhra Pradesh in September 1999 I was asking voters for five more years to be able to complete an unfinished agenda. There were many changes the TDP government initiated in my first term, many new directions that we set in motion. When you have travelled fifty years in one direction, changing course is not easy, and takes time, resources and political will. The voters in my state recognized that and gave me another term.

This book is about the changes we are attempting, the challenge ahead, the lessons learned. It is also about what governance demands in the world's largest democracy from both the politician and the bureaucrat. In the twenty-one years that I have spent in public life, since I was first elected an MLA at the age of twenty-eight, I have been both in the government and outside it. I have seen the government from the perspective of a legislator, including an opposition one, a minister and a chief minister. I have diagnosed the inefficiencies and redundancies, the systemic problems in the government.

By the time I came to the last job I knew where the problems lay: what I had to mobilize was the will and the resources to attempt changes that would go against the grain for voters, government employees, even politicians. In this century we cannot afford to continue in the old way: the government will go both bankrupt and collapse under the weight of its own administrative failures. And one billion people in a country with many resources will have to continue to suffer poverty, poor education and ill health for no fault of their own.

So what are the new mantras for the twenty-first century? As far as India is concerned, very simple ones. Better planning, intensive training for both politicians and bureaucrats, strategies that will empower the poor and women in particular, and a hard look at what the government should do and what it should withdraw from. We need to put in place policies that will help create jobs, and develop those sectors of the economy which will lead to growth.

If the 1990s for India was a decade of economic reform, in the next decade we urgently need to consider political reform. Who should be a politician, what his or her role should be, and how to bring about far greater involvement of citizens in governance are issues for us to ponder.

The third set of priorities involve technology: how it can improve government systems, deliver citizen services, and enable the country to compete globally for employment in the information technology sector which has a potential of growing from $5 billion in output in India today to $100 billion in the next ten years. Andhra Pradesh has also ventured into promoting biotechnology because of the potential it holds.

To move forward I believe any country must have leaders who can first scrutinize the existing balance sheet of assets and liabilities and then devise strategy with clarity and commitment. I have been saying from the beginning that in

India we have all the resources, natural and human. India is the biggest democracy in the world. It has a large domestic market. It has a free press and an independent judiciary. It has a large pool of scientific and technical manpower. But we are not able to give its politics a direction, or able to create the proper climate for achievement. Yet Indians have achieved striking success abroad.

There are two ways of looking at the fifty years behind us: you could either look at how far India has got as an independent nation emerging from colonial bondage or at how much remains undone. By the end of the twentieth century India had the fastest growing economy in the world. But it also had a huge chunk of people who had no access even to the most basic services. That is the challenge of governing this nation.

Few countries have hung on to democracy so tenaciously, despite an increasingly divisive electorate. But the quality of democracy we offer our people leaves a lot to be desired. India ranks low in the United Nations Development Programme's Human Development Index, but high up in Transparency International's Corruption Index.

Few countries have populations that spell such extremes in terms of human resources. We have more unlettered people than the entire population of every country in the world barring China. But at the other end of the spectrum, our institutes of technology are becoming recruiting grounds for the world's leading corporations.

One level of Indian society has achieved so much purchasing power and become such a sophisticated market that imported goods are flooding neighbourhood stores in our cities. Yet at another level there are millions of Indians who have today less calories available to them per capita than at the beginning of the last decade.

At one level our industrialists and entrepreneurs are listing their stocks on the world's premium exchanges. But at another level, our artisans are losing their skills to join the ranks of landless labour. And between these extremes we have a growing middle class, which is vocal and increasingly demanding better governance from the leaders.

If that is the balance sheet, what is the strategy? To govern in such a country you cannot take up one challenge at a time. A range of problems have to be tackled simultaneously. You need to both think very big and very small. You have to nurture savings groups of village women who put aside a rupee a day, so that they can generate marginal capital to improve their lives. But you also have to go out and woo foreign and Indian investors who will help create infrastructure and jobs. To meet the range of people's needs you have to make available both electric power for pumpsets and optic fibre cable for telecommunications. You need industry for growth, but also environmental safeguards so that health hazards are minimized.

All this is true of both Andhra Pradesh and India.

In the last four years I have been grappling with these challenges at the level of my state. Being chief minister in contemporary India is a tough proposition. States can no longer look to the Centre for resources, they have to fend for themselves. At the same time the demands made of a state are increasing. As populations continue to grow, and the aspirations of an expanding middle class continue to rise, people are becoming more aware of their rights and less willing to put up with shoddy governance. They demand better civic amenities. There are more graduates looking for more jobs. People want better education for their children.

There has been a dramatic change in the role chief ministers have been called upon to play. Gone are the days when industrialists had to wait upon the government to get licences. Today states are competing aggressively with each other to attract industries to their states. We need the jobs, so we try to offer incentives better than those offered by other states. A politician who wants to deliver cannot have an ego. He has to lobby with the Central government for funds, using every persuasion he can think of. He has to woo industry and sell his state as an attractive investment destination. He has to woo foreign investment. He has to impress upon funding agencies that he can deliver.

I began to focus on several key areas as soon as I took over as chief minister in 1995. IT was one of them, because 23 per cent of the country's software engineers are from Andhra Pradesh. We were the first to set up a department of information technology in the country. We then started looking at the task of inviting leading IT companies to the state.

We heard Bill Gates was coming to Delhi and Mumbai. Gates is somebody I admire. Within twenty to twenty-five years he has reached the top of the IT world. His name is synonymous with information technology. I wanted to request him to come to Andhra Pradesh, to tell him that we would extend all the cooperation he might want.

When my officials approached his office they said his time was already booked. When they insisted the Microsoft people relented and said I could have an exclusive meeting in which only a few select people would be present. How exclusive? Highly exclusive. It transpired that highly exclusive meant a group of 75 to 100! I could not broach the subject of his investing in my state at such a meeting. Fortunately for us, at that time the US ambassador to India, Frank Wisner, was visiting Hyderabad.

I told him I wanted a one-to-one meeting with Gates and he said he would arrange it. What was the best way to get him interested in Hyderabad as a place to invest? Microsoft did not have a major presence abroad at that point.

We thought we would make a presentation on a laptop and focus on just three issues. A Microsoft software development centre, a strategic partnership between Microsoft and AP Technology Services, and the participation of Microsoft in the Indian Institute of Information Technology. These three issues were flagged for discussion and a lot of effort went into preparing a highly focussed presentation that would catch his attention.

When we arrived at the ambassador's residence with the laptop he suggested that we skip the presentation and have a verbal interaction with Gates. I knew I had to make the presentation to interest Gates, so I insisted. Finally the ambassador gave in. Instead of the twenty minutes promised Gates listened and asked questions for forty. He said later that he had put Hyderabad on top of his list because we were the most aggressive of those wanting Microsoft to locate in their country or state.

That meeting was an important milestone in the whole process of taking IT forward. The demonstration value of that one coup was considerable. The confidence level of other would-be investors in Andhra Pradesh received a big boost. They felt that Microsoft must have done a thorough analysis of the pros and cons before choosing Hyderabad. Which was indeed the case, because they did send a number of teams. They got a lot of input from these and only after processing and analysing this they took a decision. So in a sense this raised the visibility of Hyderabad in the IT world and it also encouraged others to make investments here.

At that point Microsoft was looking globally for alternative places where they could expand. They were looking at China, Israel and India. Gates promised at that meeting that he would send a team to Hyderabad and shortly after a team came. They went around the location chosen for Hi-Tec City. There was nothing on the ground as yet. When they came back two months later the building was two storeys deep. When they came back yet again five or six months later, the structure was up. Larsen and Toubro put up Hi-Tec City in a record fifteen months. And it demonstrated to

Microsoft that the Andhra Pradesh government meant business.

Finally, each of the three points I discussed with Gates at the US ambassador's residence were finalized. And the Microsoft Software Development Centre was inaugurated on 28 February 1999 in Hi-Tec City.

I recount this here only to show that an Indian chief minister in today's global economy has to be a salesman. If he rests on his pride nothing will be achieved. He also has to be like a chief executive who makes things happen. Speed is of the essence. As Klaus Schwab of the Davos World Economic Forum puts it, 'We have moved from a world where the big eat the small to a world where the fast eat the slow.'

Once you get someone interested in your state you have to demonstrate that the government moves, takes decisions and implements them quickly. Otherwise the opportunity will be lost. Not just in the rest of the world, in the rest of India too there is competition, waiting to capture investment that is getting harder and harder to come by.

The major challenge for all of us in India for some time to come will be economic. At the beginning of the decade of the 1990s the Central government recognized that the country's economy was in a crisis and drastic changes would have to be made in its functioning. Most state governments faced that realization by the end of the same decade. Their finances had deteriorated alarmingly, many were borrowing to meet current expenditure, and the interest on debt incurred was showing up as a substantial percentage of revenue expenditure.

One after another, states are reaching the point where they find bankruptcy staring them in the face: and then the day arrives when there is no money in the treasury to pay salaries.

Then a frantic search for a bailout begins. Development

takes a back seat to finding resources for current expenditure. The reason why state finances have come to such a pass are dealt with elsewhere in this book.

This is why the major priority in India for the new century is that both old-style politics and old-style governance have to change: the country can no longer afford them. Since its inception eighteen years ago there has been tremendous change in the Telugu Desam's approach to governance. When N.T. Rama Rao founded the party, there was a commitment to populist measures because the social condition of the people warranted it at that time.

Today, with the state exchequer bled dry, the mandate is more for effective governance. When my opponents in the last election held out the promise of free power, I told voters that they could choose between free power and uninterrupted power. Producing power is as expensive as it is vital. But all across the country states charge little or nothing for it. The mounting debts of the state electricity board were one reason for the state of bankruptcy that Andhra Pradesh was reduced to four years ago. People have to be educated on this issue.

The era of free handouts as a part of electoral politics is over. We have seen several decades of such politics, but the country's economy can no longer afford it. Hard decisions need to be taken if revenues are to be mobilized to reduce government deficit. But the art of politics is to make such decisions palatable so that they are not rejected outright by citizens, who are the voters. First, people should be convinced that such steps are necessary.

In 1999 two prominent reformers of the Congress party and the Tamil Maanila Congress failed to get re-elected. That does not mean that reformers cannot win a popular mandate. I have implemented economic reforms in Andhra Pradesh and been re-elected in that state. It does mean that people's support for reforms cannot be taken for granted. I have made it a point to prepare the people and to change their psychology, because that is the only way to gain acceptability for increased user charges in several areas.

There will be strikes, but the government has to have consumers on its side. In order to enlist public support for reforms it is necessary to educate public opinion, as was done in Andhra Pradesh for each major programme of reform taken up. White papers were published, public meetings were conducted, a debate in the print and electronic media carried out, issues were discussed threadbare in the assembly and a concerted drive was taken up to educate the public about the necessity of reforms.

If I have opposed hikes in the price of kerosene, diesel and foodgrains in the public distribution system it is because I feel this process was not adopted by the Central government in respect of various decisions taken recently. These measures were introduced without preparing people adequately for them.

For three years we had an appalling position financially, and in terms of growth, Andhra Pradesh was ranked below the all-India average. Our financial crisis is still there, but we are spending huge money on development. The productivity of our people will have to be rapidly increased through investments in health and education. It will take some more time for these investments to yield dividends.

My goal is to take care of two things. One is development, the other is fiscal discipline. Meanwhile we have to continue to open up the economy, and create conditions that investors welcome. We have to have speedy and transparent decision making and rapid implementation. We have to honour commitments made to the industry so that it can come in and create jobs that any state with a population of seventy-five million people needs. All of this requires a mindset different from that of the past. Industrialists doing business in my state will affirm that there is a marked change in attitude on the part of the bureaucracy in the last few years. They behave less like rulers and more like facilitators. Among the states in the country, Andhra Pradesh has moved from being twenty-second in investor perception rankings in 1995 to third in 2000.

In Andhra Pradesh we have produced Vision 2020 because I felt we must have a long-term vision for how we want to develop the state. For a vision, a reasonable time-span is twenty years. Today planning is for five years at a time and so it cannot be sufficiently long term.

More than half the people in my state are illiterate. Despite improvements in the health sector, Andhra Pradesh still lags behind many states in the country on key health indicators. Our urban infrastructure and services are still inadequate. Until recently our annual economic growth rate was lower than the country's average of 5.2 per cent.

To change all this we have to take stock of what the needs are in the social sector, what the assets of the state are which can be leveraged, in which areas economic opportunity can be created, and what the demands for infrastructure will be in the future. The Vision 2020 exercise has identified those sectors of the economy which will effectively stimulate growth: agriculture, industry and services. To realize its goals there have to be clearly set targets: yearly, quarterly, monthly.

It has also identified those tasks that should be undertaken by a government, and those which should not. The philosophy that the AP government as an organization is attempting to internalize is that any organization needs to rethink and reform itself on a continuous basis. Reform cannot be a one-time effort that is over once you have taken some steps. Change and reform is a continuous process.

At the heart of the administrative reform we are attempting is the change in role for the government from being actor, to enabler and facilitator. The government must stop trying to do things which it does badly and install a policy framework which gives it the role of a facilitator.

The vision document gave us a macro plan. At the other end of the spectrum we also need micro plans. Right at the beginning of my second term as chief minister we began to work on this. We initiated a debate at the village level on micro-level planning. We will follow this up by preparing suitable plans. What are the local resources available, natural and human? How can poverty be eradicated in five or ten years' time? On the basis of the plans prepared we will have some clarity on what we are going to do for the next five years.

In this manner, village by village, we will be able to set small goals for population control, for school enrolment, for the growth rate, for the identification and exploitation of natural resources, for assessing and augmenting local employment. Students and lecturers were drafted to assist in this village-level planning process because to prepare micro plans in all rural habitations and municipal wards we needed a lot of hands. There was some criticism that their course work was being affected. But I feel that confronting the country's rural reality should also be part of a young Indian's education.

From the beginning of my political career I have used students to conduct surveys. And in this micro-planning exercise we roped in universities and institutionalized student involvement by giving them academic credit for the work they did in conducting household surveys, prioritizing local needs, finalizing micro-plans and getting them approved by household committees.

Apart from economic recovery and detailed planning, administrative reform is another must for better governance in India. We can no longer afford departmental inefficiency and the enormous waste that is typical of the government machinery. Nor can we afford to continue with endemic corruption. So new systems have to be put in place, new solutions explored.

One solution is information technology. In the last four years we have focussed on this because I strongly believe in the transparency it brings. Without technology you cannot have progress. We cannot achieve things any more in the traditional way. Apart from transparency IT brings about accountability and removal of discretion. Misuse and wastage will become less, corruption will go. In terms of cost we may spend 5 per cent of the budget in introducing it, but now 50 per cent of that budget is wasted for lack of accountability. Today with information technology we can analyse where we have spent, how we have spent, what are the priorities.

New systems and solutions are also being attempted in rural development. These involve allocating state funds for development to people in the villages to manage and utilize. In two areas, irrigation and school education, we have passed legislation to enable devolution of state funds to people's committees to execute works that were earlier done in the government sector. Money is now disbursed by committees of farmers and parents. They are the stakeholders: we want to involve them, train them and give a legal basis to their involvement in governance.

This has been a major shift in rural development spending and execution of works during my first tenure as chief minister. The presence of six self-help groups in every habitation ensures accountability of the government functionaries who have to execute works in these areas. I have been repeatedly asked why we need self-help groups when there are panchayati raj bodies at the village level which can perform the same function of ensuring accountability. I believe people's direct participation in governance is different from representative democracy.

Panchayats have been in existence for many years. Central government schemes have been there all these years, yet there has been no dramatic change in the quality of life in our villages. There is still not enough water reaching their fields, or enough teachers in primary schools, or any medical facility within reasonable distance. My hope is that there will be results because of motivation; stakeholders will be motivated when they are directly involved.

I have been asked what has changed in the villages of Andhra Pradesh from the time I grew up in a rural area in the early 1950s. The biggest change has been attitudinal. There used to be participation, there used to be honesty, people in the village were not overly greedy. They were not so dependent on the government. Today they are far more dependent on the government. And because of political promises, the dependence has only grown.

In my village the irrigation sources were once all maintained by the villagers, but over a period of time all these responsibilities have been taken over by government departments. Now, nobody bothers to clear the irrigation channels leading to their fields. We have tried to revive that system through the water users' associations. It is working.

For the millennium the challenge is to re-inculcate the old culture of participation. We have to tell the citizens, this is your responsibility, this is our responsibility. In India people have become very conscious of their fundamental rights. But no one has asked, what are his or her fundamental duties? Not enough people are bothered about that today. I want to discuss that with people at every level. This is your duty, this is your right. Both have to go hand in hand. Governance is beyond the capacity of the government alone. Civil society, the private sector, local communities—all have to play their part.

Finally, if there is a sense of hope in a country as beset with problems as ours at the turn of the century, one should be happy. That in itself is a tremendous achievement. Today many Indians have reason for hope when they look to the individuals who do the country proud on the world stage— whether it is Amartya Sen or Dr Raj Reddy or Arundhati

Roy. Individual Indians are beating the system and achieving tremendous success.

In the last few years, the newborn competitive spirit in our federal polity has also contributed to this spirit of hope. State governments are now competing with each other to put progressive policies in place, to attract investment, to develop their human resources. They are racing each other to get on to the information technology bandwagon. They are looking around for ideas to bring a fresh approach to the persisting problems of illiteracy, infant mortality, unemployment and underemployment. They are struggling to fend off the bankruptcy in their exchequers. All said and done, things are happening, not just in my state, but in others as well.

I am sure we are seeing the beginning of a turnaround for the nation.

I am bombarded daily with e-mail from people within the country and outside, anxious to be reassured on this question. Is there hope for the Indian state, they want to know. Will we achieve success in what we are attempting in Andhra Pradesh? Will the rest of India be able to emulate that success? Can India fulfil its potential as a nation-state in the twenty-first century? We can, but for the political class, the bureaucracy and the people, it is a tough call.

2

REINVENTING POLITICS

Now that economic reform in India is set on an irreversible course, it is time for the political class to take a hard, practical look at how politics in our society can be made more purposeful, less self-serving and less fractious. I don't say this out of self-righteousness but out of a hard-headed recognition of the fact that the country has paid a heavy social and economic price for too much politicking and too little governance. The failure on the part of parties to learn coalition behaviour has led to three general elections in a little over three years, each of them costing the exchequer a thousand crore rupees.

The Telugu Desam is a regional party with a national outlook. There are three fundamental departures from traditional Indian politics that we are attempting within the party. The first is to recognize that the end of politics is governance, not mere ruling. It has therefore to introduce an element of professionalism so that the quality of governance can be enhanced.

The second is our belief that the politics of populism can be replaced by the politics of development. The latter too can be made to pay electoral dividends. People have begun to recognize that it is not viable for governments to continue providing goods and services for free. They do, however, want better service from the government of the day and are willing to pay for it.

The third change that the TDP is attempting, and one that I sincerely believe in, is our effort to delegitimize the vulgarity associated with Indian politics. It is important to make politics respectable, to dissociate it in the minds of the younger generation from corruption and incompetence.

My party's agenda for the next five years in Andhra Pradesh, therefore, is to redefine politics along these lines. Some clear steps have to be taken. First, we need greater professionalism in politics. Legislators need training to keep abreast of the latest issues and contemporary trends. I believe the idea of training politicians was first attempted in India in Andhra Pradesh, when N.G. Ranga started a school for politicians in Guntur in the 1950s. We attempted it in the TDP in N.T. Rama Rao's second term as chief minister.

My party has constructed a four-storey training institute with a regular faculty to conduct training for legislators and other party functionaries, such as members of the mandal praja parishads and zilla praja parishads, all round the year. There is a dormitory that accommodates 500 trainees at any given time. In addition to this central training institute, we have divisional training institutes in the districts.

We train newly elected members of the legislative assembly in their duties, including the importance of attending assembly sessions. We train party leaders at all levels on how to conduct themselves. We will train market committee chairpersons, who are political appointees, on what their role should be, how to solve the farming community's problems, what are the innovative methods of crop storage, and so on.

We also train the state's council of ministers. Each election brings its crop of first timers, both into politics and into the cabinet. Every good cabinet, both for reasons of political representation and to induct new professional blood, will have people who have not been ministers before, and may not even have been members of Parliament or of the legislature before. Having an orientation course for them becomes a common-sense thing to do.

We did it systematically for the first time in October–November 1999, with the intention of exposing the new ministers to a whole range of ideas, goals and practices that they may not have been familiar with. All of us in the cabinet were also exposed to some yoga and meditation, because learning management of stress is as useful to a minister as acquainting herself or himself with the allotted portfolio.

During this orientation course I did a two-hour presentation for the new cabinet members on transforming Andhra Pradesh. The focus was interdisciplinary, because every minister, regardless of his or her portfolio, should be aware of the government's entire programme in all sectors. It also placed the challenge of governance and leadership in global perspective.

At the turn of the century, training an Indian politician in a leadership position is a management training exercise. A politician in the Telugu Desam Party has to be a professional leader who understands what good governance should consist of, what the international experience on governmental reform has been, and what stage the Indian economy is at as compared to other East Asian economies. He or she should also comprehend what range of strategies and initiatives will deliver poverty eradication, a better government–citizen interface, and a sustained high level of growth.

The orientation I gave my cabinet spelt out the lessons we have to learn from East Asia. First you have to see India in relation to these countries to understand our mistakes in the way we have run our economy: in thirty years, from 1965 to 1995, the gross domestic product per capita in relation to the US grew by 69.3 per cent in Singapore, 39.8 per cent in

South Korea, 22.5 per cent in Malaysia, 7.6 per cent in China, and 1.3 per cent in India.

What were the factors behind East Asian growth? Several important ones: the transformation of agriculture through irrigation and power, private sector-led development, export-led growth and high savings and investment. These countries invested a great deal in infrastructure and today their roads and ports would put ours to shame.

Similarly, I emphasize the transformation of the public sector that has taken place in countries such as Australia, Britain and New Zealand. New Zealand's Ministry of Public Works had 12,000 employees at one time, and built most of the airports, bridges, power stations, roads, canals, dams and railways in that country.

Today it no longer exists. First it was split up, and all policy advice functions transferred to other departments. Commercially oriented services were converted into state-owned enterprises. These were reorganized along business lines and required to raise capital on the market. At the same time, they were freed from government regulations. Over time each of these was sold to the private sector. New Zealand no longer has any government in-house capability to design, build or repair infrastructure. When these services are needed, they are purchased on the open market.

In its first term the TDP government set administrative reforms, growth plans and human resource development initiatives in motion. Every member of the cabinet needs to know what the strategies and objectives in these areas are. I reviewed the TDP's manifesto commitments with them, and outlined IT and Internet goals for both the government and society in Andhra Pradesh. Very shortly, many areas of government–citizen interface will be able to take place through information systems, rather than directly.

Who should be the inspiration for a twenty-first century Indian politician? In any century, Mahatma Gandhi's precepts and his dream of an equitable Indian society will remain universally relevant. For my partymen and women, N.T. Rama Rao's instinctive vision also remains very relevant, based as it was on an articulation of regional aspirations and a clear empathy with the backward and downtrodden.

But beyond that, because providing a range of services for millions of people across different income groups is such a complex job, politicians must read management thought, must be acquainted with the managerial wisdom of Peter Drucker and Jack Welch, the legendary CEO of General Electric, and must study how politicians in other parts of the world have succeeded in delivering growth and governance.

They have to become familiar with concepts such as deregulation, citizens' charters and sunset laws because after five decades of crippling regulation, frustratingly poor services and resource-sapping growth in government employment, India can afford to lose no more time in bringing such concepts into practice.

The second element of redefinition is that politics should draw professionals from other fields, so that as a vocation it acquires both respectability and commitment. Politicians have come to be regarded as crooks in modern India—antisocial elements have entered the political arena in all states. When teachers, doctors, lawyers and executives come in to join its ranks, this stigma will go.

During the 1999 assembly election we had an influx of young and educated people into the ranks of MLAs. Doctors, engineers and postgraduates came in. A few rural leaders with journalism or NGO backgrounds were also given tickets. They won. Only about a fifth of the total have studied less than the intermediate level. A former senior police officer joined the party, was elected and is today a cabinet minister.

In these elections I launched a movement called Praja Deewena. We told the people, if you are expecting a good government, your contribution should be there in achieving it. A lot of administrative experience has now been introduced into the party after retired bureaucrats, professors, economists and industrialists have been persuaded to join it.

I am firmly of the opinion that to meet the challenge of bringing about a qualitative change in a billion lives, millions of ordinary citizens have to join the effort. If you leave politics to professional politicians and governance to professional bureaucrats, you have only yourself to blame if things around you do not change much.

If nearly 40 per cent of enfranchised Indians habitually do not vote, and by all accounts these are the better educated section, it reflects a degree of cynicism and indifference which has to end if we have to change the face of India.

We have some evidence that in the 1999 elections, persons who had never voted came to the polling booth. It is a change in attitudes that we are trying to bring about in the minds of the people. We cannot say we have totally succeeded. But we have made a beginning and are going to pursue it.

Third, there should be a way for ordinary citizens to participate in development activity on a regular basis.

We are trying to motivate the people through programmes like the Janmabhoomi to contribute both in cash and kind and to participate in supervision. This programme takes up infrastructure creation at the village level. The local community decides in gram sabhas or village meetings what works to take up. We are appealing to them that these are the kind of assets we are trying to build up for their children. Indeed, they will be useful for generations to come. You involve yourself, you participate in the change that we are trying to bring about.

Fourth, politicians should be given all the facilities they need to perform their job well. If an MLA needs to tour his constituency and does not have a car, he will either neglect his constituency or accept a favour from somebody whom he later will have to help with contracts. We should work towards reducing such nexuses by enhancing a politician's facilities, and perhaps even his salary. If a politician is to be a professional, he must be treated like one.

A recent survey of salaries across Asia in *Asiaweek* magazine showed that with the exception of China, salaries of the head of government, of the finance minister and of members of parliament were considerably higher than those in India in Indonesia, the Philippines, Singapore, Thailand, South Korea, Malaysia, Japan, Australia and Hong Kong.

Fifth, a political party must have a source of income, so that it does not have to solicit contributions at election time. Every contribution that it accepts binds its hands a little more when it is in power. During the last elections we thought of appealing to the common man for contributions, with the slogan one vote, one note. But given the political slander our opposition was already indulging in, we felt our intentions would be vitiated.

In both Malaysia and Taiwan, political parties run businesses to raise money for their needs. In India, where politicians are perceived as innately dishonest, there may be difficulty in convincing people that the idea is sincerely meant. Nevertheless, other ideas are worth exploring.

Changing the image of the politician is a necessary prelude to changing the way politics is practised. To begin with, political conduct will have to be put under scrutiny, so that public opinion exerts it own pressure. In recent years we have had some fine televised debates in Parliament. At the other end of the spectrum, we have seen mikes and furniture being hurled at one another in a state assembly.

We began permitting the televising of assembly proceedings in Andhra Pradesh two years ago, so that people could see how their elected representatives behave. Now they can see their language, their presentation, their appearance, their attendance. It is a move towards transparency. Anybody can film the assembly proceedings. There is no preview of the footage any more, though in the beginning there was.

We are also inviting the common man to involve himself in governance. The weekly Dial your CM programme on Hyderabad Doordarshan offers the citizen a chance to interact with the head of the government on different issues and schemes. When the ruler and ruled interact, politics becomes a lot healthier and such a trend leads to a responsive government.

That is also the logic behind institutionalizing gram sabhas as a part of the Janmabhoomi programme. People have to come to these sabhas, voice their opinions regarding programmes to be taken up, and question both government servants and their own representatives on the quality of implementation. If the gram sabhas are not functioning effectively, Janmabhoomi will not achieve its objective of decentralized planning and implementation.

Political accountability occurs once in five years at election time. That is not good enough. In the TDP, we do a constant evaluation of how our elected representatives are fulfilling their public roles. For example, if we have constituted hospital advisory committees with MLAs as chairpersons, we analyse their performance and grade them. There is pressure on them to perform.

However, we are also experimenting with election-time accountability. In the September 1999 assembly elections we attempted, for the first time, to poll the opinions of the entire six lakh active membership of the party on which candidates should be renominated or dropped. We sent computerized forms to all active members seeking their opinion, without revealing their names. The filled forms were brought by party observers in sealed envelopes and processed in the TDP headquarters. We used this as one source of information in deciding which candidates should be nominated or renominated. And it was a means of keeping the opinion of the party worker in mind while choosing candidates.

For a party leader, contact is the best form of ensuring accountability. If you do not continuously keep in touch with a wide spectrum of people, you will not have your finger on the pulse of the state. I travel a great deal, visiting each district in the state at least once every two or three months.

This achieves several things. I get a first-hand look at how development schemes are really being implemented. Has the work been done, and if so, of what quality. In a culture where there is precious little bureaucratic accountability, this helps, however marginally, to drive home the point that people are expected to deliver.

I can get feedback from the people themselves, so that I do not have to depend on my partymen or my officials for the accurate picture. Besides, I can make public contact. Every meeting I address, whether it is at a street corner or at a big, organized rally, gives me an opportunity to explain to people what the government is trying to do, and if taxes or user charges are being raised, why this has to be done. It gives the people access to the chief minister.

It also brings the chief minister in contact with those far-flung party cadres who might never otherwise have access to him or her. Usually when I am travelling across the state to take part in the Janmabhoomi rounds or inaugurate upgraded primary health centres or training camps, the days are spent looking at schemes and talking to officials, and party meetings with local cadres are held at night.

There are many other ways in which I try to maintain contact with the men and women who are executing our policies and schemes. We have many large review meetings in Hyderabad of the presidents of self-help groups, or of rural development functionaries. I often spend a whole day attending these. Thousands of men and women from the districts come, camp in Hyderabad, and share their experiences with each other and us in government. It gives them an opportunity to meet others who are implementing similar programmes and may have adopted a different approach.

After the assembly elections in 1999, I convened a meeting in Jubilee Hall in Hyderabad with all the IAS and IPS officers in the city. The objective was to set out the agenda for the government's next five years, and to solicit ideas from the bureaucrats. What can we do differently this time around? My cabinet members were also present. Several officials offered their views, and I took notes. We aim to have these interactions once in three months. I learn from my officers' experiences: they are the front line, implementing the decisions we take. They know what the stumbling blocks to implementation are.

Similarly, in the Telugu Desam Party, we go to great lengths to maintain contact with thousands of party workers in the mandals and villages. Once in two years we conduct the Mahanadu on NTR's birthday. All around the year we have review meetings and training courses. We give them questionnaires to solicit their views.

I also try at election time to contact as many voters as our finances permit. In the last elections we mailed sixty-six lakh letters to voters describing what had been done for them by the government which was seeking re-election. I doubt that any other political party in the country has attempted anything similar. It is part of the TDP's philosophy to continually reach out to citizens, to attempt to rope them into the exercise of governance.

Finally, part of redefining politics is bringing a greater sense of responsibility into the conduct of the opposition in any legislature. Its behaviour should not be a free-for-all, as it often is now, both in the state assemblies as well as in Parliament. Being in the opposition brings its own challenges and responsibilities. It gives you time to build your party, to study issues that have to be projected in the assembly. Between 1989 and 1994 we were in the opposition, and we treated this as a period of consolidation for the party. There were many issues to take up: law and order, corruption, people's programmes. We exploited them to the maximum, but not irresponsibly.

People are watching the political conduct of the opposition. It is an area where you can create a good impact, if your approach is positive. Now that TV cameras are present during assembly sessions, people can see and judge for themselves how legislators behave, what is the quality of the debate. The audiences will certainly appreciate a positive approach, not a negative one.

In 1989, when the Telugu Desam lost the elections, I was elected by a margin of 6000 votes. In 1994, after five years on the opposition benches, my margin of victory in the next election increased to 60,000 votes. In the 1999 assembly elections, when the leader of the Congress Legislature Party was defeated, it was a reflection of how they conducted themselves in the opposition.

In terms of their opposition conduct in Parliament or in the assembly, there is not that much difference between one political party and another. They speak one language when in power, another when out of it. Even when they see merit in the ruling party's programmes, they cannot bring themselves to admit it, because if they did, they would jeopardize their own chances of being re-elected. It becomes their dharma to oppose, failing which they may not have an existence.

The role of the opposition should not be to oppose the ruling party's schemes but to monitor their implementation. Constructive criticism keeps the government of the day on its toes. There are accusations about Janmabhoomi—that contractors put in the 30 per cent contribution meant to come in from the general public so that they can win the contract for road or building works in that village; or that the gram sabhas are not attended by the scheduled castes because word does not reach them; or that there is corruption and misuse. It is a massive programme and lapses will occur. Nevertheless, we have appealed to the opposition also to bring such misuse to the notice of the government.

The other aspect of opposition behaviour and its impact on governance relates to major policy changes that have to be ushered in through Parliament with its cooperation. In our bicameral legislature the ruling coalition is often without a majority in the upper house. Major legislation such as the opening up of insurance to the private sector cannot be passed without support from the opposition benches.

Yet parties have been known to oppose such legislation when in the opposition, and then seek to introduce the same legislation when in power themselves. However, this trend has begun to change, and it is a welcome change. Developing a coalition culture involves rising above partisan considerations to pass legislation that will help take reforms forward. And it also becomes a demonstration of the fact that political reform is beginning to take root.

3

CHANGING EQUATIONS

In Indian politics stability has given way to constant change, particularly at the level of state governments. Since 1967 chief ministers have, on average, been in office for only 2.65 years. Uttar Pradesh has seen twenty-seven governments in forty-four years.

Between 1989 and 1999, 77 per cent of the incumbents in all states were defeated in assembly elections. If you take only major states with ten or more Lok Sabha seats, the figure rises to 82 per cent. Parties and politicians are also changing alignments on an annual basis, so that cabinet ministers in successive governments can end up representing a different party each time.

The same party also represents different electoral constituencies in different states. In the three states where it has a base the Janata Dal represents three radically different social groups: the dalit and lower OBC (other backward castes) in Bihar, dominant peasant proprietors in Karnataka, and a cross-section of social groups with an accent on the upper castes in Orissa. Similarly, the Congress is the party of the downtrodden, as opposed to the BJP's support base in states like Uttar Pradesh, but in West Bengal it represents the better off in comparison to the constituency of the Left Front.

Psephologist Yogendra Yadav, who has delineated the above trends, also points out that whereas the political participation of suppressed groups like the dalits, scheduled tribes and women is rising, that of the educated elites is shrinking. That too affects electoral outcomes and there is a consequent shift in power, localized though it may be.

In the 1950s and '60s urban areas recorded higher voter turnouts; today rural areas do so. Turnout in both Lok Sabha and assembly elections has risen from around 45 per cent in 1952 to around 63 per cent in 1998. All these rapid changes are further compounded by the rise of regional parties.

From the point of view of a regional party, the instability in current Indian politics is a positive phenomenon. What is seen as instability is actually an assertion of pluralism. After three decades of domination by the Congress party the country's ideological spectrum is widening to reflect linguistic, ethnic, caste and regional identities. That is why elections are no longer yielding decisive mandates.

In the Telugu Desam Party we see the current period of shifting coalitions and unstable governments as a manifestation of more fundamental changes taking place in the national polity. The backward classes and dalits are asserting themselves. There is a steady decline in the base of national political parties like the Congress. Thanks to its failure to accommodate dissent in a democratic manner within the party, the diverse classes and communities that were accommodated within the Congress have split up into separate parties. The Congress remains a major party, but the Congress era, when it was presumed to be the natural party of governance, is over.

In the Hindi heartland, despite the rise of the Bharatiya Janata Party, not a single major party has been able to fill the vacuum. In the aftermath of Mandal, caste alignments have resulted in myriad political formations. Many of these have regional rather than national bases.

This construction of new political constituencies has created enormous space for regional parties to emerge as a strong force. Parties like the Telugu Desam and the DMK reflect the grassroots aspirations of people in their states. This is true not just of the southern states, but also of Haryana and Orissa. In 1989 this trend was already in evidence at the Centre when Devi Lal of Haryana and Biju Patnaik of Orissa emerged as major political players after the defeat of the Congress. Ten years later it seems that both the formation and survival of national governments depends on regional parties.

When my father-in-law, N.T. Rama Rao, founded the Telugu Desam in 1982 and was swept into power, he provided political space to constituencies that were so far under-represented in the dominant political party at the state level. This included certain sections of the backward and forward classes, women, and educated professionals such as doctors, lawyers and teachers.

With the formation of this party he was also capturing and capitalizing on the feelings of both pride and resentment that the Telugu people had. He promised to set right the neglect of more than thirty years of Congress rule and restore Telugu pride. He often said that Andhra's pride need not be pledged to Delhi but could be upheld in Hyderabad.

NTR set up the party and united it under his charisma, I organized and consolidated it under his leadership. We made it cadre based and gave it a solid organizational foundation. Like the older Dravida Munnetra Kazhagam and Anna Dravida Munnetra Kazhagam in Tamil Nadu, this was a monolithic party under the leadership of a strong personality. It spoke the language of the region and its top leaders were within reach: in Hyderabad, instead of in Delhi.

Because of its smaller, more homogeneous regional base,

building an identification with the people of the state was easier. Over close to two decades our regional party has consolidated and expanded its membership in the state. It has been in power for two and a half terms since 1982 and was re-elected in 1999 to a third.

Even back in 1984 with thirty members of Parliament it was the single largest opposition party in the Lok Sabha.

In the decade of the 1990s several regional parties have been voted into office with convincing mandates even as the electoral clout of the national parties is being increasingly regionalized. In 1996 the United Front government at the Centre reflected for the first time a coalition of several national and regional parties. Since then the Telugu Desam itself has twice played a crucial role in the formation of the Central government.

In March 1998, when no coalition was able to summon the requisite numbers, we decided to offer issue-based support to the Bharatiya Janata Party-led coalition so that a government could be formed and could proceed with the business of governance. And in October 1999, we once again offered unconditional support from outside to the National Democratic Alliance so that the country could have a government.

The current phase of instability in the national polity is part of a polarization process that will see the emergence of two alternative and competing coalition groups. The contours of these were already present in the 1998 and 1999 Lok Sabha elections. Our effort in the Telugu Desam is to catalyse political alignments around a dominant ideology of development.

The number of poor in India today exceeds the total population of India at the time of Independence. They have remained fairly untouched by the development process. Increasingly, people will vote on the basis of the ability of parties to squarely address issues of food, clothing, shelter, health care, education and jobs.

So what does all of the above portend for the next decade of Indian politics? What implications does it have for Centre–state relations? For a political culture unaccustomed to the sharing of power at the Centre? And what demands will these changes make on the Indian Constitution which was drawn up at a time when the political situation was very different?

These are vital issues that cannot be ignored or wished away.

Restructuring of our federal system is now taking place. State politics will dominate national politics. As the number of seats held in the Lok Sabha by national parties decreases, the new contenders from the regional parties will increase their clout enormously. It is for that reason that recent general elections have seen such hard bargaining between regional and national parties in seat-sharing arrangements. At the time of the formation of a coalition government, the more seats a regional party has to contribute to an alliance, the greater its ability to win a hearing for its state's problems.

The TDP as a regional party has a clear-cut approach towards national issues and state issues. It is committed to secularism, national unity and federalism on the one hand, and the rapid development of Andhra Pradesh on the other. Effective federalism does not, in my view, mean a weak Centre held to ransom by coalition partners from among the regional parties. Ideally, it should mean a strong Centre and strong states.

To reach that goal, there is a whole agenda of Centre–state issues that are repeatedly brought up at every Inter-state Council Meeting year after year but remain unresolved. The Telugu Desam Party's role in the United Front government contributed to better Centre–state relations, improved financial and administrative devolution to the states, and led to the flow of a record quantum of funds under various sectors to Andhra Pradesh. A number of long-pending issues were resolved and many projects received clearance. This, we believe, is as it should be.

It is not healthy in the long term for regional parties to merely acquire political clout at the Centre so that they can cash political cheques in a situation where all states are competing for bigger slices of a fast-dwindling Central pie. Effective federalism should mean that they become strong economic entities on their own. Central policies have to facilitate this process. The states should be able to plan for their own economies and raise resources.

Economic liberalization has helped: private investment has become an engine for growth that state governments can tap as much as the Centre. But the Constitution places restrictions on borrowings by states which are anachronistic and should be removed. These will be dealt with a little later in the discussion in this chapter on constitutional reforms. Ultimately, it is economic strength that will deliver political stability in the states by creating employment and enhancing the quality of people's lives. It will also reduce the states' dependence on financial flows from the Centre.

State governments which have realized this have been competing to attract fresh investment. Today Andhra Pradesh is one of four states with a credit–deposit ratio which is well above the national average. This means that the utilization of credit is high, utilization of money in the productive sector is high because the investor feels it is less risky to invest in this state. Credit will increasingly be available in those states which are putting progressive policies in place.

The success of economic reforms has financial implications for the states which have not been fully appreciated. For reforms to succeed we need to focus on more effective provision of public goods and merit goods. Public goods are those funded by taxation, such as roads, municipal services, street lighting, even free-to-air broadcasting. Merit goods are beneficial services such as welfare or education which the government is expected to provide.

Under the constitutional division of responsibilities between the Centre and the states the provision of all public goods except defence is with the states. Provision of merit goods is the exclusive responsibility of the states. As such the reforms imply higher expenditure commitments for the states in a variety of ways—notably to implement safety-net programmes for protecting the poor during the transition.

States also need to invest in building and maintaining infrastructure to facilitate the private investment that will come in once reforms have begun. Without roads, airports and telecommunications, expansion of industry and consequently employment will not take place. They need money for this. With no fresh investment by the Centre in public enterprises, the responsibility for backward area development too has devolved entirely on states. Experience shows that the only effective instrument of backward area development is investment in the agriculture sector, which makes a large claim on state resources.

For all of the above, financial demands are made upon state governments which are already sorely strapped for cash.

Then there is the forceful lesson of the East Asian miracle emphasizing a strong commitment to human resource development. Towards this end, states need to invest in primary education, public health, female literacy and family planning to create a workforce equipped to take advantage of economic opportunity. The costs of these development initiatives have to be born by the states.

This, then, is the right time to redefine both Central and state powers and discuss in depth their financial, administrative and legal aspects. Surely there can be no meaningful liberalization without a concomitant process of economic decentralization.

The Telugu Desam Party has repeatedly urged the Government of India to abolish centrally sponsored schemes and transfer the money earmarked for them to the states as an untied grant as part of tax devolution. It is neither practical nor logical for the Centre to specify, as it does today, down to the last detail, how development schemes should be designed, financed and implemented in the nearly 500 districts of the country, as culturally and geographically diverse as they are.

The Central government has also been independently administering and supervising programmes across the length and breadth of the country. Given how big this country is, how diverse its economics, culture, terrain, climate and food habits, it is surely futile to believe that the Centre can do so effectively.

To take just one example, the Centre has an exclusive and extensive machinery for preventing child labour when the entire task could have been left to the states. The delivery systems for both regulatory and development administration should be left to the states. Instead we have a situation where the Centre passes funds directly to panchayats, bypassing state governments. It also confers with district collectors, again bypassing state governments.

All Central taxes should be pooled for devolution to the states as recommended by the tenth finance commission. In a phased manner, 50 per cent of the money should be transferred to the states. They will then have better control over planning and execution.

How do you decide what a state's entitlement should be? Both the Planning Commission and Finance Commission devolutions have been heavily loaded in favour of population and poverty. In the case of the Finance Commission, 50 per cent of the devolution is on the basis of income, that is, poverty inversely related to income. Twenty per cent is on the basis of population, and the rest is made up of other criteria. The Planning Commission's criteria are 50 per cent devolution on the basis of population of the state, and 25 per cent on the basis of poverty inversely related to income.

The time has come to consider performance criteria. If the Centre continues to dole out unconditional grants and devolution on the basis of backwardness alone, no state will have the incentive to improve its family planning performance or its economic management. What kind of performance criteria would it be fair to ask states to conform to? We have some ideas that we are looking at to suggest to the Centre, in line with the improvements to our own economy that we are attempting.

By and large, devolution could in some measure be linked to improved economic practices. When you have a very low rate of economic development, the foremost requirement is what steps you take to accelerate the growth process and thereafter sustain it. But while doing so you should be in a position to do this in a financially viable manner. A very critical component of that is a good administrative structure and a positive decision-making system. When you invest you should do so in a qualitative manner to get the best possible returns.

The other aspect is controlling non-productive expenditure, which is an overwhelming part of current state spending. One criterion could be to examine what programmes a state has to control unproductive expenditure on redundant establishment, and to improve the administration of existing tax rates so that revenues improve. Better control of leakages should also be encouraged. Another criterion could be to look at the size and composition of the state's capital expenditure.

Finally, to base devolution on the basis of population of the state is to penalize those states which have done well on the family planning front. Andhra Pradesh was the first state in the country to come up with a population policy and put state funds into the family planning programme. Its performance in the area of family planning is the third best in the country. We will soon be reaching the stage when AP's population is only replacing itself, not growing. But states which may not reach the goal of achieving a net replacement rate of one even in the next sixty years stand to get a bigger share of Central tax resources on this basis.

Another issue which should be reviewed is planning. The existing planning process is overcentralized, with the Planning Commission's activities encompassing practically all socio-economic areas. This amounts to the Centre encroaching upon the autonomy of the states. There is need to reorient the planning process to provide greater freedom to states, since the Central government is not in a position to decide the correct priorities for them. In the process the quality of planning is suffering. I am of the view that Central intervention in state plans should be minimal. Even plan grants should be made discretionary and must be merged as a share of tax devolution.

The other aspect of this issue is that states should have a more effective and meaningful role in the formulation of the five-year plans. The role and responsibility of the Planning Commission should be downsized. The commission should be restricted to giving loans for specific projects to be negotiated by each state under a World Bank/IMF type of arrangement. The quantum of loans and their terms will be determined by the nature of the project, as also the specific economic and financial circumstances of the state, much like under the IMF regime. The terms and conditions for loans in various sectors could be used by the Centre to signal national priorities.

Both democracy and decentralization have to be the twin pillars of our evolution as a strong nation-state and our emergence as a vibrant economy. Instead, the record since Independence has increasingly been one of excessive and indiscriminate overcentralization. Largely because of a single party being in office both at the Centre and in the states, the states came to be treated as the extended arms of the Centre. It came to usurp control and authority over a number of areas which should legitimately be within the ambit of the states.

Governance has become inherently political. The relationship between the Central and state governments, the economic decisions taken by the former and what they mean for the latter, the translating of political support within a coalition government into economic transactions between Centre and state, the shaping of a ruling party's policies by the conduct of the opposition—all these add up to the politics of contemporary governance.

Managing these compulsions is part of the challenge of governing, and to the extent that the mobilization of resources to run a state government is vital for delivering schemes and services, it is important today for a chief minister to be a good politician in the best sense of the word. Particularly in a situation where so many states find themselves in an acute financial crisis and are competing for the limited resources of the Centre.

However, in a coalition situation this assistance has to be negotiated: when the price of political support is sought to be overtly extracted it is bad for the morale of the country, and leads to a feeling of instability among the people. Coalition partners should not be seen as holding the government of the day to ransom. The short-lived nature of coalition governments in the last couple of years has made it clear that exemplary coalition behaviour is yet to be learned by Indian political parties.

Even regional parties can provide a lead for the development of the country. A strong Centre and strong states, that is what we want. Today there is a strong Centre and weak states—that is not going to help. If you give more financial powers to states you are not weakening the Centre; on the contrary, you are strengthening the states.

The time has also come for certain constitutional

provisions to be reviewed. The Constitution of India is fifty years old. Though it has provided a durable and practical framework of institutions and mechanisms for the governance of the country, the situation at the time of the country's Independence was in many ways very different from what it is today.

In a scenario characterized by coalition governments and hung Parliaments the existing constitutional provisions have been found wanting in many respects. We need a national debate to consider the institutional mechanisms that should be put in place to tackle the new realities of Indian politics. Whether a presidential system of government is to be preferred or whether the prime minister should be elected by the Lok Sabha are matters that deserve serious examination.

The framers of the Indian Constitution adopted the 'first past the post' system for our democracy. Such a system has resulted in a distinct advantage to certain political parties. The Congress even in the best of times did not secure more than 40 per cent of the total votes cast. The voter turnout has generally been around 60 per cent during the elections. In effect, therefore, parties in power have not been representative of the majority.

We need to explore alternative systems available elsewhere in the world in order to devise a system best suited to our own country. We could consider systems of proportional representation followed by Germany, Ireland, Japan or Switzerland. It would also be useful to consider in the same context compulsory voting for citizens, as exists in countries like Australia.

Given the rising public concern about corrupt practices in politics, the time has also come to introduce public funding of election expenditure. The US Congress passed the Federal Election Campaign Act in 1974, which provides for matching contribution from the state for amounts to be raised by candidates for presidential elections. This contribution is subject to the candidates adhering to the limits specified for incurring expenses on the poll campaign.

A vital part of any constitutional review will have to be the question of division of powers between the Centre and the states as envisaged in the Constitution. A number of recommendations made by the Sarkaria Commission remain to be implemented. Of greatest concern to state governments is the use of Article 356 of the Constitution, which gives the Union the power to dismiss an elected state government. The provisions of this article are inconsistent with the spirit of cooperative federalism.

This article has become increasingly prone to misuse. Along with some chief ministers I have been arguing in the Standing Committee of the Inter-state Council that this article must be annulled altogether. Mr Karunanidhi, chief minister of Tamil Nadu, made a pertinent case for this in a letter to me some time back, pointing out that it has been misused and abused more than a hundred times. He wrote: 'Even though deletion of Article 356 is an ideal, and it has no place in a Constitution which calls itself federal, I am sorry we could not reach a consensus about it . . . The next best thing for the present is to make the misuse of Article 356 as difficult as possible.'

This article presumes that the Centre has a greater commitment to the Constitution than the states. That is manifestly not so. The states are equally committed to the constitutional principles of national integrity and secularism. There has not, however, been unanimity among chief ministers on the issue of removal of this article. We have therefore outlined to the Centre safeguards that must be followed to prevent its misuse. These are in the form of draft amendments to Article 356 which make its misuse considerably more difficult.

Another restrictive provision of the Constitution that is anachronistic and must be removed is Article 293, which restricts borrowing by the states. States should be allowed to tap the market as they like. In a market-driven economy the market can be depended upon to impose the necessary checks and balances to keep borrowing at prudent levels. In all fairness, the Centre too must voluntarily accept a corresponding discipline on a borrowing limit, as is the case of some other federations.

India is a country of one billion people. It is a country of immense talent, capability and experience. Despite such a wealth of human and natural resources we have made poor progress. We have to now put in place systems that can truly contribute to people's empowerment in every sense of the term. For this reason, we have to seriously address all systemic weaknesses and devise mechanisms for restoring life, vigour and vitality to our democratic polity.

II

THE INNOVATIVE GOVERNMENT

4

SIMPLIFYING GOVERNMENT

Being in the saddle gives you an insight into what ails Indian governance. By the time the crisis of bankruptcy hit us I had already been a minister in three different governments handling a variety of portfolios. I knew where the problems lay; I also knew that half measures would no longer suffice. To rescue Andhra Pradesh from the morass of indebtedness and inefficiency into which it was sinking we in the government would have to begin looking inward.

The machinery which attempts to run the state needs an urgent overhaul itself. It is huge and self-perpetuating. It is slow and accountable to nobody. Above all, it is obstructive. It essentially exists for itself, not for public service.

In Andhra Pradesh we surveyed people's perception of prevailing levels of corruption and found that people thought 66 per cent of the Andhra Pradesh State Electricity Board employees were corrupt, 65 per cent of the civil supplies personnel were perceived to be corrupt, 64 per cent of the revenue officers and 62 per cent of the police force. Fifty-two per cent of the employees of local bodies were also perceived to be corrupt.

At the beginning of the millennium, then, the question

really is, how much government do we need and in what areas?

David Osborne and Ted Gaebler, authors of *Reinventing Government*, write that 'the central problem of governments today is not what they do but how they operate'. Changing technologies make the old approach of people-intensive government redundant. Information technology can make a huge difference to citizen–government interfaces. It can also usher in transparency and flatter organizations.

A simple three-point diagnosis of the systemic malady in Indian governance points to too many employees, too many levels and far too many files leading to excruciating delays. From these follow the manifestations of the malady: poor or no delivery of services, tremendous delays in decision making, absence of accountability, and corruption.

What this added up to was the need for drastic administrative reforms. Many attempts had been made in the past to introduce them, but with limited results. From 1957 onwards in Andhra Pradesh, five committees had been constituted on this subject until 1990. The objectives of such reform also seemed self-evident: to cut red tape by streamlining systems, minimize delays in the processing of files and papers at all levels, address public grievances effectively, cut down wasteful expenditure, control corruption and improve the quality of governance.

Between 1986 and 1997 there were another nine committees looking at specific aspects of administrative reform. Despite these exertions, the inadequacies and inefficiencies of government have only grown. And the financial crisis the state found itself in was in no small measure due to the fact that the government itself was sapping huge resources, even as it failed to deliver on governance.

Increasingly, earnings from taxes and other sources go mainly into paying bloated wage bills. State governments are bankrupt because of the accelerating growth of revenue deficits. Revenue receipts have failed hopelessly to keep abreast of revenue expenditure. To put it plainly, what the government earns is much less than what it spends. And certainly the most overwhelming cause of the deficit is the state government's expanding role as employer. In 1984-85 expenditure on salaries and pensions of employees accounted for 76.98 per cent of tax and non-tax receipts in Andhra Pradesh. By 1996-97 this had grown to 94.5 per cent.

This did not include the cost of maintaining the employees of municipalities and public sector undertakings. If those directly employed in government departments numbered 53,205 in 1996-97, the latter accounted for 2.96 lakh employees with an approximate bill on salaries and other allowances of Rs 1531 crore. (And these categories do not cover yet a third sector whose salaries come from the government: those employed by panchayati raj institutions). Both kinds of employees are paid salaries from budget support provided by the government as well as the organizations' own sources of income. But the PSUs are not generating enough revenues to meet their share of the salary bill, with the result that they have become a steady drain on the state government, which can ill afford this additional burden.

What's more, the money can be more productively employed in other sectors of the economy. Somebody recently calculated that the cost of maintaining one public sector employee for a year is roughly the same as what it costs to run a primary school. Need I say more?

The overall picture is fairly horrendous. In 1996-97 the salary bill and interest payments together amounted to 108.6 per cent of the state's own tax and non-tax receipts. And if you took into account total revenue receipts, including tax devolution and grants from the Centre, the expenditure in that year on salaries and interest payments alone was 65.5 per cent. Where then was the state government to find the resources for productive spending and growth?

The galloping growth in expenditure on the pay, allowances and pensions of government employees has unleashed processes leading to a debt trap. As the wage bill grows the revenue deficit grows, and as it grows borrowings have to be made to bridge the gap. The interest cost of these borrowings entail further borrowings. It is a vicious circle. Reducing establishment costs is crucial for restoring the fiscal balance.

The growth in wage and salary bills is a direct result of increase in emoluments and perquisites, as well as an increase in the number of employees. The latter does not make for increased efficiency; on the contrary. Even as a large number of staff have been identified as redundant in Andhra Pradesh, pendency is increasing. There is no shortage of manpower, but productivity is low. There is also a mismatch in demand and supply of personnel, which cannot be overcome because of rigidities in redeployment.

From 1988 to 1993 education accounted for the greatest increase in employment. Universities, an increase of 22.65 per cent, and aided government institutions an increase of 16.34 per cent. The next biggest chunk to register an increase was state government employees, and the third, employment in public sector undertakings. The judiciary saw an increase of 8.02 per cent.

Between 1984-85 and 1996-97 the overall increase in the state's establishment cost amounted to 368.2 per cent. Some departments were heavier spenders than others. The council of ministers accounted for the biggest percentage increase in costs accounting for pay, allowances, wages and transport allowance—766.7 per cent. This was accounted for entirely by the pay of officers. The second-most expensive department was medical and public health, with an increase of 653.5 per cent, followed by the police, the judiciary and education.

How do we begin to tackle the problem?

In an effort to curb this unbridled growth of employment in the state government the Andhra Pradesh Regulation of Appointments to Public Services and Rationalization of Staff Pattern and Pay Structure Act of 1994 was brought into force. It was supposed to prevent government departments, corporations, universities and local bodies from making unauthorized and irregular appointments through the back door of nominal muster rolls, daily wagers and appointments on consolidated pay. It was the first Act of its kind in the country.

Following its enactment, a staff review committee was appointed by the state government to review existing staffing patterns. Its labours were quite illuminating. It began by reviewing the engineering establishments of three departments: irrigation, roads and buildings, and panchayati raj. The government in its munificence was employing more than twice as many people than it really needed.

Whole divisions were found to be surplus. A hundred and sixty-four divisions out of 340 in irrigation, 48 out of 102 in roads and buildings, 34 out of 107 in panchayati raj.

And what was the cost of this form of welfarism? The surplus staff per annum in the irrigation department cost the government Rs 157.42 crore. For roads and buildings and the panchayati raj departments together the cost was Rs 84 crore per annum.

By the time the staff review committee completed its task, its report ran into several volumes. In essence its findings can be compressed into a single sentence. Out of 2,70,000 posts reviewed, 1,96,740 or 40.62 per cent were found to be surplus. The overall gross surplus percentage over the existing number of posts was 40.53 per cent posts. After accounting for the deficit posts identified, just over one lakh jobs were found to be surplus. Some 35,000 of these were in the irrigation department alone.

How are surplus jobs created in the government? There

are different ways. In some cases schemes are wound up but jobs cannot be terminated. When a disease has been eradicated, the health department cannot terminate the jobs of the staff attached to the eradication programme because they have a permanent tenure, according to the terms of their appointment. When a huge irrigation project is completed over several years, there is a category of labour employed on it called work charged labour who should technically be discharged when the work is over, but are not discharged.

Another way is when a court decrees that daily wagers should be regularized. There are several Supreme Court judgements in this regard. A common source of surplus staff is the sanctioning of a new scheme. Every new scheme creates a department.

Then there are recruitments conducted by political appointees who are not accountable to anyone, such as the chairmen of public sector units. The office of the chairman of one public sector unit in Andhra Pradesh had twenty-three typists because several preceding chairmen had appointed one or two during their tenure, and each of their successors wanted to bring in their own people. This was despite an official ban on recruitment!

Has the situation begun to be remedied as an outcome of the redundancy appraisal exercise? Only partly. Identifying surplus jobs is easier than doing away with them in a democracy. You can abolish posts, but people have to be redeployed, they cannot be sacked. We do not have a safety net in place as yet. While with the advent of the 1999 elections the government was forced to postpone taking a formal decision on whether to accept or reject the staff review committee report, some changes have taken place.

Recruitment in low-skill categories has stopped, but recruitment of skilled personnel such as paramedical staff is continuing. The composition of government staff in the state is therefore undergoing a shift. The number of skilled people in the government essential for running basic services like health is growing; simultaneously the proportion of non-skilled employees in the overall scenario is shrinking. The overall numbers are not declining just yet; however, the composition is changing in favour of a better service delivery system.

Both at the Central and state government level the only viable approach to begin downsizing is to freeze existing posts so that when the incumbent retires there is no fresh recruitment to the post.

In Andhra Pradesh more posts have been frozen at the lower levels because people want their promotions. The other concomitant move is to offer a voluntary retirement scheme, which we have begun to do where public sector enterprises are concerned.

In the second term of the TDP government, with a convincing mandate for change from the electorate, it may be possible to take more concrete action on the recommendations of the staff review committee. Each department will have to discuss the recommendations given to it in detail before deciding what action is to be taken. What the exercise has done, however, is made the departments of finance and administration acutely aware of the redundancies and their financial implications.

Meanwhile, the time has come for governments in India to incorporate sunset laws as a general practice. What are sunset laws? They are statutes which deal with the self-perpetuating tendencies of government agencies and programmes by providing for their periodic review. They ask the basic question: do this agency's or department's functions continue to be needed? Such laws automatically terminate a state regulatory agency or board or function of government on a certain date. To continue that agency or function beyond that date a state legislature must pass a bill. If you have a sunset law for every scheme and policy it gives greater clarity to your implementation.

The second fundamental problem was too many levels of staff in too many departments. This has the effect of slowing down decision making. If less governmental presence overall is the goal, it has to begin with drastic pruning. Departmental committees recommended the abolition/disbandment/merger of certain departments. There were 180 commissionerates or heads of department. A committee appointed under a previous government was already looking at the reorganization of these.

For instance, the home department was found to be dealing with the police, prisons, passports, sainik welfare, arms, Acts and rules, printing, cinematography and courts. General administration was dealing with the film development corporation. Should cinematography and film development be under different departments? Should youth services remain with tourism and culture or should it be clubbed along with sports as part of higher education?

The expenditure sections of the irrigation department were variously scattered under finance, works and projects. Logically land acquisition for house sites is a subject that should be clubbed with the housing department. There were three commissioners and one special commissioner dealing with land. It was decided to abolish two of these four posts after redesignating the jobs.

Job levels also needed to be rationalized. The commissioner of civil supplies had the following levels below him: a director of civil supplies, an additional director of civil supplies looking after administration and the public distribution system, a deputy director grade I, a supply officer, an assistant supply officer, a grain purchasing officer, a grain purchasing assistant, a deputy tehsildar, and a checkpost deputy tehsildar. After some deliberation the districts of East Godavari, West Godavari, Krishna, Nalgonda and Guntur decided to scrap the posts of grain purchasing officers.

As for level jumping or cutting down the number of officers who had to see a file, every department had to examine the existing procedures and arrive at some conclusion on how much of the red tape could be eliminated. Special committees which had on board experts from outside, in addition to concerned departmental people, spent a good deal of energy on examining this and other rationalization measures.

On the basis of their recommendations a cabinet sub-committee formulated an approach paper in November 1999 which suggested the introduction of a desk officer system in the secretariat for the identification of priority and non-priority files. A priority file would go through only two levels before reaching the minister. A non-priority file would travel through three levels before reaching the minister. The current average of the number of levels through which a file travels is six.

■

Figuring out how to track files has consumed a great deal of our government's recent attention. Files are meant to embody decision making. But the rate at which they travel through the government hierarchy is more representative of government inertia. They are symbolic of many things. The seemingly innocuous piece of cardboard and string with sheafs of papers within it symbolizes obfuscation, deferred responsibility and corruption. Today a decision cannot be taken in the government without perusing the notings in the file. And if a clerk should choose to lock up a file and go home, even the secretary of the department cannot do anything about it.

Files are generated within the government at a prolific rate. If you stacked them up you could build a staircase to heaven. At last count there were 1,08,000 files pending in the secretariat, two and a half times that number with heads of departments, and seven times that number in the districts.

For the secretariat, at least, a goal has been set: by September 2000 the number of files is to be brought down to 50,000.

The cabinet sub-committee on administrative reform has drawn up a specific agenda for reforms in file management in its report of January 2000. A computerized file monitoring system has to be quickly implemented, a mechanism has to be developed which will discourage the generation of new files and the multiplication of files on the same subject, and the monitoring system for file disposal has to be reviewed and strengthened. We have arrived at a profound realization: just about any piece of paper coming to the government does not necessarily have to be converted into a file!

Our analysis of file disposals in the government was fairly illuminating. While those categorized as 'public importance' did form the single largest category of files, 'service matters' formed a sizeable chunk of files generated and circulated in the government. In several departments they constituted the single largest category. The files related to transfers, promotions and disciplinary actions. Not only does the scale of employment within the government sap its resources, managing the employees also consumes much of the government's working hours.

Court cases was the third largest identifiable category.

The irrigation and command area development departments had the largest number of files pertaining to court cases, all relating to either land acquisition or the claims of contractors who had not been paid.

What was illuminating was the snail's pace of disposal in most departments. Compared to pendency at the beginning of a sample fortnight (the last fortnight of 1999), disposal worked out at a departmental average of 13 per cent. Those relating to the finance and planning departments moved the fastest. We have to see whether the effort to cut down the number of levels through which a file moves reduces pendency significantly.

We are also looking at another way of speeding up decision making within the government. One of the major issues the cabinet sub-committees examined was the delegation of powers, in order to reduce delays in decision making and increase the speed of implementation of government orders. An officers' committee was set up thereafter to make specific proposals on the delegation of powers to district collectors and other officers.

Based on its recommendations the cabinet took a few decisions and orders were issued delegating powers of the government to the commissioner, land revenue officers and collectors for the alienation of government lands, delegating powers of collectors to joint collectors in respect of regularization of encroachments and land reforms, nominating joint collectors to various district purchase committees, and so on.

Collectors were given financial powers to engage private agencies to execute works they deemed necessary. Substantial delegation of financial powers has been effected in the irrigation department. Engineers and chief engineers can sanction works costing much larger amounts than they could sanction before.

Finally there is the business of rules. In this country, most rules and regulations are outdated. Nobody knows what the rule is except the concerned clerk. So a revision and updating of these has become fundamental to the administrative reform exercise. Fresh manuals are being prepared containing laws, rules, regulations, codes of conduct, and role definitions. Outdated rules and regulations are being removed. We want to conduct this exercise every year.

Other aspects of slow decision making were considered. Shouldn't the government work harder? Should it have so many holidays? The state government had twenty-five holidays, apart from weekends. In a review exercise we scaled these down to fifteen holidays, carefully retaining religious holidays of every community. The government offered twenty-seven optional holidays, again many of them related to religious observances. These were scaled down to twenty. Government employees are entitled to take any ten of these a year. They could take fifteen days casual leave, we whittled those down to ten. Finally, however, though the exercise was done, the proposed reduction could not be implemented. There were too many sensitivities involved.

5

INNOVATING WITH THE BUREAUCRACY

On the 26th of January 2000 we put out an innocuous-looking white, grey and blue leaflet titled Citizen's Charter of Hyderabad Metropolitan Water Supply and Sewerage Board. Even our most strident critics will have to admit that it represents a quantum leap in the relationship between the government and the citizen in India. It seeks to formalize a contract between the two, which affirms that the citizen has a right to service. This in a country where millions of citizens spend much of their productive time waiting inside or outside government offices for government employees to attend to their requests.

The opening page of this leaflet reads thus: 'The aim and purpose of this Charter of HMWSSB is to confirm publicly the rights that customers, who pay their bills regularly, have in receiving water and sanitation services from the Board and also confirm the standards that the Board has set for itself with regard to providing services to its customers, stating the customers' obligations.' This charter came into effect from 26 January itself.

It lists the services to be provided by the board, and the minimum and maximum redressal time for each. If there is no water supply it has to be restored within three days. If it is not restored at the end of the second day the customer will be supplied 250 litres per connection per day by tanker until it is restored. It also promises that a new water supply connection will be released by the board within thirty working days from the date of payment of connection fee in full.

Similarly the charter lists the customer's obligations: to pay water bills promptly, to not tamper with the water meter, to not dump building material near sewer manholes, and so on.

After the charter was initiated the number of complaints being recorded by metro customer care increased substantially. The number of complaints redressed within the given time frame also increased. But with the increase in complaints the efficiency in percentage terms went down initially. The board has now initiated ways of improving its performance. There has also been a sharp increase in applications for water connections, and in the number sanctioned.

Similar citizen's charters for other services are being introduced in stages. The one for the municipal corporations in the cities of Andhra Pradesh gives the time frame within which citizens can expect garbage cleaning, or removal of carcasses, or the issuing of birth and death certificates. It details the names and office and residence phone numbers of the officials responsible for providing these services.

Governments around the world are looking seriously at improving their efficiency and reform. Some of them have adopted a mission-driven, market-oriented approach treating citizens as customers, others have introduced the concept of citizen's charters in public organizations, which stipulate the standards of service citizens can expect, as also the compensation they will be paid if they do not get it. British Rail's Passenger Charter offers passengers delayed for more than one hour a voucher worth 20 per cent or more of the ticket price.

Our first citizen's charter also breaks new ground in India by pledging a token compensation of Rs 20 to a customer who does not get a service in the time frame stipulated by the citizen's charter. The amount, I stress, is a token one to begin with. It is intended to underline the concept that the ordinary citizen has a right to service from the government, and is entitled to compensation if he or she does not get it.

At the centre of much that is wrong—as well as right—with the government is the bureaucratic framework, starting from the secretary in the secretariat down to the mandal officers in the mandals. Their training and level of motivation and the systems within which they operate have all been put under scrutiny as we tackle administrative reform on an ongoing basis. For instance, in Hyderabad there has even been an extreme case where a government utility has had to be petitioned thirty-nine times in eight months just to give a bill so that the citizen could pay the utility what he owed it!

When there are enough committees working on something, at the very least you end up identifying the problem. We found that there were several, so a gamut of responses was called for. A central problem was accountability, or the lack of it. It affected both service delivery and productivity. If the government has to become genuinely accountable, its systems of working have to be examined for inadequacies and flaws.

Do these systems have accountability built into them? Do they leave too much to discretion? Do they offer enough incentives for performance and disincentives for non-performance? Both inefficiency and corruption can be reduced if correctives are brought into the system.

Towards this end certain interventions are being made in the state. These involve procedural reforms, including reforms in the tendering process, transfer policy reforms, and specific measures to remove discretion from the decision-making process.

Discretionary powers are a fount of corruption and misuse, yet discretion is allowed in all sorts of government processes. When you recruit teachers or doctors and have an interview as part of the recruitment process, you are leaving room for discretion. Solution? Drop the interview requirement and recruit strictly on the basis of marks. We are doing this in respect of both teachers and doctors. And the process has been made completely transparent.

On the day that the recruitment is to take place for doctors, candidates come, look at the list of vacancies displayed, and apply for the posts on the spot, giving their MBBS marks. The selection committee processes these applications and appointments are announced then and there as their forms are processed and the selections are made. Earlier it could take up to a month for a selected doctor to get his orders.

Discretion was also part of the government transfer process. People are willing to pull strings at the very highest level to avoid a transfer. The system of transfers by counselling was evolved because even as chief minister I was subject to pulls and pressures by all and sundry: thousands of requests for favourable decisions regarding postings used to come in.

Counselling means drawing up a marking system on the basis of which applicants for transfers are awarded points according to quantifiable criteria. Committees are set up according to laid down norms, and these then execute transfers on the basis of the points earned by each candidate. As it turned out, everybody it seemed, had a relative who was being transferred to a place he did not want to go to. How we eliminated discretion from the transfer process and how counselling works is described later in this chapter.

In undertaking a massive road widening exercise in Hyderabad without paying compensation in cash, the question of discretionary powers again came up. We gave people who surrendered land for the road widening compensation in kind. The chief minister used to have the powers to allow changes of land use, and to raise the heights of buildings. I delegated these powers to the commissioner subject to the condition that he could only exercise these powers for road widening.

Wherever a road was to be widened we asked for sacrifice of horizontal property and allowed vertical construction. If people gave up a 1000 square feet, they were allowed to construct a 1000 square feet vertically. The commissioner was also given the authority to convert land use from residential to commercial.

We also tackled the discretionary practices prevalent in the matter of building regulations and floor space index rules. This was one area we identified for comprehensive changes and proper rationalization. It was found that the existing system had a lot of scope for subjectivity, discretion, delays, misuse and corruption.

A white paper on the proposed regulations on FSI (floor space index) or FAR (floor area ratio) was prepared and placed in the Andhra Pradesh assembly in September 1996. Suggestions were sought across the board: from residential associations, builders and real estate developers, engineers and town planners, architects, legislators, the media, and organizations like the Housing Board, Metro Board and State Electricity Board.

In 1998 the new FSI policy came into effect. Its main purpose was to make the process of granting building permission simple, quick, transparent and people friendly, with no discretion for anyone. Issuing permissions for building was made quick and time bound. Applications had to be disposed of in fifteen days for individual residential buildings and thirty days for other buildings.

The new policy laid down the new FSI rules and allowed for no discretion, choice or option to anyone in authority, including the government. No requests for relaxations of

FAR or zoning regulations were to be considered by the government, which simply gave up its discretionary powers. While doing so it rationalized and introduced comprehensive changes in the existing regulations. It removed the height restriction on the construction of buildings and liberalized the provisions for allowing multi-level parking. It was decided that change of land use cases would be taken up by the government once a year.

Transfers are a necessary evil in the government. They become necessary because vacancies arising from promotion and retirement have to be filled. But there are some postings that are more desirable than others, and people use influence and bribes to get these. They also use influence to resist transfers to places they do not want to go to, with the result that regions of the country—particularly tribal areas—that desperately need good administrators seldom get them.

Those officers and staff who want to enhance their income also display considerable enterprise in organizing transfers for themselves to the well-lubricated departments, such as transport or commercial taxes. We thought it worth our while to try and bring some method, transparency and linkage with performance into the area of transfers.

Our effort to systematize transfers began with rural schools, which were invariably short of teachers because they wanted to be in the cities or near their families. When it yielded results, we began to apply a system called 'transfers by counselling' to other departments as well.

Transfers need to be based on clearly defined parameters, and when we undertook to develop these we consulted those groups with a stake in the issue: the different service associations. For instance, when we introduced a system of performance-oriented transfers and postings in the forest department, we did so after taking the views of the AP Forest Officers' Association, the Forest Range Officers' Association, the non-gazetted officers' union and other relevant unions.

In arriving at a candidate's total marks due consideration is given to length of service in various wings of the department, to whether husband and wife are working in the same department, to past performance in respect of achievement targets, and marks are deducted for past punishments that might have been given to the candidate.

But the maximum importance is given to performance. A performance evaluation pro forma is prepared by the relevant department. A forest ranger who is employed on raising plantations would get a hundred marks in his counselling pro forma if the survival of saplings in his range was more than 90 per cent, and twenty-five marks if it was between 25 and 50 per cent. He would get negative marking for punishments imposed, or for acts of negligence such as unreported encroachment of forests.

Government orders have been issued in respect of those departments which have already switched to this method of conducting transfers and they anticipate eventualities such as two applicants with the same marks applying for the same posting.

The third initiative which has begun to yield some results is the attempt at wide-ranging reforms in the tendering process. In India the state is a compulsive builder, constructing projects that take decades to complete, raising buildings which are unaesthetic and poorly constructed, and laying roads that forever need to be relaid. All infrastructure construction having been in the public domain, state governments plough a substantial part of their budgets into public works that are substandard in execution and run into massive cost overruns. The experience in AP was no different.

We had projects that were begun in the 1970s and completed in the 1990s. We had contractors undervaluing bids in order to bag contracts and then sending in escalation demands or abandoning the works midway. They often went to the extent of bidding 50 per cent less than the value of the contract. Of course they also did the opposite: inflating bids to as much as 150 per cent more than their actual value to make money on a contract.

There were inadequacies in existing procedures which resulted in the collusion of contractors at the time of submitting tenders, the work they did was of poor quality, often works were abandoned after the profitable portion had been completed, and the whole process was replete with litigation and malpractices. It was an area of governance that was crying out for comprehensive reform. Even contractors were eager to see changes in the system.

We decided to examine the whole area of tender reform, and identify the loopholes with which the process of tendering was ridden. And we decided that in attempting to streamline the procedures of sanctioning and tendering we would involve all concerned: engineers and officials as well as builders and contractors. We began by setting up an inter-departmental committee which came up with a set of recommendations. These were then discussed, and concerned ministers of the government presided over a meeting of builders and contractors with the technical people of all the concerned departments participating. Following this interaction the recommendations were further modified.

Cost overruns are in considerable measure due to the fact that the land acquisition is often not complete when the project is started. The delays that result often hurt both the builders and the government. We decided to make project implementation and approval a two-stage process whereby the permission for work to begin would not be given until all preliminary procedures including land acquisition were complete.

Then we did something that had not been done before: we introduced a process of registration for contractors, classifying them according to the monetary value of works they were competent to execute. We enhanced these limits, which had not been revised since 1984. We also started a process of reviewing contractors to weed out and blacklist those who had defaulted or adopted unethical practices. Among the more colourful practices indulged in was that of burning tender boxes or pouring acid into them to destroy competitive bids.

To safeguard the interests of the government we put in clauses in the tender schedules that provided for bank guarantees in the case of discount tenders, at the rate of 50 per cent of the differential between the estimated contract value and the tendered contract value. Rates for different works were fixed, no price negotiations were permitted, thereby eliminating discretion. The powers of executive engineers and superintending engineers to accord technical sanction were enhanced.

We worked in incentives and disincentives for contractors, awarding merit certificates for timely completion of works that also ensured good quality. Contractors with good records now receive preference at the time of awarding tenders. The entire process has been long and complex, involving protracted negotiations. But the system now has transparency and the number of works being completed on schedule has gone up sharply.

Project by project, we have been able to estimate the crores of rupees saved thanks to reinvited bids within the 15 per cent ceiling. Under the AP III Project it was Rs 8.07 crore, for the six works of the KC Canal it was a savings of Rs 4.08 crore, and for the D Bund of the Telugu Ganga Project the tenders received in the first call were cancelled on grounds of collusion.

A contractor will overbid, his fellow contractors will refrain from putting in competitive bids, and when the government is forced to accept his bid, he will share the profits with his fellow contractors. That used to be the practice. The second time the tenders were submitted for the Telugu Ganga Project they were still not within the 15 per cent ceiling. But the second bill amounted to a soaring of Rs 6.88 crore.

In addition to the exercise of discretion and the lack of accountability, there is the problem of low productivity. The central problem of too much government is not just that there are too many people, it is also that cumulatively they do very little. The notion of security and permanence that is built into a government job in India has been a disincentive to performance.

Because the nature of the work is not contractual, people do not work. A fair amount of disciplinary action is taken within the state government in Andhra Pradesh, but this is more likely to be for acts of commission than omission. The state may penalize an official for misuse of his powers or for proven charges of corruption; proving inefficiency is more difficult.

In the new century, the government will have to continue to provide services which will bring jobs in their wake, and create employment but not necessarily permanent employment. The shift in the latter will have to be to contractual work where the renewal of jobs is linked to performance. It cannot continue to be the government's business to create permanent employment without accountability.

Increasingly, state governments will have to begin examining options to the present permanent tenures of employment. In our state a small but significant beginning has been made in the social welfare department, which manages the residential schools for the scheduled castes. Since 1996-97 the society which runs these schools has stopped appointing teachers to permanent jobs. Instead they are selected on contract basis for one academic year. At the end of the year the performance of the teacher is assessed, and if found satisfactory, an offer of renewal is given. Otherwise it is denied.

These teachers are assessed on a monthly basis on the basis of their punctuality, regularity, coverage of syllabus, classroom preparation and performance of students. Teachers have been made liable for poor results obtained by the students in public examinations.

Until 1998-99, 547 teachers had been appointed on contract basis. Out of these, 477 had their contracts renewed while in 70 cases the contract was terminated. The consensus opinion in the department is that the performance of these contract teachers is better than that of teachers recruited under the old system.

This experiment is relevant for the future because, as was mentioned in the earlier chapter, educational institutions in the state make up the single largest category of government employment. In other areas of government as well, moving to the contract system will have positive implications for cost efficiency and performance levels. If the government employed fewer people it could make them more accountable and pay them better.

Government employment has to become increasingly contractual. We have also made a beginning in Hyderabad city by outsourcing municipal services.

For two decades there was no recruitment for conservancy workers in the Municipal Corporation of Hyderabad, while the city's population rose from 20 to 50 lakh. New colonies came up, the city expanded both horizontally and vertically, traffic increased on the roads, garbage generation increased exponentially. In 1994 a first attempt at privatization was launched and 10 per cent of the area privatized.

In 1996 more colonies were privatized for sweeping and garbage lifting and the extent of privatization of the MCH area went up. By September 1998 it had gone up to 25 per cent. But the systems of privatization we had opted for were not foolproof; both systems had shortcomings. It took us another two months of detailed discussion and deliberation to evolve a satisfactory system whereby a composite contract was given for both material and manpower.

With a contract system you can enforce a degree of accountability. The system of monitoring the privatized services that was worked out envisaged monitoring by both the MCH supervisors and also by citizen's committees. The latter have to certify satisfactory performance; without this certification their bills are not passed. In addition detailed performance indicators have to be met by the system of sweeping and garbage lifting that has been adopted.

There are still areas of the corporation which are served by the regular sanitation employees. The expenditure on the regular establishment is slightly more than on the privatized services.

In my first term I felt it was important to push people personally to deliver. All over the country politicians make inspections at hospitals, government service counters and at public places like markets and roads. The media cynically terms these photo opportunities. I worked suprise public inspections of roads, drains, government offices into my daily routine, insisting on results.

I also insisted that it become part of the routine for senior officers in the secretariat. We expect them to take the lead in ensuring better public sanitation. Regardless of which department they belong to, they are supposed to participate in the clean and green programme and carry out regular inspections. I have been participating in these regularly.

Members of Parliament, MLAs and party leaders are also regularly expected to participate in cleanliness drives.

The idea is to send the message all the way down the system that people in the government, from the lowliest karamchari to the head of department, are expected to perform the jobs given to them. If cleaning drains is somebody's responsibility, he has to do it. The same is true of cleaning offices. And if clearing files that come to him as quickly as possible is the job of a section officer, he has to do it. If he does not he may be suspended.

Reform has to start from the top. From 1998 we experimented with asking secretaries in the secretariat to fill in pro formas looking at how they spend their time in office. But having generated a lot of pro formas we did not have time or manpower at the senior level to process them. However, it was a useful exercise for the officers themselves inasmuch as they could see how they had spent their time. They found that they were spending an inordinate amount of their time in meetings.

We are devising fresh systems for grading people on their performance. While it is easier to assess a head of department, for whom you can have clear performance parameters, it is not that simple to assess the performance of a secretary who provides guidance and motivation to his department. How do we measure whether he has motivated them enough?

The Government of India's rule is that the confidential reports of government officers should be kept secret from them, but it is now our thinking that every month or every quarter the senior officer should talk to officers whose CR he writes, and discuss with them his assessment of their work, so that the officers will have some idea of what is going into their CR.

The system so far has also not devised a way of making people accountable for inaction. If a field officer did not visit all the villages in his area he was not penalized for it. On the other hand, if he was enthusiastic in implementing a decision that affected somebody important adversely he was victimized. The message that went out was that it was safer to do nothing.

While the process of ensuring accountability began in the rural areas with Janmabhoomi (see chapter 13) in 1997, in the year 2000 we are taking up the issue of accountability in the urban areas. We are working on a system whereby the heads of public utilities such as the municipal corporation or water supply or police will have to take complaints and queries from the public and answer them over a cable TV channel once a week.

The commissioner of police, Hyderabad, has made a beginning. The district collectors of Chittoor and Anantpur have also begun to answer questions from the public over cable television. In the US, cable television broadcasts meetings of the local town council. That is another innovation we will consider emulating.

Increasingly, in the new millennium, public administrators will operate in an environment which is significantly different from the top-down approach of the past. Furthermore, increased citizen pressure for a responsive government will result in greater citizen participation, in a bottom-up approach where communities and neighbourhoods have a voice in determining how public funds are allocated. This is a worldwide trend. Both elected representatives and officials of the administration will be required to participate in a policy-making process in which citizens are included in the discussion on public policies.

Such a model of government may result in a loss of control and power for elected representatives and appointed administrators. Nevertheless, the plus point is that greater community involvement may result in more responsive policy making and, more important, better implementation.

In my second term as chief minister I have accelerated efforts at systemic change. It will take time, but new systems are being put in place, and some of them are already beginning to deliver. Whatever changes we initiate, we do so after an elaborate consultation process. That is necessary for acceptance. There will still be strikes; however, if we have consulted all sections of society, public opinion will be on our side.

At the beginning of the government's second consecutive

term in October 1999 I convened a meeting of all class one officers in Hyderabad. Over two hours, with members of the state cabinet present, we listened to bureaucrats suggest ways of improving ongoing programmes.

We solicited ideas and fresh approaches to old problems. Several officers got up to suggest improvements and solutions which ranged from innovations in present practices to a stress upon better use of resources. Waste, in the government system, is enormous. A number of suggestions emerged from this meeting. Someone proposed that for Janmabhoomi to be effective at the grassroots you need a resource group to evaluate it constantly, look at ways to link it with other programmes at the village level, and conduct action research on effective decentralization.

Another proposed that the empowerment of women in Andhra Pradesh would be more effective if there was a mahila shakti campaign that consciously disempowered men at the same time time, starting from Hyderabad down to the grassroots level.

A forest service official suggested that the present concept of joint forest management, which is confined to degraded forest land, should be extended to the 2.5 million hectares of government wasteland in the state. Somebody else suggested that with some Rs 4000 to 5000 crore of funds flowing into the state for non-governmental organizations, there was need for an institutionalized mechanism such as a state coordination cell to work with NGOs to eliminate duplication of effort between NGOs and the government. There was also a suggestion that bureaucrats should be retrained as social workers. And that there should be multi-functional roles so that people in one department could give ideas arising from their experience to other departments.

A bureaucrat made the pertinent point that centrally sponsored schemes today work out guidelines that are so detailed that they leave no flexibility to the states. They tell you exactly how much money to spend on what component of the programme. And if you do not adhere to these because they are not practicable, audit objections are raised at the local level. Sanctioned staff also remained after the programme was wound up, adding to the state government's bloated wage bills. He felt that while the Central government might have a vested interest in seeing that states implement programmes in the Centre's way, it would be more practicable for it to give greater autonomy to states to implement these programmes.

A senior officer felt that the system of checkposts run by the transport department should be abolished, since these led to a great deal of corruption and the tarnishing of the government's reputation. He also suggested that the state transport department should revamp its bus routes, which currently left 60 per cent of district routes unserved. In some cases, though the road network had grown considerably, the routes had not been revised in more than thirty years. In the same vein, another officer suggested that if more villages were linked with buses the quality of panchayati raj administration could be improved.

Another bureaucrat talked about wasteful expenditure in the secretariat: waste of lights, power, fans, air-conditioning and geysers. The government consumes a phenomenal amount of energy and wastes much of it. It also wastes a great deal of paper. His estimate was that 4000 to 5000 tonnes of paper was consumed annually in a government department alone, and many trees could be saved if such waste could be averted.

He also pointed out that 40 to 50 per cent of human consumption of water was for flushing toilets, and urban society ought to follow the lead of countries in Europe which had redesigned their systems to ensure that bath and kitchen water were recycled for flushing toilets.

Other suggestions concerned the more efficient use of

natural gas that is presently being flared in the state, as fuel. The suggestions both demonstrated the range of activities that governance today encompasses and the capacity for critical inputs that a thinking officer can have. I took notes because my government puts a premium on ideas. They will serve the government better than greater financial resources. We have already attempted to implement many innovative ideas in the state and we would like to continue doing so. We have planned to hold such meetings on a quarterly basis.

Inevitably effective administrative reform has to mean a degree of introspection on the part of the bureaucracy and the political class regarding their respective roles. A study on the Indian Administrative Service has shown that its officers's perception of themselves was considerably at variance with the perception of other professionals working with them. 'IAS Profiles', a study conducted by P. Singh and R. Bhandarkar in 1994, looked at this question of perception. A total of 289 IAS officers from ten states were interviewed. The category of non-IAS persons interviewed included politicians, police officers, technocrats and others.

The difference in viewpoint was illuminating. Sixty-one per cent of IAS officers thought of themselves as action- and result-focussed, but only around 32 per cent of the others saw these qualities in them. While 67 per cent saw themselves as being of intellectually high calibre, only 23 per cent of the others thought so of them. Sixty-nine per cent of the others saw IAS officers as being focussed on their own career, but the IAS officers had a more charitable view of themselves: only 21.54 per cent of them thought this was their primary concern. Fifty-two per cent of the IAS officers thought of themselves as innovative and creative, only 9 per cent of the others saw them that way. While 54 per cent of the others thought the IAS officers were arrogant as a tribe, only 19 per cent of those in the service thought so.

In the book *Governance and the IAS*, written by an IAS

officer, R.K. Dhar, the writer concludes that while stepping into the next millennium the IAS has to 'transform its stance from being power-focussed to service-focussed. The country has to shift from governance through regulation and control to enabling forms of development administration, from a planned to a liberalized economic system, from maintenance of the status quo to the catalysing of change—in short from rowing to steering.' That is indeed well put.

Where politicians are concerned we do not even have any systematic data on how they perceive themselves, or whether, collectively, they feel any need to improve their conduct and performance. Bureaucrats and politicians are the human resources of a government. They have to be constantly motivated and trained. If all my ministers are more efficient the total state will be transformed. There are more than thirty ministers, 294 MLAs, and 641 officers from the all-India services. If all these eight or nine hundred people work with sincerity and if you manage resources with utmost efficiency, you can do wonders.

In Andhra Pradesh intensive training has been taken up for both bureaucrats and politicians, and government procedures and manuals are being reviewed and revamped. The state government is training all levels of bureaucracy and the Telugu Desam Party is systematically training its own cadres. Both the government and the party have to come up with creative solutions for better governance in the new millennium.

6

INFORMATION TECHNOLOGY
IN GOVERNANCE

For every task that needs to be done in the government, industry or in the social sector, there are two ways of doing it. The conventional way, and a better way. Finding the latter is the challenge.

In 1998, during a drive to Tirupati, a ministerial colleague hit upon an idea which we had not thought of before. Why not computerize the process of having a darshan of Lord Venkateshwara, he said, and let people book slots so that they don't have to wait for many hours in hopelessly long queues? It was an excellent idea.

I thought about it and I didn't see why it could not be done. Think of the harassment it would save the millions of people who come to Tirumala on pilgrimage each year.

When they arrived in Tirumala they could go and book a darshan timing, and then be free to look around the town until their turn came. We decided to implement it.

Today visitors go to a counter and get a bar-coded wristband which tells them what their time slot is and puts in identification details. They can go around the place and come back just in time for the darshan and identify themselves. Now that the State Wide Area Network has come up in Andhra Pradesh, providing digital connectivity throughout the state, it will soon be possible for people within the state to book their darshan timings before they leave home.

Information technology in government is about finding a better, more efficient and faster way of doing the same things. The world is changing around us; if we don't change with it we will get left behind. In the last four and a half years we have focussed on information and communication technologies (ICTs) because I strongly believe that they are indispensable for the future.

My logic is simple. What you think of as a luxury today, will become a necessity tomorrow, and that applies to all the latest technologies available. Particularly information technology. It will provide better service, better governance, better facilities, better comfort. Even the critics who carp today will find their time better spent in the near future when IT-enabled conveniences take the drudgery out of their encounters with government service counters.

The Andhra Pradesh state government has an older history of office computerization than many others, with computers already being used in some departments at the beginning of the 1980s. At this point computers were just seeping into the private sector. Today, the state can boast of having probably the largest computer presence internally inside government departments. This is making it easier for us to move over to the next level of service.

The concept of Hi-Tec City was also at the planning stage before I became chief minister. What we have done subsequently is to build on what already existed and draw up a structured framework for making the state a premier IT centre of India. The goal is both to make it a hub for the IT industry, as well as a hub for developing electronic governance applications. We have entered the race late in the first instance but are catching up fast. Where electronic governance is concerned we have been first movers.

This chapter is about electronic governance. To make it possible enabling processes are being put in place, and a dedicated group of enablers within the government is being created. The state government is identifying, training and motivating a highly committed set of officers who will combine understanding of technology with a high level of expertise.

The basic requirement is an overall IT architecture which should be defined early on. This ensures consistency and inter-operability of the databases of different government agencies and departments, with open standards being adopted as far as possible. All databases requiring distributed access will be web-enabled.

A Central Data Repository together with Government Information Locater Services will be set up to provide information support to citizens, as well as public and private agencies. All Acts, rules, regulations, manuals and government orders are being digitized in order to ensure electronic access. And base maps of the state have been digitized to ensure uniform adoption by government departments and agencies.

The success of the electronic government initiative will depend upon the training and motivation of personnel. We are revamping the training programmes for government employees to familiarize them with information technology. We have now set up a training facility in the Dr Marri Chenna Reddy Human Resources Development Institute of Andhra Pradesh where everyone, from ministers and secretaries down to section officers, has to undergo computer training.

Apart from familiarizing people with computers, change management skills will be needed to address issues which will arise with the induction of IT. We are working on this too. This is important because the idea is to use IT not just to automate processes but also as a strategic tool to simplify procedures and revamp processes. Meanwhile, to guarantee citizens quality services we are working on citizen's charters which will spell out the standards of service government departments are expected to maintain. These will be electronically available.

At the core of electronic governance will be a range of citizen services made possible through value-added network services. Some of these have already gone on-stream. To distil my own experience and that of my state government in the last four or five years, I would say that there are four dimensions to using information and communication technologies in government. The first is personal: it is an invaluable tool for a head of government. It enables him to keep track of different sectors, get feedback and suggestions from people who have no access to him, and it enables him to seek relevant information on the Internet.

The second application is for citizen-related services, saving people a good deal of harassment in their day-to-day dealings with the government. The third is to use IT as a tool within the government. It helps you process decisions faster, helps you see where the money is going and how your schemes are working, and it helps you do away with the conventional inter-departmental baggage—piles of files that gather dust and peons who carry them up and down corridors and floors when they could be more gainfully employed elsewhere.

The fourth application we have evolved in our state is the use of IT for planning, for creating a citizen database and for monitoring land use in conjunction with remote sensing.

Once the data is available many applications are possible. I shall describe what we are doing in Andhra Pradesh in each of these categories.

Why does a chief minister need information technology

to help him function? Because the dimensions of the job have changed over the years. The government has grown a great deal in size and almost every sector of it is in crisis. The flow of resources that an administration needs to function with can no longer be taken for granted. A chief minister has to personally set targets for revenue earning departments such as commercial tax, excise, transport and motor vehicles tax and push for them to be met. He cannot do so unless he has performance data at his fingertips.

The power sector is in crisis and since power is so critical to the functioning of every sector, close monitoring from the top is necessary to ensure that outages and transmission losses are minimized. Besides, each chief minister has his individual style of functioning. I have been accused of running an overcentralized administration and being far too hands-on, personally supervising schemes in the districts by interacting with collectors on a daily basis.

I believe this kind of overseeing is necessary to set the tone of the administration. There have been decades of laxity that have to be made up for. There is no institutionalized system of accountability yet in the administration, though we are working to introduce this. In its absence I have chosen to personally enforce accountability. The officers may not like it, but my first obligation is to the people of my state.

I have on my personal monitoring system 132 categories under which information is continually updated. Eleven of these pertain to the state electricity board. By personally tracking every aspect of generation and distribution I have been able to ensure better availability of power to farmers during the sowing season, and to students at examination time. During such periods when availability of power is critical the number of teleconferences we have on power with district collectors is stepped up. At these, officials from AP Transco and the department of energy are present, the different collectors explain the times at which they want power, we tell them what the availability position is, and we coordinate it on the spot.

Tracking water levels in the state reservoirs is another sector of information which has served a crucial function during past monsoons. We were actually able to determine the optimum trade off between generating hydro power and meeting irrigation needs.

To ensure availability of food to the poorest and to keep track of food prices so that they do not spiral out of control I track eight categories of information under civil supplies. I also receive incoming revenue information under six categories from finance and planning. Many of the items on my computer in my office at home may not require daily reviewing, but they help me check the veracity of occasional media reports on those sectors. I also keep track of projects for which we have received loans that have to be repaid with interest. I want the officials implementing these to set their targets on a daily basis.

Covering up poor performance is less possible when the chief minister has an efficient data retrieval system at his fingertips. One day I noticed that the plant load factor in the Rayalseema Thermal Power Project was unusually low. When I asked why I was told by a quick-thinking officer that the unit was designed for high calorie coal whereas what they were actually getting was low calorie coal. I then scanned the pif for that unit in the past months and found that on a particular day the plant load factor had been as high as 84 per cent. Where did you get the coal from on that day, I asked them. There was silence. The truth is that this unit gets its coal from only one source. Obviously the poor performance was not related to coal supply.

Similarly, during a review meeting of commercial tax officers I asked one of them why his performance was poor. He said there had been a cyclone in his area and all the coconut trees had been damaged. I looked at the commodity break-up for his circle and found that coconuts did not even figure in the top ten commodities for this circle. I told him that. Silence again.

In addition to the items on the chief minister's information system, important issues that appear in the print and electronic media each day are computerized by the information and public relations department every morning for my use. I treat the press as an important avenue of receiving feedback on the performance of my administration. I begin my working day each morning at 6.30 a.m. by reviewing the updates on my computer, but not more than an hour is spent on this.

How much administrative work do I do on computers? Not much as yet, but I have asked the department of industries to develop a work-flow automation application. This will use Lotus Notes software and will enable online movement of files, recording of views and issue of orders. My secretariat is also working to put in place a system which will enable me to use e-mail to communicate instructions to departments on action to be taken regarding news items appearing in the media.

I have been using e-mail from the early days in my tenure as chief minister. We set up a website which invites people to e-mail me. I receive a vast number of messages each day. Initially the bulk was from non-resident Indians of Andhra origin who were excited by the initiatives our government was taking. But increasingly these are also from people in India and in the state. I find this is the most rewarding aspect of e-mail. It transcends the security barrier between a leader and his people.

People in the districts have begun to e-mail me with their complaints as well as feedback. One of the farmer's committees of the water users associations used e-mail to complain to me about their president. I am very keen to give a thrust to the development of digital content in Telugu, because once we have electronic kiosks all over the state from which people can communicate in the language they know, they will be able to ventilate their grievances directly to their representatives, whether it is the chief minister or members of Parliament or members of the legislative assembly.

Industrialists in the state and elsewhere in the country who want to draw my attention to certain issues also use e-mail. I am not able to reply to individual messages but there is a cell for electronic correspondence in my office which scans and responds to all the mails I receive, bringing a number of them to my attention. Often we receive ideas from people across the world, which are duly noted.

I am fascinated by the Internet, particularly by the wealth of information on it. Heading as I do a state which has a long cyclone-prone coastline, I discovered early on that I could even use the Net to track cyclonic storms in the Bay of Bengal. It enabled me to push my administration into taking preparatory action.

The Internet has also been an invaluable resource in the entire exercise of undertaking administrative reform in Andhra Pradesh. As a firm believer in borrowing ideas on best practices evolved anywhere in the world, I urged the Vision 2020 team to use the Internet extensively to obtain such information while drafting the document. In the formative stages of making plans for revitalizing the government my bureaucrats download reports on modernizing the government for my use.

My secretariat also uses the Internet to equip me with information relevant to meetings with diplomats or representatives of companies interested in doing business in Andhra Pradesh. I like to make Power Point presentations for my interactions with specific sectors: it makes for targeted and focussed communication. The Internet is a good resource for researching facts and figures to highlight points we wish to make. I am aware that this is not the mode of communication usually followed by governments within the country, but as these governments assume the role of modern-day organizations they too will have to present a businesslike face to the world.

The Andhra Pradesh government uses the Internet in down-to-earth, practical ways. Apart from the official state government website www.andhrapradesh.com, departments have their individual websites. We use the web to post tender notices, pro formas, departmental news, information about water levels in reservoirs, and circulars and government orders. The Andhra Pradesh Pollution Control Board posts industry standards and guidelines on its websites. It gives information about pollution control technologies, uses the web to register public complaints against polluting units, and posts the status of complaints received.

These then are the applications of information technology that a head of government can use in his/her personal capacity.

What are those which the citizen can use? Where he or she is concerned, information technology boils down to one word which the citizen understands: convenience. What we are attempting is a fundamental change in the way people interact with the government: the harassment, the queues, the bribes.

People come into contact with the government when they need birth, death or registration certificates, when they have to pay taxes, obtain land records, register deeds or apply for passports, or when they have to apply for permits and licences. More often than not, they dread the contact. In Andhra Pradesh we've decided that the citizen should be made the focus of information technology applications in the government.

IT can provide what good governance needs: speed, efficiency, transparency, consistency and reliability. It can smoothen the interface citizens and business have with the government, by making the latter more responsive. With information technology it becomes possible to improve internal efficiencies, integrate services, and to introduce new services. Some applications have already gone on-stream in the state.

One of the first citizen oriented applications was the computerization of the registration and stamps department. People come here to get their immovable properties valued, to register sale deeds and then pay the stamp duty on sales. They come to register property transactions, and obtain non-encumbrance certificates. They also come to register societies, firms, chit funds, and non-trading companies. Statewide, this department services some 50 lakh citizens a year and earns substantial revenue for the state through stamp duty sales. In 1998-99 gross revenue from it was Rs 650 crore. It employs 4000 people in 387 sub-districts across the state.

In physical terms the logistics of this department amounted to a phenomenal amount of record keeping, and record checking to obtain the details on the basis of which non-encumbrance certificates were issued. It involved queueing up over several days. A registration of a land or property transaction took, on an average, seven days, and may well have entailed a bribe to the clerk to get the job done. Getting a non-encumbrance certificate could take up to five days, and for the clerk doing it, it meant going through cupboardsful of ancient registers to get details of all the transactions that might have taken place over a period of time over a particular piece of property.

In August 1996 we decided to computerize the entire process, throughout the state, at some 387 sub-registrars's offices. Some straightforward objectives were set: to demystify the registration procedure, to enhance the speed and reliability of the system, to provide transparency in valuation, to replace the copying and filing system with imaging, to preserve the documents on CDs, and to automate all back-office functions. Above all, the purpose was to smoothen the citizen–government interface.

The project took fifteen months to implement. It involved transferring all the existing records to electronic databases, training some 1,600 personnel (many of whom had never handled computers before) and using project management techniques to effect the transition. The project was divided into tasks and sub-tasks, and outside agencies such as NIIT (National Institute of Information Technology) and NIC (National Informatics Centre) enrolled as major partners. Altogether twenty-six private agencies were involved in procuring the software and hardware and getting the project off the ground. The computerized application was renamed CARD: Computer-Aided Administration of Registration Department.

We tried to quantify the effort in terms of man-years. The software development took eight man-years, site preparation twenty-five, training seventy-six man-years and data entry 500 man-years, that is, it would have taken one skilled person that much time to accomplish these tasks! The same men and women who used to manually enter data and process applications were retrained to do the entire process electronically, including the scanning of documents. The project went on-stream in November 1998. A registration process that used to take up to a week, now takes one hour. The clutter is gone. In one sub-registrar's office in Hyderabad, a single CD, representing 500 registrations, sits in a steel cupboard that is otherwise empty. Back-up copies of all CDs are stored at the district registrar's office.

CARD now provides a transparent method of valuation of properties and calculation of stamp duties. It simplifies registration procedures. It enhances the speed, reliability and consistency of the system. Scanning of documents has replaced copying. The manual systems of copying, indexing and accounting have given way to a state-of-the-art document management system. And there has been a sea change in the ease with which documents can be retrieved and copies made available. The service is invaluable because of its reliability. Nowadays the quality of record keeping has deteriorated, since people are less meticulous. This project does electronic verification of transactions in order to issue the non-encumbrance certificate, effortlessly, for everybody, all the time.

In the first phase 249 out of 387 offices have been computerized. Anywhere in the state today a man or woman who walks in to register a document encounters a transformed environment. We ran a campaign to build up public awareness. People were told to go straight to the counter, to avoid brokers, and to question the department in the case of nonfulfilment of a commitment. I am consciously raising the expectations citizens have from the system. Convenience is a drug on which once hooked, they will not settle for less. And thanks to information technology, the services can be centrally monitored.

There has been a measurable change in the time taken to deliver the same service in CARD offices compared to non-CARD offices. Registering deeds used to take three days, now it takes sixty minutes. Encumbrance certificates that used to take from one to five days to prepare now take ten minutes. Certified copies of documents which used to take three days to issue can be done in fifteen minutes. A market value check slip used to take an hour to issue. Now it takes ten minutes. Sale of stamp paper used to take thirty to sixty minutes. This has come down to fifteen to thirty minutes. The system provides several layers of security and back-up.

Our future objectives are to introduce the Telugu version of the CARD software and network these centres so that records for any town can be obtained without actually going there. The AP State Wide Area Network (APSWAN) which has now been commissioned and which will be discussed later in this chapter, will make such networking possible.

Once it is linked up, you can disaggregate point of delivery of service from point of performance of service. Eventually, we intend to add to the convenience of the citizen by actually putting the registration process on the Internet.

The service charges fees according to transactions and is independent of treasury support. The project cost Rs 18 crore to implement.

■

To innovate in this country you require more than resources: you require political courage. Go beyond ideology and talk technology and the opposition bears down upon you thick and fast, hurling accusations of wastefulness, of misplaced priorities, and of producing a white elephant. It happened with Hi-Tec City, it has happened with APSWAN and will doubtless happen with the Knowledge Park. You have to try to convince those opposing the changes and stay your course. Ultimately the citizen is the best judge of what we are attempting.

Apart from executing the transformation of registration services described above, we had also planned similar transformation of twenty commonly needed citizen services by computerizing them. Apvan.com was to have been a joint venture between the state government and a consortium of Singapore companies to offer online services such as the payment of electricity, water and telephone bills, and issue driving licences.

It proposed a major innovation: the concept of anytime, anywhere government services. It would allow citizen–government transactions at a convenient time or place throughout the day and year, as opposed to the existing system of transacting business with government departments only during office hours. It would usher in non-stop 24-hour government.

It also proposed to integrate services, which again is a powerful new concept. Millions of Indians spend as many man-hours each year queueing in front of one government window after another. If you want to get a driver's licence you have to go to a transport authority, but that office will require documents for which you have to go to another government office. Through Apvan.com we envisioned cross-departmental integration of information which would provide a one-stop interface for all transactions between the citizen and the government. A single window to interact with all the government services available. This would increase the convenience of citizens enormously. A change of address provided to one government department would be automatically incorporated in the databases of other departments without the need for multiple correspondence.

Apvan was to begin operation with the Twin Cities Integrated Network Services which was called TWINS. In the summer of 1999 it ran into opposition from worker unions. Employees threatened to go on strike fearing heavy retrenchment. The assembly elections were just four or five months away and the opposition parties fuelled fears of redundancies in government employment. We had repeatedly tried to assure the unions that there would be no retrenchment, but they would not be placated. We gave the unions a commitment that we would not force it down their throats.

TWINS was to begin with a pilot project in Banjara Hills which would facilitate the payment of utility bills and the obtaining of certificates, permits and licences. Though we put the joint venture called Apvan.com on hold until after the elections we went ahead with the pilot project on our own. By the end of the year we had it up and running. On Road No 7 in Banjara Hills, you can walk into a small building and experience a qualitative difference in the kind of citizen–government interaction offered. We call it an integrated citizen service centre.

It is sparkling clean, fully air-conditioned, and there are no queues. You pick up an electronically generated token number and sit down in the waiting area. When the token display flashes your number you go to the counter it indicates. You fish out all the bills you want to pay and the person at the counter processes them. All the counters handle all the services offered. It operates on Web server-based technology with a central hub and a Web server linking it to as many departments as the applications covered require.

At the Banjara Hills pilot the following applications are operational: payment of electricity, water and property tax bills, issuance of birth, death and caste and vehicle registration certificates, and renewal of driving licences. Eventually a range of information and facilitation services will also be offered. This service centre works on two shifts and is open from 7 a.m. to 9 p.m. It may have operational glitches, but it is light years removed from the inhospitable ambience of government payment counters all over the country.

Apvan.com was to extend the TWINS model to the rest of the state. The concept is that eventually the point of delivery of a government service or its front end can be anywhere. It could be electronic kiosks or it could be cable TV or even a hand-held device or cellular phone. It could be manned or unmanned service terminals. It could be dial-up Internet access. Or it could be an ideal combination of any of these.

The apprehension in the mind of the government employees was that the back-end, which is the point of decision regarding a service, would be taken away from them. But that is not the case at all. Apvan was just going to provide a secure, reliable, and controlled interface between the departments and the citizens through a network. Even without forming the joint venture we have envisioned we are going ahead with the concept.

Are such innovations just for the urban elite? No, certainly not. The following rural services are to be offered and are indeed already operational: land registration, utility payments and commercial taxes. The roll-out plan of the project envisages that by the third year the services will be penetrating almost 70 per cent of the state. By year four onwards, the entire state is to be covered.

Has the transition to electronic delivery of citizen services meant an abrupt end to the culture of corruption and bribes? Probably not everywhere in the rural areas. Nevertheless, as the public sees how easy it has become now for the same job to be done it will be increasingly reluctant to give bribes. I expect our party cadres to educate people on this issue. Before long the existing culture of corruption will dry up, because with automated services the demand for a bribe will no longer be possible to sustain. As for urban centres like TWINS, which has twenty service counters in a row in an open hall, demanding a bribe for a service done becomes virtually impossible.

Apvan, when we are able to implement it in its full form, will deal a major body blow to corruption. It will mean, for instance, the computerization of all transport checkpoints, which will increase our revenue collections and reduce leakage. I want to reiterate that information and communication technologies bring transparency, accountability, and removal of discretion. Misuse and wastage will become less. Corruption will be eliminated.

■

The third facet of our experience so far is putting IT to use in the running of the government. And here too, the investment is worth it. In terms of cost, we may spend 5 per cent of the budget, but in some cases as much as 50 per cent of the budget for development expenditure is now wasted. There is no accountability. Today with information technology we can analyse where we have spent, how we have spent, what are the priorities. That is the advantage.

In 1996-97 we set up the first department of information technology in the country. Just four years into our commitment to bringing IT to bear upon governance we seem to have convinced other state governments by example. Today, even in states like Bihar and Uttar Pradesh, I see politicians and bureaucrats anxious to seek some of the advantages of this technology for their own states. IT as an idea has more than caught on.

Even as we had launched our statewide area network late in 1999, I read of a new district in Uttar Pradesh, Fatehabad, where a young district collector has put a wide area network in place for his own district, feeding information to his district headquarters from twenty-two sites in the district.

Karnataka is launching many schemes similar to the ones in Andhra Pradesh. Kerala has taken an e-governance initiative which unleashes the power of the Internet on the state's 152 development blocks, through a programme called RD-Net. It enables rural folk to access government data, apply for loans and lodge complaints from their remote villages.

Tamil Nadu and Karnataka have introduced computers in government schools, Goa, Madhya Pradesh and Delhi have IT policies in place—the scenario is certainly very different from just five years ago.

We are working on overcoming the resistance labour unions have shown to our efforts to introduce IT in government. In the case of CARD we simply retrained existing personnel. We are not destroying jobs—we are changing the tools with which people worked.

And finally, we have a genuine commitment to popularizing IT in society at large. Already Hyderabad has a burgeoning cyber parlour culture which has helped to make the use of e-mail a janata phenomenon. People from all walks of life, including women in burqas, walk in, pay ten rupees and send or receive e-mail. In other cities in the country cyber cafes charge by the hour, in Hyderabad they charge a rupee a minute. But this should become true of not just the capital city but also the mandal headquarters.

The IT revolution is not elitist, it is first and foremost of use to the common man, but to drive this point home, we have to make its access easy. How this can be achieved in Andhra Pradesh and elsewhere is our primary concern in our IT policy. CARD and TWINS are an example, but other applications are also being worked upon.

Let me first explain in simple terms what levels of computer networking we are attempting to introduce in the government. Computers with their memory (information storage) devices can be interconnected in an office (called a local area network, LAN); several offices in a city can be interconnected (metropolitan area network, MAN) and several cities can be connected (wide area network, WAN).

The interconnection utilizes telecommunication systems which can be linked by radio or optic fibre cables. The latter can carry vast quantities of information in multi-media at the speed of light, and most inexpensively. It is a technology that is far removed from the speed and efficiency with which the government, with its files and peons and dispatchers, works today. Poor or rich, every society should benefit from it.

Infrastructure for information technology involves broadband connectivity. We are wiring up the state with fibre-optic cable, right down to the mandal level. We would like this to be extended to the village level. The more fibre is installed, the more people in the state can become connected citizens. Some of this connectivity has been created by the Department of Telecom (DOT), but we have also encouraged private sector participation.

What is required is reliable and secure bandwidth. The government requires this for its own multimedia needs: to transfer files between districts and the state government headquarters, for video-conferencing by ministers and bureaucrats at all levels, and for the use of public sector organizations providing citizen services, such as the state road transport corporation, which can provide return booking of journeys.

The private sector will also require this to facilitate teleworking, provide Internet connections, online education and a variety of other services. Small entrepreneurs in the districts should also be able to lease bandwidth for their operations.

Eventually, we hope that farmers who now take their produce to ryotu bazaars will be able to get online information from different bazaars on the prices being offered there—perhaps through kiosks near their villages—so that they can decide which one is offering a better price for the product they want to sell.

The Andhra Pradesh State Wide Area Network was formally inaugurated on 1 November 1999. It is essentially a statewide intranet. Data, voice and video connectivity has been established with all twenty-three districts in the state. By March 2000, 1125 mandals—an administrative unit peculiar only to Andhra Pradesh that covers several panchayats—will also be linked. To make this intranet possible, the Department of Telecommunications has laid more than 20,000 km of optic fibre connecting the mandals to each other and to the district and state headquarters.

The work in various offices, in different cities, towns and panchayat villages is getting computerized. Officials are informed, educated and trained to dispel fear of change. Personal computers in offices are inter-worked in a local area network and the Hyderabad secretariat network with several hundred is the largest.

What has APSWAN cost us? It is a Rs 25 crore 'Build-Own-Operate' work, awarded on the basis of tenders to a private company. The state government has guaranteed on the basis of its traffic, a quarterly payment for five years. We have put no capital in the project and the extra capacity can be used for per-transaction priced applications. Besides, there is provision for a joint venture company should the government opt for it.

The expenditure on infrastructure, maintenance and operation, including staff, are the responsibility of the private company. For the services they provide the state government we will pay Rs 1.10 crore per quarter over a period of five years to the company. This agreement is being adhered to and their obligation is to provide minimum time of 99.99 per cent at the secretariat and 99.90 per cent at each district network centre.

For APSWAN 2MB bandwidth was provided to us free of cost by the Department of Telecommunications. We managed to get this sanctioned at the intervention of Prime Minister Inder Gujral in 1997. I was keen on getting a dedicated network cleared by DOT because it was meant for a pioneering project which was being undertaken for the first time in the country.

As I recall, I spoke to the prime minister when he and I were both attending a meeting at Vigyan Bhavan, and he summoned the officials concerned over there and asked them why it could not be given free of cost. They said they would suffer a loss of revenue.

Upon which Mr Gujral took a decision right there that since this was going to be the first project of its kind in the country money should not come in the way. He asked his officials to issue orders and communicate to Hyderabad that they would be doing it free of cost. We got their communication the same evening. The cost at that point of time of the bandwidth we were asking for was Rs 18 crore. If we had had to pay for it the cost of APSWAN would have been several times what it is now.

In the first phase, work in all the twenty-three district headquarters towns and in Tirupati and Vijaywada is being computerized. The LANs of individual offices (for example, sales tax, revenue, treasury, public distribution system and electricity) within a city are all inter-connected with the collectorate as the district node (DN). This constitutes a MAN (metropolitan area network). Every district node is connected to the state capital, Hyderabad, over an optic fibre communications circuit, to constitute the State Wide Area Network or SWAN.

All the twenty-five nodes are equipped for video conferencing. At short notice, the chief minister, ministers, commissioners and directors in Hyderabad can hold statewide conferences, avoiding travel, time and related expenses; groups of collectors, inspectors general of police; education or electricity or treasury officers can hold discussions by e-mail, or voice telephony, and access vast quantities of information, all simultaneously on the information highway.

What kind of difference will APSWAN make to current government operations? Let us take a few examples. The AP State Financial Corporation is basically a bank which provides credit for industries. Now, industries may be located at Adilabad, or Visakhapatnam, or Chittoor, and the APSFC would service them through branches in these towns. When an industry submits an application at a branch office, the latter has to submit a proposal to the head office at Hyderabad.

Disbursement is not done at Hyderabad, it is done at the branch, which has to disburse the amount and keep track of repayment. The approval therefore goes back to the branch and it disburses the amount. A lot of manual intervention is involved in this process, such as physically tracking the application from the district to Hyderabad, as well as its return journey to the district. And this back and forth part of it takes a lot of time.

With the APSFC having connected its branches to

Hyderabad through our wide area network an application filed at a branch at the district headquarters can at the same moment be forwarded to Hyderabad. The Hyderabad office can take a decision on whether the proposal is all right or not and how much loan amount can be sanctioned. As soon as it is sanctioned it goes to the branch, which means there is a possibility of reducing actual travel time of the application by fifteen to twenty days.

Now take, for example, another application, this one relating to cyclones, which are the scourge of coastal districts in both Andhra and Orissa. The World Bank has given assistance for a Hazard Mitigation Information System which has already been partly implemented in 230 mandals. This uses software which receives information from the satellite as well as from the meteorological department and forecasts what is going to happen in those two to three hours when a cyclone is likely to hit. It can tell you which pockets will be hit, as well as what the inland situation will be. There are various packages available which can tell what is going to happen when a pocket is affected. When it will happen, how many people are going to be affected, what type of crops will be damaged.

Similarly in the case of floods, when the river water is rising, let's say at two centimetres per hour, there are models available which can tell which pockets are going to submerge, and the area that will be affected over the next few hours.

These kinds of forecasting are of a complex nature and difficult to operate at the mandal level or even at the district level. They require data from many sources to come out with the final projection of what is going to happen. So we are planning that the forecasting operation will be at Hyderabad, but the pictures and information will be made available in real time to district collectors through APSWAN. With regard to the level of the river, they can be informed, this is how much it will rise in the next half an hour, this much in the next one hour, and so on.

They can also send us feedback on what is happening in the field in real time. They can tell us: this is my position, the river level now is such and such. And the central operation will do its forecasting on the basis of that data. When you are connected and have the latest information, the quality of decision making will be better.

APSWAN will soon become an invaluable tool for us for in-house administration. Progress reports from every district to headquarters can reach Hyderabad much faster. Andhra Pradesh Technology Services Limited is developing a software for the finance department. All the treasuries are already computerized, but there is no way to communicate the data from the districts to Hyderabad. It comes by floppies or by hard copy or by courier. If they are online to Hyderabad the state government will know its financial position in real time: how much is the outflow, and how much revenue is coming to the government. It helps to manage resources better.

As far as its applications for ordinary people is concerned, one example is the computerization of Tirupati darshans and the booking of these from other parts of the state via APSWAN. Another is that it will now be possible for people travelling on the buses of the AP Road Transport Corporation to book their return journey at the same time as the outward journey. The beauty of information technology is that IT conquers time and distance. There are no limitations to the number of applications, the only limitation is funds. We have to decide which applications are to be taken up first.

It lends itself to educational innovations. If there is a very good teacher at a particular school who is strong in certain subjects, it is possible in theory to transmit that live class to other institutions. Bandwidth is not a problem. The question is how many applications you can run over that. You could do agricultural extension online for farmers at the mandal level by getting them to gather at a pre-determined point and have an expert talk to them and take questions from a district headquarters or from Hyderabad.

Apart from the kind of networking applications that APSWAN represents, our district rural development agencies have been discovering that they are able to efficiently track their performance under dozens of Central and state government programmes since their own operations have been computerized. It is one thing to have mountains of forms or files on beneficiaries. It is entirely another to have all the vital statistics of hundreds of beneficiaries on a computer which can give you categorized printouts which clearly highlight patterns and trends.

At the District Rural Development Agency at Nellore, for example, they discovered only after they were computerized just how poor their recoveries under the Integrated Rural Development Programme were. They were able to track recoveries thereafter mandal-wise. Similarly, under the Podupulakshmi scheme, by entering data about every single savings group in every mandal on the computer it was possible to check the status of the groups and intervene accordingly.

■

In Andhra Pradesh the chief minister can now hand his cabinet ministers a CD-ROM of the locations where the schemes under their charge have been implemented in the state. And by combining our Geographic Information System with remote sensing data we can give all MLAs CD-ROMs locating the house sites, sanitary latrines, borewells and other allotments in their constituencies. This will be done soon and they will be expected to verify that these have been properly allotted and check on the implementation.

We have two kinds of IT-enabled databases with considerable significance for planning applications. One is the Geographic Information System which has been created by digitizing maps of revenue villages and mandals, and also constituencies. Maps dating back to 1939 have been digitized since they are the only ones available, and revenue village demarcations have not changed. The other database which can be used in conjunction with this is a citizen database.

In a wired society citizen databases are created to make it possible to generate data on demand. This could be for planning purposes, or for individual certification needs. The latter becomes very simple once the data exists. Andhra Pradesh has built up in the past few years a multipurpose household survey database, MPHS, which contains information on each citizen such as age, sex, educational qualifications, household income, nature of occupation, the nature of shelter each household has, and so on. In 1995 the Election Commission of India ordered a survey of all voters with a view to issuing electoral photo identity cards. We used this opportunity to capture some more citizen data by conducting a multipurpose household survey. We carried out this survey polling-station wise, covering the entire population of the state. By the end of 1999 data entry for the 59,000 polling stations in the state was almost complete.

Once such a database is in place, issuing date of birth, caste, income and nativity certificates becomes quite painless. It will form the core around which a large number of citizen-related applications will be developed. It will also feed into the Data Warehouse Project, which AP Technology Services and CDAC Pune are jointly developing, using a Param supercomputer. This project has two core objects: person object, and land object. The main sources of data are the multipurpose household survey data and land records data. The first is available and currently being validated, while the land records data is being entered at the respective district headquarters and will be available for integration soon. Together, this Web-enabled data will be available for planners and analysts to arrive at better decisions.

In December 1999 we unveiled the State Planning and Development Monitoring System which has been developed through the convergence of two technologies, the Geographic Information System and remote sensing. The entire state has been digitized: all 23 districts, 1,125 mandals, 294 assembly constituencies, 28,245 revenue villages, and 67,505 habitations. The imaging for this system was obtained from IRS 1C and IRS 1D in March 1999 with a 23 metre resolution.

If you combine the capabilities of this system with the data from the multipurpose household survey it gives the administration details not only about every habitation, but also about the socio-economic condition of each family.

The virtual Geographic Information System that is a component of the larger system enables the person using it to get a three-dimensional feel of any part of the state he or she chooses, however remote and however small the area may be. If there is a flood in the Godavari river the system will inform you how many and which villages will be submerged.

The state's entire road network has been digitized, and concerned officials have on their computers a roads database which is useful for planning roads and monitoring their quality. Our effort is to make all kinds of data Web-enabled so that not only the district collector, but also citizens can access it. Mandals already have online access to the multipurpose household data.

We have our own remote sensing applications centre which does regular watershed monitoring and applies remote sensing to the monitoring of cropped area. It also reveals the real state of forest area vegetation, and tells you whether the groundwater level in a particular watershed is improving. The AP State Remote Sensing Applications Centre has developed a way to apply geographical information systems to assembly constituencies so that we can produce the kind of CD-ROMs described earlier. We transpose information received from the rural development department upon digitized maps of the area that a legislative constituency covers. This project is the baby of the state planning department.

Technology today makes any kind of information possible: you can get slope maps to identify areas having steep slopes. This also tells you which areas are vulnerable to soil erosion, and what the demographic pattern and fodder demand in such areas is. You can get yield estimates for any cropping area in the state, siltation studies for reservoirs, and data which tells you where to locate a rural water supply project depending on where the need is greatest.

With so much information on tap, alibis for doing nothing about alleviating poverty and backwardness are fast disappearing. With a wealth of meteorological data that is available on the Internet both droughts and floods, which continue to take a heavy toll of many parts of the country, can surely be anticipated and countered in time.

That brings us back to the unfortunate truth before the information society: technology by itself is never the answer. It needs to be propelled by political and administrative will. We have not spent crores on our impressive new geographical information system: it has cost Rs 75 lakh to install and commission. But even that would be Rs 75 lakh too many if we fail to get the public representatives and the administration to make full use of these monitoring systems to deliver results on the ground.

That's our next battle, already under way.

III

FINDING THE MONEY

7

STATE FINANCES: GETTING GRIMMER

When a state government discovers that there is no money in the treasury to even pay salaries it is a moment of reckoning. Uttar Pradesh found in 1998 that its entire revenues were not enough to pay the salaries of its employees. In 1995 we in Andhra Pradesh were in the same situation. And in 1996-97 our expenditure on salaries and pensions as a percentage of the state's own tax and non-tax receipts was 94.5 per cent!

Other states are not too far from the day when they will find bankruptcy staring them in the face: some have already reached that stage. If the beginning of the 1990s saw the Central government recognize that the country's economy was in a crisis and drastic changes would have to be made in its functioning, most state governments are facing that realization by the end of the same decade. Their finances have deteriorated alarmingly, many are borrowing to meet current expenditure, and the interest on debt incurred is showing up as a substantial percentage of revenue expenditure. This percentage has more than doubled over the last five years and has actually crossed 20 per cent of revenue expenditure in a few states.

Things did not come to such a pass unexpectedly. There were stages on the route to rapid deterioration. For more than a decade and a half the gap between revenue earnings and expenditure has been growing in the finances of most state governments. In other words, between what they earned through taxes and user charges and what they spent on running the state. For low-income states this was always a problem, but the more developed states never had a problem until the early 1980s. Andhra Pradesh, for instance, did not have a budget deficit before 1982.

In many states fiscal imbalances set in after the Central pay revision on the basis of the Fourth Pay Commission recommendations and were further aggravated after the Fifth Pay Commission recommendations came. It has been difficult for state governments to resist pressure from employee unions to pay Central scales, and many have succumbed.

But the burden of pay revision has been considerable–unbearable for the poorer states and tough even on the rich ones. Even Maharashtra found that the impact of the Fifth Pay Commission would take its expenditure on administrative services up from 10 per cent of its total revenue expenditure to about 25 per cent. As for the poorer states, as in the case of UP, more and more of them are finding that their entire revenues are not enough to pay the wages of their employees.

Throughout the 1990s fifteen major states which account for over 93 per cent of the country's population saw a steady increase in their budgets of the share of revenue expenditure, and a corresponding decrease in the share of capital expenditure. In other words, thanks to resources increasingly diverted into paying salaries and pensions, there has been less and less available to invest in building infrastructure and other assets.

Even as state governments have been grappling with their own resource imbalance, resources from the Centre have been progressively drying up. With the Central government's own tax revenues declining, the Finance Commission-mediated tax revenue devolution (the proportion of Central taxes given to the states) has stagnated, not increased in the last two years. Until 1996-97 the annual growth in the total revenues devolving to the state was between 12 to 20 per cent per year. In 1997-98 this might have registered an absolute decline had it not been for the Voluntary Disclosure of Income Scheme. The budget estimates for 1998-99 put the amount to devolve at the 1997-98 level. In other words, no increase at all.

The poorer states have been hit hard because they depend even more on such devolution. Whereas for all the states taken together the devolved tax revenues account for just about one-third of total tax revenues, the share of such devolution is as much as 60 per cent in the budget of Bihar and 50 per cent in the case of Uttar Pradesh and Orissa.

An analysis by the Planning Commission's Adviser for State Finances, N.J. Kurien, shows how states are being affected by the increasing financial stringency. The ability of state governments to finance their own plans has suffered. Not all states have been able to realize their projected Eighth Plan outlays. Whereas overall plan realization for fifteen major states was 83 per cent, individually Bihar was able to realize only 36 per cent of its plan outlay, Orissa 51 per cent and Haryana and West Bengal 67 per cent each. Realization can be defined as coming up with the resources projected. At the other end of the spectrum, in the case of Andhra Pradesh, Kerala and Tamil Nadu realized plan outlays exceeded projected plan outlays.

But the manner in which states have been finding the resources to realize their plan outlays is also a reflection of how desperate their financial condition is. The sources of financing for state plans fall under three broad heads: Central assistance, own funds of the state and borrowings of the states.

In the case of some of the poorer states the drop in
Central assistance was quite steep from the annual plan of
1997-98 to that of 1998-99. A 19 per cent drop in the case of
Uttar Pradesh, and a 12 per cent drop in the case of Madhya
Pradesh. Among the wealthier states, Goa, Haryana,
Maharashtra and Punjab also saw a decrease in the percentage
share of Central assistance in their state plans.

As for its own funds that a state could mobilize to finance
the plan, these were derived from current revenues,
contributions of state public sector undertakings, non-debt
capital receipts and additional resources mobilized. In the
case of many states, including Andhra Pradesh, this has been
a negative percentage, particularly in the annual plans. The
share of borrowings, therefore, has been going up.

In 1997-98, for all the major states taken together, Central
assistance accounted for 40 per cent of plan financing, and
borrowings accounted for 78 per cent. The contribution of
states' own funds was –18 per cent. What this means is that
about 18 per cent of the borrowings and Central assistance
was diverted by the states to meet current expenditure on
non-plan account. In 1998-99 the situation worsened in this
respect. About 25 per cent of the borrowings and/or Central
assistance were expected to be diverted by the states to meet
non-plan revenue expenditure.

Karnataka was the only state in the country which
expected to provide its own funds for plan financing. Goa,
Haryana, Punjab, Tamil Nadu and Rajasthan were projecting
more than 100 per cent borrowings to finance the approved
annual plan.

Why are state revenues in such a bad shape? Their own
tax revenues are supposed to be the main source of revenue
receipts, but these vary considerably across states. Maharashtra
collects more than twice as much as most states in the
country, and Tamil Nadu with less than 40 per cent of the
population of Uttar Pradesh collects more tax revenue than

the latter. The varying collections depend on per capita income as well as the degree of tax effort. Haryana's own tax revenue was less than that of Bihar in 1996-97.

Sales tax is the main source of own tax revenue, with other sources being excise, registration and stamp duty, motor vehicle tax, electricity duty, profession and entertainment taxes, and so on. In the wake of economic reforms several states competed with each other to announce tax concessions that would attract investment: they only ended up losing revenue while not attracting commensurate investment. Andhra Pradesh and Haryana experimented with total prohibition and finding the excise losses difficult to bear either repealed it after a year, or went in for partial prohibition, as in the case of Andhra Pradesh.

Kurien's study also shows that tax revenues are more a matter of administrative will than anything else. West Bengal and Tamil Nadu are economies of comparable size, but Tamil Nadu collects 50 per cent more sales tax revenue than the former state. A higher rate of tax on motor spirits alone fetches an additional Rs 1000 crore in Tamil Nadu. With partial prohibition in force, Tamil Nadu collects three times as much excise revenue as West Bengal, which has no prohibition at all. Punjab, with one of the highest per capita consumption expenditures in the country, has sales tax accounting for only 40 per cent of its tax revenues, compared to 60 per cent for most other states.

Central taxes also contribute to a state's tax revenues, but the Centre's own collections have been going down. Under the Tenth Finance Commission Award, 77.5 per cent of Central income tax revenues and 47.5 per cent of Union excise revenues are distributed among the states with a 60 per cent weightage given to per capita income and 20 per cent to population.

The non-tax revenues of the state consist of the state's own non-tax revenues and grants from the Centre. The former head comprises interest receipts, dividends and profits, and user charges for economic services, social services and other general services. User charges are a largely untapped source since governments have until now lacked the political courage to exploit even a fraction of their potential. It amounts to charging sensibly for electricity, water, transport and irrigation.

The record is dismal: a 1997 government white paper on subsidies estimates that the all-India average recovery rate for non-merit services is only 10 per cent. We are talking of an average subsidy rate, then, of 90 per cent. Frequent elections have meant that parties in power have put a hold on raising user charges for amenities such as water, power and state transport.

The tide is turning now, because having touched rock-bottom, state government finances have to look to user charges for succour. In the last few years thirteen states have raised state transport rates, eleven have raised power rates. But nobody has yet raised all rates for all categories of users to a point where the revenue matches costs.

If serious shortfalls in revenue are one aspect of state finances, the non-asset creating nature of most state expenditure is another aspect. Revenue expenditure far outstrips capital expenditure. For all fifteen major states taken together revenue expenditure accounted for 89 per cent of total expenditure in the year 1996-97. The heartening trend, however, is that of the total expenditure about 70 per cent was on development expenditure as opposed to non-development expenditure.

The widening revenue gap and the decrease in capital expenditure has meant a steady increase in borrowings. With financial sector deregulation state governments are also having to pay market-related interest rates which are considerably higher than the earlier fixed rates that prevailed in a regulated money market. The combination of these two factors has meant a soaring interest burden on the states.

While there has been overall deterioration in finances of all major states, a few low-income states are exceptionally badly affected and Bihar is even worse off than these. Today we should be concerned not just about the growing fiscal imbalance but also about the growing disparities between better off states and those that are fiscally much weaker. The fifteen major states, given their diversity of size, population and income, display tremendous variations in per capita income between them. It varies from approximately Rs 20,000 in Goa to Rs 4000 in Bihar.

If you divide these fifteen states into three approximate groupings of high income, middle income and low income, the population weighted average per capita income works out to around Rs 16,000 for the high-income states, Rs 10,000 for the middle income, and Rs 6000 for the low-income states, which account for 43.4 per cent of the population of the country. The high-income states only account for 19 per cent of the population, and the middle-income states for 31.3 per cent.

Even among the low-income states the variations are considerable. Rajasthan's per capita income is 220 per cent more than that of Bihar, and even Orissa, which is the second poorest state in the country among the major states, has a per capita income that is 60 per cent more than that of Bihar.

Such inter-state disparity is only growing. It was lower in 1990-91 as compared to 1996-97. Whereas the per capita income of Goa was only 3.3 times that of Bihar, by 1996-97 it had risen to 5.1 times. The poorer states seem to be sinking further under the weight of their rising costs and poor financial management. The gap between them and the better off states widens because private financial flows and investments are clearly biased towards developed and better administered states.

Some specific financial indicators affirm this trend. One

is the credit offtake. Today Andhra Pradesh is one of four states with a credit–deposit ratio which is well above the national average. This means that the utilization of credit is high, utilization of money in the productive sector is high because the investor feels it is less risky to invest in this state. Credit will increasingly be available in those states which are putting progressive policies in place.

The credit offtake is highest in the middle-income states, with the exception of Maharashtra, which also has a high credit–deposit ratio. It is lowest in the low-income states.

This is not the only indicator of investment, another is the distribution of institutional credit across states. Up to the end of March 1997 Maharashtra and Gujarat between them accounted for 35 per cent of the total financial assistance disbursed by all-India financial institutions within the country. Bihar, Madhya Pradesh, Orissa, Rajasthan and Uttar Pradesh together accounted for roughly half that figure.

Credit has thus been flowing into those states which are relatively more developed, possessing better infrastructure and administration, and are more reform oriented than the others. So has foreign direct investment and domestic investment. Gujarat with its smaller population received over a fifth of all private investment proposals in 1998, whereas Bihar with a tenth of the country's population hardly got 5 per cent of these proposals.

Data provided by the Secretariat of Industrial Approvals in the Ministry of Industry showed that the four southern states accounted for more than 34 per cent of the proposals approved in that year. Trends such as these will only widen the gap between the poorest states and the rest.

The solutions to combating the growing indebtedness and inequity in the states lie in controlling government expenditure, raising tax revenues, drastically revising user charges upwards, and restructuring the finances of state electricity boards. The losses they incur severely burden state finances. Finally, as has been discussed in the chapter on Centre–state relations in this book, the Eleventh Finance Commission will have to consider introducing performance criteria to be fulfilled by the states to make them eligible for their share of Central government finances.

In their analysis of reforms in the states, Nirupam Bajpai and Jeffrey D. Sachs of Harvard University make a case for economic policy making to be decentralized so that states can make crucial economic decisions on their own. They point out that policy making at the sub-national level is essential for state governments to be able to follow development strategies suitable to their socio-economic, cultural and geographic characteristics.

Thus, coastal states can follow a more focussed export-led growth strategy, whereas states with a large pool of trained manpower can lay more emphasis on IT and the service sector.

However, at present crucial fiscal, infrastructure and regulatory decisions on economic management are not in their hands; they remain at the Central level. This has to be remedied if the economies of states are to acquire greater dynamism.

8

FENDING OFF BANKRUPTCY: THE ANDHRA PRADESH EXPERIENCE

By the most fundamental standards of management, the economics of present-day governance spells disaster. Our expenses bear no relation to our resources. Several states are now resorting to large borrowings just to meet current expenditure. We hire several times more people than we need. And over the years we have turned into employment agencies, setting up state enterprises which end up primarily creating employment rather than producing goods and services.

When the state provides a service for the people—be it irrigation, electricity, road transport, primary school education or municipal water supply—it is usually constrained to give it away free or at heavily subsidized rates. The reason for this economically aberrant behaviour is quite simply called politics.

I studied economics in college, and was doing my Ph.D. on the economic policies of the eminent parliamentarian N.G. Ranga. Being an economist by training and a politician by experience, I can see quite clearly that political populism in recent years has in many ways been bad for the economy of state governments. We got away with practising this kind of aberrant management for some years, but as our population grows and our costs and inefficiencies mount, the spectre of bankruptcy looms ahead for many state governments.

The more fragmented the electorate becomes as caste and communal divisions come to the fore, the more political parties have to resort to populism to win their vote. Frequent elections have made matters worse: they have made responsible public finance extremely difficult. Political parties are constrained to promise that they will write off bank loans to farmers, or give them free electricity.

When a state government's resources run out it begins to borrow, when its credit rating falls it borrows at increasingly higher interest rates. But at no point can we pass on our costs to the people to whom we provide various services. User charges have stagnated. For that reason we never have the capital to invest in improving and extending these services so that water supply can actually improve in urban and rural areas and power become plentifully available.

That is not how one would run a company or corporation. If it gave services free or heavily subsidized, it would have to shut down before long, because there would soon be no resources to produce the services. But in the government all of this has been the norm rather than the exception. And it has proved very expensive.

In the 1980s, in its first term in power in Andhra Pradesh, the Telugu Desam Party was voted in on the platform of Telugu pride and the promise of rice at Rs 2 a kg for those below the poverty line. But it is difficult to implement the targeting of a subsidy like this. With even the relatively well off sections of the population accessing the subsidized rice, it proved to be a very costly promise in the long run.

When we introduced it the cost to the government of providing this subsidy was 43 paise per kilogram adding up to Rs 78 crore a year.

By 1990, the subsidy per kilogram had risen to Rs 1.74,

and its annual cost to the exchequer was Rs 368.54 crore. This was after the Congress had come to power. In 1992 they raised the price of subsidized rice to Rs 3.50 per kg from Rs 2. In 1994 N.T. Rama Rao came back to power as chief minister and reduced the price to Rs 2 again. By 1996 the annual cost to the exchequer was Rs 712 crore. When I became chief minister and we found that the cost was not sustainable we revised the price to Rs 3.50 again and at this rate the subsidy per kg by 1999 was Rs 6, and the total cost per year Rs 1100 crore.

Thus the cost of providing a subsidy begun in 1983 had multiplied fourteen times by 1999. But providing a subsidy is like clambering atop the proverbial tiger. The conventional wisdom is that you can withdraw it only at considerable risk to your government's popularity. The truth is that a subsidy gives diminishing political returns. Despite rice at Rs 2 a kg, the TDP government of N.T. Rama Rao was voted out of power in 1989, and despite continuing the subsidy while raising the rate somewhat, the Congress government that came in was voted out again at the end of its term in 1994.

The same is true of subsidies on power, fertilizers and irrigation given to farmers by successive governments, not just in Andhra Pradesh but in other states as well. Today there are some states in the country which supply power to farmers free of cost. They have never succeeded in completely nullifying the anti-incumbency vote. This was demonstrated in Punjab in 1999, where despite fulfilling an election promise of free power the Akali Dal government fared very poorly in the Lok Sabha elections. Yet both at Centre and state, the political courage to withdraw subsidies is in short supply.

Another major reason for the severe strain on state government finances is the cost of maintaining an army of employees. As the Planning Commission's adviser on state finances has described it, 'State governments are becoming governments of the employees, by the employees and for the employees.' Rising wage bills spell disaster for state government budgets because, through the 1980s and '90s, the gap between earnings and expenses or between revenue receipts and revenue expenditure has been growing. We borrow money to meet the gap. And as our debt grows we replace low-cost debt with high-cost debt. This debt begins to eat substantially into revenues.

In 1995 we in Andhra Pradesh found ourselves headed for bankruptcy, with the situation so difficult that we were finding it difficult to even pay salaries to employees. There was a tenfold increase in interest burdens on debt over the last decade. The commitment on subsidies was shooting up. Salaries, pensions, and establishment costs had increased fivefold and user charges had stagnated.

I was finance minister for ten months before I took over as chief minister, and I could see that a major crisis was building up. Meanwhile a political crisis was also brewing in the Telugu Desam Party over my father-in-law N.T. Rama Rao's inability to get a grip on urgent issues of governance. The state legislators felt there was an urgent need for a change in the party's leadership and elected me as leader. Having taken over as chief minister in September 1995 I found that the economic crisis would have to be handled without any further delay. Drastic remedies were needed: there was no other option.

We decided to publish a series of white papers on the state's finances because it was obvious that hard decisions would have to be taken urgently, and the people of the state would have to know why. The free ride was over, money would have to be raised from the public, and the sooner they got some straight talk from their government the better. Though the situation in Andhra was not different or necessarily worse than that in many other states, continuing in the same manner was certainly not a feasible proposition.

Over the next few months we prepared and published

white papers on the following subjects: state finances, revenue receipts, establishment levels and costs in the state, patterns of expenditure on the welfare sector, public enterprises and cooperatives, the financial status of the Andhra Pradesh State Electricity Board, and the patterns of expenditure in the irrigation sector. Together, they explained the reason for the collapse of state government finances.

The crisis had been building for more than a decade. Though the state has considerable natural resources and a long coastline, though its irrigation potential and fertile soil endow it with a rich agricultural base, though it has significant mineral resources, skilled manpower and the potential for industrial development, its growth performance has been poor. Between 1980-81 and 1996-97 its gross state domestic product (GSDP) grew at an annual average rate of 5 per cent. This was lower than the all-India growth rate of 5.7 per cent. This was mainly because of the poor performance of the industry and service sectors.

In fact in the industrial sector there was a decline in the growth rate, from 5.4 per cent between 1980-90 to 3.8 per cent between 1990-97. There was a decline in the all-India growth rate also during this period, but it was less, from 7.2 per cent to 6.6 per cent. Services grew only marginally in Andhra Pradesh, and agriculture was stagnant.

The state's per capita income reflected the stagnation in the growth of the economy: compared to an all-India growth rate of 3.4 per cent, the average annual growth rate of per capita income in AP during this period was 2.8 per cent.

The composition of the economy was marked by the fact that between 1980 and 1997 the share of the service sector in the gross state domestic product grew slightly, the share of agriculture declined, and the share of industry in GSDP remained stagnant at 19 per cent. The economy did not exhibit the kind of structural transformation in terms of shift of inter-sectoral shares of GSDP that would be characteristic of growth and development.

The chief minister, N. Chandrababu Naidu, with a constituent.

A canal that was re-excavated by farmers belonging to a water users' association in West Godavari District. Such associations are playing an important role in irrigation management.

A wasteland that was made green again under the watershed development programme in Mahabubnagar District.

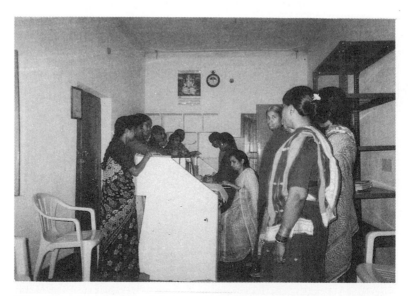

The Adarshya Mahila Sahakara Samakhya Ltd runs a bank in Moolapet, Mahabubnagar District. It has 30,000 members.

The children's mothers have taken the contract to build this anganwadi in Mahabubnagar District.

Human resource development begins in village schools like this.

The human touch.

Bazaars such as this one are helping farmers to reach consumers directly and earn more for their produce.

The government wants students to get involved in Janmabhoomi and village-level planning and earn college credit in the process.

Naidu with Bill Gates, who has set up a Microsoft software development centre in Hyderabad.

With Tony Blair, prime minister of Britain, at the World Economic Forum meeting at Davos in Switzerland.

The chief minister's information monitoring system.

As a step towards greater accountability, villages throughout Andhra Pradesh have begun to display how money received from the government is being spent.

The chief minister uses impromptu roadside meetings to explain to people what the government is doing.

Chandrababu Naidu in an open jeep making contact with local people.

A significant pointer to the global interest in Andhra Pradesh's initiatives was the visit of US President Bill Clinton to Hyderabad in March 2000.

Through the 1980s and '90s the broad trend has been a growing gap between the state government's earnings from tax and non-tax revenues and its expenditure on the cost of running the government. Between 1984 and 1997 there were just three years when there was a revenue surplus. The net result was a rapid shrinking of resources available for capital expenditure, which is used to fund infrastructure.

If a state cannot find money to develop its infrastructure it cannot attract investment from industry, or even expand its agriculture and services. Hence the stagnation. In 1996-97 our capital expenditure was the lowest among fifteen major states. During 1984 and 1997 the share of capital expenditure in total expenditure fell from 13.4 per cent to 7.6 per cent, which meant that the share of revenue expenditure grew from 86.6 per cent to 92.4. The main elements of the latter were salaries, wages and allowances, grants-in-aid towards salaries, pensions, interest payments and subsidies.

Revenues, meanwhile, shrank because tax collections were poor, and non-tax receipts such as user charges for irrigation or government-provided medical services were not sufficiently exploited. The imposition of prohibition in 1994 as fulfilment of an election promise to women voters in the state took away excise revenue, which accounted for as much as 19 to 20 per cent of government taxes. At the same time, the revenue flow from the Centre to the states did not grow. We have been as affected by this as any other state.

Thanks to stagnation in collection of Central tax revenues the tax revenue devolution to states has not increased since 1996-97, though until then it was growing annually by 12 to 20 per cent. Revenue gap grants recommended by the Tenth Finance Commission are front-loaded, that is, given early on in the stipulated period, and scheduled to taper off by 1999-2000. The Centre, faced with its own resource crunch, has been unable to maintain a growing rate of assistance to state plans.

A major reason why tax revenues in the state have not grown is because of the accumulation of arrears over the years. Sales tax arrears alone were Rs 765 crore by the end of the financial year 1996-97, cumulative evidence of poor tax efforts over many years. Poor collection of taxes is not a problem limited to Andhra Pradesh—collections vary widely from state to state. Andhra Pradesh's collections were the sixth highest.

Increasingly one has had to set stiff revenue collection targets to improve this performance. In terms of non-tax revenues we fare almost as poorly, with only Haryana and Gujarat performing far better than other states. These are supposed to come from user charges in a variety of sectors, but again collections are insignificant and growth over the years has been negligible. The only significant growth in sources of non-tax revenues has been in forests and royalty on mines and minerals.

With revenue receipts not keeping up with expenditure the revenue deficit continued to grow until it reached Rs 3199 crore in 1996-97, from Rs 188 crore in 1986-87. The state's debt position also worsened, from a little over Rs 5000 crore in March 1991 to over 25,000 crore in the budget estimates for the year 2000. Persistent revenue deficits, low recovery of user charges, low productivity of plan investments and poor performance of public enterprises resulted in a sharp increase in public debt. Between 1984-85 and 1996-97 the burden of interest payment increased over twelve times, reflecting both increasing recourse to debt financing and increasing cost of debt.

It seemed that we had come to the end of the road, and there were no soft options left. In June 1996 we released the white papers, intended to take the public into confidence about the parlous state of the exchequer. In August the same year we announced a fresh set of taxes designed to help reduce the deficit. This included a fivefold increase in profession tax, an 8 per cent entry tax on motor vehicles purchased outside and brought into the state, and a 5 per cent luxury tax on cigarettes at the point of first supply. Water rates for irrigation were raised three to four times. The state-owned transport corporation raised bus fares and the electricity board increased power tariffs.

During the annual plan discussion for 1996-97 held in Delhi we found there was a gap of roughly Rs 1000 crore in our projections. One of the Planning Commission officials present suggested that a partial roll-back of prohibition could probably yield excise revenues to fill that gap. We followed up on that and decided to do the partial lifting of prohibition. It was already becoming untenable because of increasing criminalization, and because AP was surrounded by states which did not have prohibition. Though it had been an election promise in 1994, we had no option. We also rolled back the rice subsidy to some extent by raising its price from Rs 2 to Rs 3.50.

It was a harsh way to proceed, but there really had not been much choice left. If we had carried on with the state of affairs that prevailed we would not have been able to pay salaries. Tax revenues quickly picked up as a result, from Rs 4120 crore in 1995-96 to Rs 4882 crore in 1996-97 and Rs 7346 crore in the revised estimates of 1997-98. Raising revenues was one part of the story, cutting establishment costs was another. Between 1984-85 and 1996-97 expenditure on salaries and pensions as a proportion of the state's own tax and non-tax receipts increased from 76.9 per cent to 94.5 per cent. Subsequent to the taxation measures, this percentage was expected to come down.

Even if the percentage comes down, establishment costs as a major area of expenditure remain to be tackled as part of administrative reform. The problem of treating public enterprises as part of this establishment also remain. By the end of 1995-96 the state government's investments in public enterprises amounted to Rs 2569 crore, while the outstanding loans to these enterprises amounted to Rs 2447 crore. The amount of dividend received by the government in that year on its investments in public enterprises was a return of 0.0005 per cent. By the end of that financial year the accumulated losses of public enterprises amounted to Rs 1278 crore.

Among public enterprises the most critical problem was the Andhra Pradesh State Electricity Board. Its health was vital to the well-being of the state since it functioned in the core area of power which affects every single citizen. By 1996-97 it had come to a stage where the more power it produced, the greater were its financial losses, because of the large share of its output going to low tariff sectors.

The average cost of generating and distributing one unit of electricity was about 183 paise. This represented the pooled cost of thermal and hydel power, the purchase from Central generating stations and other state electricity boards, and the distribution cost of making it available to the consumer. As against this 183 paise, the average realization from the sale of power to the agricultural sector was only 3 paise!

In the year 1995-96 we provided a subsidy of Rs 1530 crore on a sale of 8500 million units. In addition to the agricultural sector, industrial units set up anywhere in the state except within the municipal limits of Hyderabad, Vijaywada and Visakhapatnam were given a 25 per cent rebate on power bills for a period of three years from the date of commercial production.

Theoretically there was a system of cross-subsidization in place whereby industries and other high-tension consumers were supposed to subsidize the agricultural and lower segment domestic consumers. But since 1992-93 this system was failing to balance the books of APSEB. An increasing proportion of power was going to agriculture and domestic sectors. Finally we had to resort to financial restructuring to tackle the insurmountable losses. Outstanding loan was converted into equity amounting to Rs 1357 crore. Then, in order to cover losses and ensure the prescribed 3 per cent rate of return on capital by the end of the financial year, we had to further write off the state government's equity in APSEB to an extent of Rs 944 crore.

Apart from power, other subsidies eat substantially into a state government's revenue expenditure. In the category of direct subsidies the two-rupee rice scheme proved the most expensive. Until we cut back in 1996 by raising the price to Rs 3.50, it constituted the largest subsidized programme among state governments in the country.

Housing for weaker sections was another costly component in the susbsidy bill, accounting for Rs 105 crore a year by 1996-97. For a house costing Rs 12,000 the state government provided Rs 4750 as subsidy and another Rs 7000 as loan. All the beneficiary had to contribute was Rs 250. Concessional bus passes and in some cases free travel facilities provided by the state road transport corporation to students, physically handicapped persons, freedom fighters, serving and former public representatives and journalists cost the exchequer four to five crore annually, but it also cost APSRTC Rs 74 crore a year. That affected its ability to balance its books.

Then there were indirect subsidies that have been traditionally given, and become more expensive each year to sustain. The single largest item in this category is poor recovery of user charges in canal irrigation. The aggregate water rate taken at Rs 60 per acre did not even cover operation and maintenance expenses, let alone yield a return on the huge investments made. In fact, taking into account cumulative investments made in major and medium irrigation projects, the interest rate, depreciation of investments and actual operation and maintenance charges, the cost per acre of canal irrigation was working out to Rs 1094.

The recovery, as mentioned before, was Rs 60. At current costs, the capital cost of providing canal irrigation was working out to Rs 8150 per acre. The total annual subsidy bill on account of canal irrigation was Rs 818 crore at historical cost, and Rs 2751 crore annually at current cost. These are 1997-98 figures.

There is a third category of subsidies on account of non-recovery of loans given to cooperatives, public sector undertakings and individuals. Recovery under the weaker sections housing scheme was very poor, recovery of loans provided to cooperative institutions was also miserable. The state government found that its tax breaks and cash subsidies to the film industry to promote its growth in the state were also entailing a subsidy of Rs 40 crore a year. It could ill afford the subsidy.

Given this larger background of uneconomic expenditure, soaring indebtedness and the total unavailability of money for critical social sector needs, drastic remedies were called for. It was clear that economic restructuring would have to be undertaken. It was also clear that money would have to be found for neglected social and infrastructure sectors. Overall, state finances had to be put on a sustainable path.

We had approached the World Bank in 1997. I made a presentation to its president, James Wolfenson, when he visited India. We were asking for assistance in the following sectors: irrigation, roads maintenance, primary education, child development, primary health and public enterprises. The World Bank showed interest because of the commitment we had already shown in terms of initiating fiscal correctives.

Even as it was processing our request, the nuclear tests at Pokhran happened, bringing in their wake US and Japanese sanctions. But despite these the bank approved the AP Economic Restructuring Project in June 1998 for a total of Rs 3320 crore. In February 1999 we signed the agreement with the bank. Out of the total project cost, the World Bank assistance was to the tune of 65 per cent, and the share of the state government was 35 per cent.

Why did we need the money? The irrigation component was meant for reversing the decline in irrigated areas by better maintenance of the irrigation channels. We formulated a scheme to involve farmers in the process. This has been discussed in the chapter on stakeholders and self-help groups. This mammoth effort at rejuvenation would benefit all major, medium and minor irrigation schemes which had become increasingly unproductive for want of maintenance. What was at stake was a combined command area of 6.15 million hectares for which irrigation had been provided in earlier years at huge cost to the exchequer.

The road maintenance component was intended for the maintenance of some 1200 km of state highways and major district roads and for the upgradation of 2800 km of panchayati raj roads in three districts. As in the case of irrigation canals, the maintenance and upkeep of roads and other infrastructural facilities had suffered over years of financial stringency and their use and utility were therefore not optimal.

The assistance asked for from the bank to meet requirements of investments in education, health and nutrition was to help us tackle the accumulated problems in these sectors. Andhra Pradesh was lagging behind the national average in some of the key human development indices. The literacy rate of 44 per cent in the state was one example. The low female literacy rate of 33 per cent was also a matter of serious concern. Dropout rates have to decrease considerably for the improvement of overall literacy, which is why we have mounted a huge recruitment of teachers.

The primary education component of the World Bank project was intended to benefit some 7.9 million children by extending the district primary education project to fourteen educationally disadvantaged districts in the state. The primary health component had the basic objective of improving the performance of the primary health care system through improvements in quality, effectiveness and coverage of services. Under this, 500 PHCs in the state were to be upgraded, and buildings constructed for 626 more.

Similarly, though our state was going to be the third state in the country after Kerala and Tamil Nadu to achieve a net reproduction rate of one, the relatively high infant mortality rate of 63 per thousand was going to be a problem area. This required focussed attention. The nutrition status of children and mothers needed considerable improvement, particularly in the rural areas. We also needed to strengthen our rural health care system so that more babies could be delivered in hospitals instead of in homes.

Even before the World Bank assistance was negotiated we had already stepped up our efforts to improve human resources in the state, because without this we cannot have sustained growth. The expenditure in elementary education has been stepped up by 126 per cent from 1995-96 to 1999-2000, compared to a 44 per cent increase in the previous four years. More strikingly, we stepped up expenditure on women and child welfare from 8.16 per cent in the previous four years to 645.28 per cent between 1995-96 and 1999-2000. Similarly investment in rural development has gone up sharply from 6.20 per cent to 217 per cent. We have gone in for borrowing to step up increase in these sectors out of a firm conviction that no real development is possible unless public health, elementary education and rural infrastructure are tackled. The capability enhancement of ordinary people will turn our large population from being a liability into an asset.

Whenever a World Bank loan is taken a good deal of apprehension is generated about what the corresponding conditions will mean for the people of the state. This project came with two fiscal conditionalities for Andhra Pradesh. One was related to controlling the deficit, the second stipulated reorienting government expenditure.

The deficit had to be brought down from 3 per cent of GSDP in 1998-99 to 2.5 per cent of GSDP in 2002-03. The revenue deficit had to be taken from 0.4 per cent of GSDP in 1998-99 to a surplus 0.8 per cent of GSDP in 2002-03.

Regardless of who was stipulating these reductions, these were desirable steps that could only improve the health of state finances in the long run. In fact some of the fiscal consolidation measures called for had already been initiated by us before the Economic Restructuring Project began to be implemented. In 1996, after the white papers on the state of AP's finances had been published, correctives had been put into motion which brought down the fiscal deficit (as percentage of GSDP) from 3.8 in 1994-95 to 3 in 1998-99. The revenue deficit was brought down from 1.2 to 0.4.

The second conditionality of the AP Economic Restructuring Project involved reorienting government expenditure more in the direction of social and human development areas, such as education, nutrition and health. These priorities too we had already set in motion.

A major accusation about my stewardship of Andhra Pradesh is that I am leading it into a debt trap, particularly because of the World Bank loan. In actuality the terms we have negotiated make it one of the cheapest sources of funds. As much as 59 per cent of the World Bank loan is coming to us as a grant. The effective rate of interest works out to be 5 per cent per annum only.

Compare this with the rate of interest for other sources of loans available to state governments. The LIC charges a rate of interest of 13.40 per cent. Market borrowings charge 12.50 per cent. Bonds of government corporations charge between 14.50 to 15.50 as rate of interest.

The state's outstanding public debt has undoubtedly increased sharply, more than doubling from Rs 11,670.73 crore in 1994-95 to Rs 25,018.61 crore in the budget estimates of 1999-2000. More than half of this is loans from the Central government. I make no secret of the fact that huge funds will be needed to make the quantum jump in investment in human resources and infrastructure required to set Andhra Pradesh on a path of growth, and negate the stagnation of the last twenty years.

And I would point to a comparison with other states which puts our level of debt in perspective. Andhra Pradesh's debt as a percentage of NSDP (Net State Domestic Product) is 20.39 per cent compared to 32.13 for Punjab, 26.63 for Kerala and 38.44 for Bihar. Only five states have a lower percentage: Gujarat, Karnataka, Madhya Pradesh, Maharashtra and Tamil Nadu. Our interest as percentage of NSDP is lower than that of eleven other states.

What matters is not only the size of debt but the government's capacity to pay it back. As long as our revenue base is showing buoyancy, as long as we can use the debt for investment which will give returns, the debt will not be harmful. In the case of Andhra Pradesh, the scenario is not one of sinking into a debt trap from which we will not be able to get out. We have to improve our revenues further and are taking measures to do so.

Part of the reason for the mounting debt burden of the states is that the grant-loan component of Central assistance of 30:70 was fixed in 1969. For a lasting solution of the debt problem of states the Centre must write off a part of the outstanding loans.

I have also long been representing to the Central government that the time has come to change the yardstick for the devolution of Central funds to states. I have presented my case to the Eleventh Finance Commission, recommending devolution on the basis of performance rather than on the basis of the level of poverty or population. States that are spending heavily on family welfare must not be penalized in favour of some states which have not been making as much effort to contain population or poverty.

State governments have been getting a smaller share of the Centre's gross tax revenue than is their due. The present and previous governments have not even implemented the 29 per cent share to states recommended by the Tenth Finance Commission. My demand is that the Eleventh Finance Commission must suitably increase the share of states in income tax and Union excise duties so that they get 50 per cent of the gross tax revenue, pending a constitutional amendment. States have to be compensated for meeting the additional commitment on account of pay revision.

Finally, democratic processes bring their own financial price. In an election year the government in power has to struggle to maintain fiscal balance while seeking to reassure voters that they will not be adversely affected. These are the compulsions of a democracy with a weak economy. The Indian electorate is very mature. They can judge if a government is sincere in its efforts to govern. But their threshold of tolerance with respect to prices of food and other commodities is low. At least twice in recent memory, in 1979 and in 1998, the price of onions has brought down governments.

The vulnerability of the poor to populist promises from competing political parties also remains high. In 1999 the Congress promised free power in Andhra Pradesh if elected, despite the calamitous financial mess the state electricity board was in. It is not, therefore, possible to do major belt tightening in an election year; some profligacy creeps in, and the exchequer bears the brunt. Tough measures can only be taken in the early years in office. Once people have been guaranteed a minimum standard of living, once a safety net is in place to insulate the poor from the rigours of economic reform, it may be possible to maintain fiscal discipline through all five years of the electoral cycle.

Meanwhile, having won the elections in 1999 we have our work for the next five years on the financial front cut out.

While not wanting to cause distress to the poorest by cutting back steeply on subsidies, our focus will be on targeting them much better so that only the really needy are covered. User charges in all sectors have to be reviewed and stepped up to as much as consumers can reasonably bear.

On the power front the regulatory commission will give its recommendations, but at the same time our emphasis will be on curtailing pilferage and transmission losses which lead to revenue losses. And to reduce the burden on the exchequer, government employment will have to be rationalized. Redeployment of staff, freezing of posts, the offering of a voluntary retirement scheme: all these are options which we now intend to explore.

As part of wide-ranging fiscal reforms, the state government also decided in the financial year beginning April 2000 to adopt zero-based budgeting as policy tool to bring fiscal discipline in all the departments. Under this concept every department would be required to justify its budget need for projected performance starting from scratch. All the existing schemes and projects would be scrutinized thoroughly and would be made subject to an in-depth questioning to evaluate their relevance to the development and welfare of the people of the state.

Every department was also being asked to evaluate each scheme under select 'performance indicators' and all future financial allocations and releases would be made by linking them to performance and to their impact on the overall achievement of the objectives of the Vision 2020.

A cabinet sub-committee of four ministers was constituted. On its recommendations the government constituted committees for all the departments to undertake and supervise the implementation of a zero-based budget. Meanwhile, instead of the budget for the year, the state government presented a vote on account during the budget session of the state legislature.

9

ATTRACTING INVESTORS

In 1998 I visited a small municipality in San Jose in Silicon Valley. It was called Milpitas, had a population of only about 50,000 people, and pulled in an annual revenue, I was told, of $40 million a year. 'How do you attract industry here?' I wanted to know.

A local official explained their approach. 'When someone wants to set up shop in this town, we ask for information on four or five counts. How much area the office will occupy, how many people will be employed, what is the proposed turnover, and so on. We have developed a computer software which tells us, when we key in the information on these four or five parameters, how much we can expect to earn from this unit by way of taxes and local spending by its employees. On the basis of that we decide what incentives we want to offer.'

In other countries even municipalities are honing their strategies for investment. It is therefore entirely appropriate that in India state governments have begun to play a major role in pulling in the money they need to help finance their development. Most of our bigger states have populations that are equal to those of some European countries and are considerably less developed. Our needs are so great that we have to attract huge investment both nationally and globally to be able to provide employment for all these people and raise their living standards.

In Andhra Pradesh alone, for instance, by 2020 the industrial sector will account for 21 per cent of its economy and will need to provide 43 per cent of the new jobs in the state. To achieve these levels the Vision 2020 exercise has estimated that the total investment needed will be of a very high level.

In the past few years state governments have begun competing with each other in this regard and that is healthy for the country as a whole. Companies, banks and institutions are now dealing directly with state governments which will increasingly become direct investment destinations within India.

The global economy is based on some fairly simple assumptions. The economies that have created wealth are not necessarily those which have the capacity to absorb fresh investment today. It is the poorer economies of the world that have this capacity. They also offer cheaper labour than do the industrialized countries.

And to the extent that they have bigger populations whose buying power is slowly increasing, these countries which can absorb investment are also the world's emerging markets. They can offer higher returns to the investor. That is why governments both state and Central in many countries of the world are wooing foreign investment, and that is why foreign investors are constantly exploring options: in India, in China, in Russia and elsewhere.

The competition, however, is as intense as the opportunities are enormous. Investors don't have to come to India. They are being wooed assiduously by other countries which have a far more market-friendly image. As Rajat Gupta of McKinsey said recently about the attitude of CEOs of Fortune 500 companies to India, it is not that perceptions are negative. India is out of mind for most of them. Though it has one of the largest consumer markets in the world, India has continuously failed to attract any sizeable portion of the foreign direct investment available worldwide.

Even if they were to come to India, they certainly don't have to come to Andhra Pradesh, which was not on any investor's radar screen until a few years ago. Maharashtra and Gujarat are the states which have attracted more investment, which have better industrial bases, and traditionally a more helpful bureaucracy. Karnataka was off the block much earlier than Andhra Pradesh where the information technology industry is concerned.

Against this background, setting out to create more employment in my state has meant three broad areas of initiative. Identifying those sectors in which there is potential, and in which even an under-industrialized state like Andhra Pradesh can rapidly develop competencies. We had commissioned Vision 2020 for this purpose, but having completed the exercise it remains a vision document which tells us what has to be done, not how it can happen. The next step for us is to come up with a road map for getting to the goals it outlines. This process has already begun.

Second, wooing investment, both here and abroad, particularly in the identified sectors. This involves issues of policy support as well as changing the mindset where the bureaucracy is concerned, and ushering in a major attitudinal change in this regard. It also means going out of the country to register a presence with potential investors abroad, and attempting to get past the mental barrier that exists with regard to India as a whole as an investment destination.

Third, examining the fiscal incentives that can be offered. We have to look at the structure of taxes and tariffs to see where these can be rationalized, so that revenues to the state increase through volume rather than through high rates of taxation, which act as a disincentive to industries wishing to locate there.

Today state governments are hard-pressed for resources.

One route is severe taxation and a sharp revision of user charges. But when the economy is in recession that is neither a politically astute nor a humane option. The better route is to revive the state's economy by creating a climate for investment, and then going out to woo investment so that jobs can be created in the state.

It does not take any great prescience to see that in a state with seventy-five million people and a gross state domestic product that is below the national average what is needed most is employment. For the first fifty years of this country's independence governments tried to create this employment themselves and failed quite miserably. The cumulative record of industrial undertakings run by the state proves that. In the present context, governments do not have the resources to do this. They have to draw in investors who will create employment, facilitate their entry into the state.

When I became chief minister and set out to revive the state's economy, I ran quite quickly into two major hurdles.

The first was that the national economy at that time was heading for a recession. Nobody was investing. The second was that even if they were, Andhra Pradesh was simply not a state they would have thought of investing in. As I have said before, in the year 1995 our ranking in terms of investor perception was 22.

Until then, we had missed the bus on industry. The state was a late starter on industrialization: as a major agricultural state we had focussed much more on irrigation and power in the early years. We did not have an entrepreneurial culture in the state.

The only course at that point was to go out and market the state. That is what I set out to do. By going to every investors' forum, domestic or foreign, and making Power Point presentations on what Andhra Pradesh had to offer. By being open to the media. By inviting ambassadors of various countries to visit Hyderabad. Everywhere I emphasized our commitment to transforming the infrastructure in the state. I did a lot of brainstorming with my officials and captains of industry and we decided that Andhra Pradesh had the potential of becoming an IT state, and we should go for that goal. By 1998, with the changes in the investment climate that had taken place in the state, we had climbed to third position in terms of investor perceptions.

When you think bigger than the rest of your competition you will set your goals higher. When your goals are more ambitious, the hardsell must be more. If I have to market my state and my stewardship of it, I have to begin by projecting both. When I went to Malaysia in 1997 potential investors said, 'But we do not know how long your government at the Centre will last.' So I would have to tell them, 'There is absolute political stability in the state of Andhra Pradesh. I can guarantee you that.' When the media begins to write about us—local, national, international—we may be accused of hardsell. But the truth is that without the publicity we would not get the attention of potential investors or get the investment that they are preparing to make.

To return to the three streams of initiative undertaken to create more employment, the most important and farsighted of these, I believe, is the Vision 2020 approach. The document has been criticized as being a catch-all exercise, but it did succeed in identifying a clear set of growth engines for the state. Under the category of agriculture these were horticulture, dairy, rice, poultry and agro-processing. Under industry construction, garment and leather products, minerals and small-scale sector industries were thought to be the areas where we could develop strengths. And under services information technology, knowledge-based industries, tourism and the creation of a logistics hub were the growth engines that the Vision 2020 document identified.

Out of these, as a first step, we are jointly examining in collaboration with industrial federations in the state the core industries on which we should focus in the short term.

For each of these we have to look at the initiatives

required to be taken to develop the sector further. In most cases these are areas in which we already have strengths.

Once we know our weaknesses we can devise strategies to tackle them.

To take information technology as a first and striking example, we already possess a huge pool of knowledge workers. But even though NASSCOM figures show that Andhra Pradesh is the state from which the highest percentage of Indian IT professionals worldwide originate, it was not until a few years ago a favoured destination for the IT industry. In the last four years the state government has worked single-mindedly to give it that policy focus.

We clearly recognized the strategic importance of information technology in creating a competitive economy that is equipped for the future. It does enormous things for the economy. If you do not have it, you cannot realize its potential. Any trade or commerce relies on this medium; you cannot be competitive globally without it. By being first mover you have tremendous advantage.

The information technology industry in India currently accounts for $5 billion in output, $2.75 billion in exports and employs about 230,000 people. But it has the potential to grow twenty times in eight years to $100 billion in output, $50 billion in exports and employ 2.2 million people. That is if India does the right things to exploit this potential. IT software and services could be India's largest export industry.

Obviously this rapid growth in IT offers tremendous opportunities for Andhra Pradesh. To capture those we mapped out a threefold strategy. We decided to publicize our intention of getting infrastructure going, and actually began to get it going so that they could come and see we meant business. Microsoft sent their team again and again, and each time they saw progress on the ground.

Then we consciously decided to go for the big names, starting with the biggest. If they came and set up shop here, we felt the demonstration effect would be tremendous.

The third prong of the strategy was to push IT education and get industry involved so that it could help create the human resources their investment in the state would require in years to come.

Implementing this strategy called for some measures. We were the first state in the country to create a department of information technology. When it became clear that the state government had a leading role to play in assisting an information technology boom in Andhra Pradesh, we formed a Special Interest Group. This comprised experts from the IT industry, the government and academic institutions. It suggested that Andhra Pradesh should have an information technology policy and accordingly we began work on a draft information technology policy for the state.

Many states in the country have now woken up to the need to boost information technology and attract investment in this sector. So there is considerable competition in announcing incentives. We have been constantly monitoring the incentives that will be required. A major growth area has been identified as IT-enabled services, or remote services. It is estimated that by the year 2008 this industry in India will generate annual revenues of US$20 billion or Rs 85,000 crore, leading to opportunities for more than 10,000 full-fledged units.

This sector, like the software industry, requires a conducive environment and access to large pools of skilled and semi-skilled professionals. IT-enabled services afford opportunity for creating jobs for large numbers of qualified, unemployed youth. In fact the value of putting in place a statewide area network is that such jobs can be pushed down to the districts, thanks to the connectivity provided.

However, globally this is an intensely cost-competitive sector, so a government that wants to attract those jobs has to come with a specific set of incentives tailored to its requirement. We worked on this, linking incentives given by the state directly to the employment generated. Deliberations with industry led to its articulating a series of demands for both incentives and procedural simplification, which we then addressed. In May 1999 we came up with an IT incentives policy.

We exempted the industry from the purview of the AP Pollution Control Act except in respect of power generation sets. We also exempted it from statutory power cuts. We extended the incentives and concessions in respect of power tariff which were applicable to industry, to this sector also. New IT industrial units were given 25 per cent concessional power tariff for a period of three years from the date of release of power, or of actually going into commercial production, whichever was earlier. We also instructed the department of energy to extend power connections to it on a priority basis.

Other incentives included total exemption for the software industry from sales tax and from zoning regulations for purposes of location. And we agreed in principle to self-certification or exemption as far as possible for the IT software industry from the provisions of a series of Acts such as the factories Act, minimum wages Act, workmen's compensation Act, and so on. We also gave permission to the industry to run a three-shift operation.

Further, we linked an incentive such as rebate in the cost of land allotted to an IT industry to jobs created, governed by a series of provisos. We formulated an investment subsidy for new IT industries, and special incentives for mega projects and pioneering projects with investments exceeding Rs 100 crore. But in addition to all these, it is the availability of trained manpower in the state which we expected would be a critical factor that companies would take into account while setting up IT investments. General Electric, for instance, has committed to taking its employment in Hyderabad up to 5000 people over a three-year time frame.

Incentives apart, to give a boost to the growth of existing companies and to the establishing of new projects we have set up a Rs 15 crore venture capital fund for software and information technology in Andhra Pradesh. When Indian entrepreneurs who have had striking success in Silicon Valley are asked why they cannot do in India what they can abroad, they usually cite the availability of venture capital as a major reason. So we decided that providing venture capital could be one way of getting young software engineers to consider setting up base here instead of emigrating.

The contributors to this fund are the Andhra Pradesh Industrial Development Corporation Ltd, the Small Industries Development Bank of India, and the AP Industrial and Infrastructure Corporation Ltd. Its purpose is to provide venture capital in projects with a high growth potential, and to provide replacement capital to purchase shares from existing equity investment. An asset management company has been incorporated to manage the fund, which is to have a limited life of ten years.

But the single biggest incentive we created to convince the IT industry of our intentions was the planning and execution of Hi-Tec City, which stands for Hyderabad Engineering Technology Consultancy City. It was conceived as a one-stop solution to meet the professional, business and social needs of high technology companies. It has been planned as an integrated township with all infrastructure facilities such as office space, production areas, housing, hotel, clubhouse, convention centre, showrooms, banks, shopping complex, captive power plant and effluent water waste management system.

The circular building that has come up in Madhapur in Hyderabad is a column-free structure whose biggest attraction is that those who rent space in it can count on captive electric supply, water supply, and a range of building automation systems. More important, however, captive telecommunication and data communication links have been provided. Videsh Sanchar Nigam Ltd has set up an international gateway for Hi-Tec city. The reason I emphasize this is because if you want the world to come to your doorstep with jobs and services you have to guarantee world-class infrastructure that is totally dependable. Hi-Tec City has become a symbol of the IT-friendly and helpful attitude of the state government.

At the same time there are those who see it as a white elephant that is not finding takers. Investors are sensitive to the political environment. There was a slowdown as the assembly elections approached because potential investors wanted to be assured that there would not be a change in the IT-friendly policy of the state in case there was a change in government. At present, however, the first phase of Hi-Tec City is fully booked and the second phase has commenced.

Having decided upon information technology as a vital growth engine we began to move swiftly to develop a world-class IT base. Once we had demonstrated that we meant business global players such as Microsoft, Oracle, General Electric and Motorola began to come in and set up significant parts of their business in the state. To create an environment where IT companies would thrive, we took several initiatives. The Hi-Tec City was one. Another was the decision to set up the Indian Institute of Information Technology to prepare outstanding professionals for positions of leadership in the IT world. We wanted it to become a global centre of excellence in IT.

After extensive discussions with industry we decided upon an innovative structure for the IIIT which is industry-sponsored, industry driven, self-financed and autonomous. It is taking the form of a core institute surrounded by a cluster of eight to ten corporate schools, operated by global leaders in the IT industry. While the IIIT is responsible for long-term and degree programmes, the schools run specialized short-term programmes. These are owned, run and managed by major IT companies with full academic, financial and managerial autonomy within the school.

Each of these schools represents the core competence

area of the company setting up that school. Companies such as IBM, Oracle, Motorola, Metamor and Satyam have already entered into agreements to set up corporate schools in the IIIT and out of these IBM's School of Enterprise-wide Computing became operational in January 1998. Oracle and Metamor Schools have already become operational in October 1998.

We intend it to be a global centre of excellence in IT education, training and research, but it is also intended to assist development of IT applications for social sectors like health, agriculture, education and rural development. The institution is expected to undertake design and consultancy services and create industry-required short-term courses for effective linkage with industry and users. It will also build linkages with leading universities of the world in the field of IT and management.

As a result of our efforts to create a growth-conducive climate software exports from Hyderabad have been growing at over 100 per cent over the last few years. Between 1995-96 and 1999-2000 their value went up from Rs 60 crore to Rs 1059 crore.

Meanwhile the growth in the number of companies in Hyderabad in relation to other locations in the country has shown a significant increase, both in absolute numbers and in percentage growth. In 1998-99 companies registered at Hyderabad increased 71 per cent in terms of their number as compared to 25 per cent in Bangalore, 36 per cent in Noida, and 51 per cent in Chennai. In 1999-2000 the number of companies registered in Hyderabad jumped fivefold, from 192 to 975. This shows the enormous potential of IT in the state.

To realize the potential we are looking at all of the following: ways to make PCs cheaper and more accessible for a far greater segment of the population, a boost to computer education for children in government schools, ways to permit private users on the statewide area network, rapid commissioning of information kiosks across the state, the issue of single window clearance for the information technology industry, and continued efforts to overcome resistance among some segments of government employees to information technology.

Where would we like to be twenty years from now? We aspire to a scenario where Andhra Pradesh becomes a premier centre for information technology software and services both in India and the world. There will be a large and thriving IT mega-hub in and around Hyderabad, with supplementary locations in Visakhapatnam, Warangal, Vijaywada and Tirupati. We expect by then that a significant number of the top 500 global IT companies will have centres in Hyderabad and that it will be a preferred destination for IT professionals.

At a parallel level we will have created in the state an information-based society in which this technology is a way of life. Andhra Pradesh will have become an established pioneer in electronic government applications as well as the IT education centre of India, and a leader in distance and distributed learning.

We have identified the steps that have to be taken to transit from what we are to where we want to be. We have to develop world-class IT infrastructure including broadband digital connectivity which will move information much faster. The measure of a country's potential in the millennium will be, 'megabits per capita'. How much installed bandwidth a country has divided by the number of potential users.

We have to make Andhra Pradesh the hub for developing electronic government applications. We need to promote Andhra Pradesh as a premier location for top-notch IT companies. We have to develop education and research institutions to make Andhra Pradesh a premier IT education centre in India. And finally, we have to bring IT into the service of people in all parts of the state.

Of these steps the first is crucial. We need an advanced communications network in the targeted IT areas and major business hubs. Several IT services of the future will need far more telecommunications bandwidth than the services of today. International networks are being contemplated by FLAG (Fibre Link Across the Globe), Project Oxygen, and by Reliance which will be establishing terrestrial networks capable of supporting bandwidths of up to one terabit per second. They will be needed to sustain the communications explosion that will come in this century. We are working to promote the establishment of broadband digital networks in the state.

Equally, creating telecommunications infrastructure will mean that the government has to provide high-band connectivity with international gateways.

A major Central policy change that will be required is removing the monopoly of VSNL over international communications. The National IT Task Force of which I was co-chairperson made this recommendation.

If Andhra Pradesh is to be a major hub for the IT business, policy changes shall be necessary. In addition, we want to extend our commitment to creating telecommunications infrastructure to promoting the use of satellite and wireless communications.

We also expect cable television networks to become a multipurpose communications medium for homes and offices.

Today Hi-Tec City is spread over less than one square kilometre whereas the US Silicon Valley is an 80 km strip and Malaysia's Multimedia Super Corridor is a 750 km strip. We plan to invite the private sector to create satellite townships near Hi-Tec City and other IT hubs so that residential facilities and other living conditions comparable to other locations in the world can be provided.

To promote Andhra Pradesh as an IT destination we are organizing promotions in Silicon Valley and Europe. We are also developing alliances with targeted countries such as Japan, Singapore and Germany to encourage companies in these countries to set up IT centres in Andhra Pradesh.

■

Besides information technology, where tourism is concerned
Andhra Pradesh has been a case of untapped potential, a
situation that the state government is now moving to rapidly
rectify. A state tourism policy was announced in 1998 and in
that fiscal year the budgetary allocation for tourism was
enhanced from Rs 1.2 crore to Rs 45 crore. We feel there is
tremendous service sector employment potential in this area
if we can attract the investment.

The strategy is to develop Andhra Pradesh as both a
destination and a hub. We have identified six special tourism
areas to be developed: Hyderabad, Visakhapatnam, Tirupati,
Nagarjunasagar which has potential as a Buddhist heritage
site, Warangal and Vijaywada. The state's assets are a unique
mix of heritage sites, a long coastline, picturesque lakes,
valleys, hill stations, ancient temples, historic monuments
and cultural sites with considerable potential for beach tourism,
pilgrim tourism, conference tourism, leisure tourism, cultural
tourism and adventure tourism. The state enjoys a strategic
location geographically.

Intensive private-public participation is central to the
state government's approach to tourism. The state government
will provide land and basic infrastructure, whereas the
investment and expertise will come from the private sector.
A number of concessions and incentives form part of the new
tourism policy to draw entrepreneurs to invest in tourism
related activities. This includes a tax holiday on sales tax,
investment subsidies for all tourism ventures, rebate on
electricity charges, exemptions from luxury tax for new hotels
and from road tax for identified tourism circuits. Large
projects of above Rs 10 crore will be eligible for special
incentives. Our policy is designed to make Andhra Pradesh
a tourism destination state in India.

The Andhra Pradesh government appointed world-class
professional consultancy firms to study the potential in special
tourism areas and make recommendations. Tirupati sees

tourist arrivals of nearly 18 million every year but the average stay is of two and a half days and the average expenditure of Rs 146 a day. The policy is looking at how we can capture value along with numbers. Schemes to enhance the tourist potential of Tirupati, Chandragiri, Kalyandam, Kalahasti, Talakona and other areas have been set in motion.

There will be considerable focus on Hyderabad and its attractions too. Development schemes for the Charminar area, Qutub Shahi tombs and other heritage sites are finalized. The Buddha Purnima project around the Hussain Sagar Lake area is expected to be a unique tourist and cultural experience.

Another area of potential employment where there are strengths that have to be leveraged is agri-business. Andhra Pradesh has shown the highest rate of growth in the country in the use of tractors, pumpsets and fertilizers. It is the leading producer of poultry products. Its brackish water prawn culture and pisciculture have taken off in a big way. In total silk cocoon production it is second only to Karnataka.

Yet the gross irrigated area in the state has come down by 1.5 per cent in the last few years. Farmers need far more financial assistance to cultivate the land they have; they also need faster disbursal of subsidies. We have to invest in warehouses and cold storage, improve transportation facilities for them, invest in farmer education, organize self-certification by seed and chemicals producers, and invest in providing irrigation facilities.

Dairying is an area in which Andhra Pradesh has some strength; it also makes a good case study of how value can be added in this sector to make it a major industry, and what needs to be done towards this end. Today, dairy is India's second largest food expenditure category after cereals, and accounts for 18 per cent of the total food expenditure of our people. The World Bank estimates that demand will triple in the next ten years with the rise in per capita consumption.

What's more, consumption of value-added dairy products will go up.

The World Trade Organization wants member countries to bring down dairy subsidies, which immediately puts India at an advantage because it is one industry in which there are virtually no subsidies. It could emerge as a strong player in export markets. There are other advantages: it is a very effective tool in the empowerment of women, it is labour intensive and increases village prosperity, and Operation Flood in other parts of the country has demonstrated the social and economic impact it can have.

The current reality in Andhra Pradesh, however, is that though it has a number of milk pockets, dairying has been dominated by the cooperative sector and unorganized individual milkmen. The cooperative sector in Andhra Pradesh has been characterized by low profitability, overstaffing, low capacity utilization, weak marketing and much else. To transform this situation a number of initiatives have been mapped out involving the entry of the private sector, development of veterinary facilities, and amending of the milk and milk products order which is restrictive.

To take just two other examples, pharmaceuticals and the health sector are areas where Andhra Pradesh already has a strong presence and where strategic interventions could make a critical difference. Today the state accounts for one-third of all the bulk drug units in the country, and has a huge pool of skilled people in the pharma sector. But its growth rate in pharma is declining compared to the national average, there has been a significant erosion of profits, and research and development facilities are inadequate.

The way forward, therefore, could include dedicated industrial estates for bulk drug manufacturing, a critical strengthening of research and development efforts, the establishment of international standard test laboratories, help in the expansion of existing manufacturing units and much else. These are the areas we have to work on. A major boost came from the commissioning in October 1999 of the Knowledge Park, certainly the first initiative of its kind in the country.

We have implemented the concept of creating world-class infrastructure facilities for research and development in collaboration with ICICI. Modular laboratories which can be hired on a lease basis have been constructed. The rationale for this project comes from the fact that a lot of multinationals are interested in doing research in India because of the availability of high quality scientific manpower. When the same Indians do research in the US costs are high, here it can be done at a tenth of the cost.

Like Hi-Tec City, Knowledge Park will have dedicated infrastructure, including power supply. It will also have single window clearance, including a customs office to clear imported drugs. The experience of Anji Reddy's Reddy Labs has been that this can be a major constraint: customs clearance through Bombay inhibits the speedy import of chemicals that may be required for ongoing research.

We are also looking at what will be required to make Hyderabad a major health care city—indeed a destination for health tourism. With reference to the rest of India it has central location, and has a large number of corporate hospitals. We need to see how these can attract patients from other states, and from other countries. We need to persuade non-resident Indian doctors to spend sabbaticals in India. Health care institutions will have to be given electricity and water at industrial rates to make them competitive enough to draw patients from other destinations.

The sectors listed above are merely illustrative: there are many others where we are examining what needs to be done to enhance investment opportunities. The chapter on Vision 2020 will deal with more of these.

Wooing investment at national and international fora is another initiative in attracting investors. Critics, particularly in the political opposition, may carp, but it has to be done. If Hyderabad has to have top of the mind recall among the investing global community we have to go and remind people of its existence, again and again. China began liberalizing in 1978. But the big money which came into China came ten years later. Creating investor confidence is not a one-off thing—it is a process. You have to go back again and again to a place like Davos, have face-to-face sessions with CEOs, make your sales pitch to them in their own countries, in short market yourself. Continuously.

People do not decide to invest the first time they meet you. They have to develop confidence in you first. I went to Malaysia in 1997, to the US in 1998, to the World Economic Summit in Davos in 1999 and then again in 2000. Investment does not necessarily follow because of one visit. But when I make a presentation to them myself, answer their questions, anticipate their doubts, it puts Hyderabad as a possibility into their minds.

The plain truth is that India's image in the investing community is poor. And every time an Enron or a Cogentrix has a bad experience, the negative fallout affects other investment destinations within the country. State governments will have to work very hard and be very aggressive in their marketing to counter these negative experiences that some companies have had.

A politician, be he a chief minister, finance minister or prime minister, also educates himself when he travels and sees how things are done in other cultures. When I visited the Media Lab at the Massachusetts Institute of Technology, it was an education for me on the possibilities technology holds for the people of any country. I see no reason why people in India should not aspire to be on the frontiers of these fields. As for Davos, the best minds in the world come there. It is a tremendous education to just sit in that forum and listen.

Wooing investment abroad is one kind of initiative. The

other one that will matter more in the long run is changing the face that we as a state present to our industrialists at home, including those within Andhra Pradesh. When I started interacting directly with industry this is what they would tell me: 'We look forward to an environment in which government does not believe they are rulers but that they are serving the state.' They would also tell me, 'Your officials look down upon industry. They treat us as the starting point of all ills in society. They mistake profit for profiteering.' Today the same industrialists will concede that there has been a major attitudinal change.

It is not only Andhra Pradesh. With the exception of Gujarat most states in the country are run by politicians and bureaucracies which have traditionally treated industry with suspicion. In the case of the bureaucracy it is a result of their training. Marketing was not meant to be part of their job, their training is in regulation and control. If their role has to change in the new economy, their training also has to take this into account.

In Gujarat the bureaucracy is entrepreneurial. Irrespective of the party in power the bureaucracy drives the industrial development of Gujarat. They are investment friendly, investor friendly, corporate friendly. Today in Andhra Pradesh we are trying to create a similar environment in which industry and government can be partners in driving the state's economic growth. But again, the mindset has to change all the way down.

I have discovered that drawing investment to your state in competition with other states is a battle you win sometimes, and lose sometimes. But if you lose, it should not be for lack of trying. Personal ego should not come in the way of making an all-out bid for a project. What is at stake is not just a few thousand jobs in direct employment but an entire range of ancillary industries that spring up over time around, say, a major automobile project. And, of course, a new and substantial stream of taxes for the state exchequer.

The big manufacturing opportunity of the 1990s was in the automobile industry. But all of this went to one of three clusters that have developed in the country for automobile engineering operations in Chennai, the Bombay–Pune belt and in the Delhi–Haryana area. Ford, Mitsubishi, Hyundai, Daewoo—Andhra Pradesh lost out on all those. With Toyota, however, I did try very hard, with the backing and support of the Confederation of Indian Industries.

They arranged a meeting for me with Mr Toyota. I made a presentation to him on my laptop which my officials had prepared. They had done a lot of research on Toyota Motors, where it is located around the world, its manufacturing facilities, its history as a company. Based on their needs we had drawn up a case for locating it in Andhra Pradesh.

We would have been able to give them the kind of land they wanted, rapid clearances, and access to more than one port for shipping the parts. But we lost out because the Kirloskars, Toyota's local partner, were insistent on Karnataka with which they already had manufacturing links. Decisions on major projects, therefore, are taken in different ways. The irony is that today the Kirloskars have almost pulled out of the project, but Toyota continues to be located in Karnataka because the factory has come up and it is too late to relocate.

With the Indian School of Business which is now coming up near Hyderabad and for which there was tremendous competition from Karnataka, Tamil Nadu and Maharashtra, we did manage to pull it off. We had heard that the decision had been taken to locate it in Mumbai. But then one morning one of my aides read in the *Economic Times* that the project was running into trouble with the Maharashtra government. When he told me I got on the phone immediately, called each of the Indian industrialists associated with the project and invited them here. When they came I made a presentation to them on 'Hyderabad as the Emerging Knowledge Hub'.

We got into the race a little later than the others, but

once we were in it we moved with the greatest speed in giving them the kind of location that they wanted and other clearances. It was important to clinch it just in terms of its sheer potential. It is a prestigious Rs 200 crore-plus project that will bring its own spin-off.

The school is a collaboration between the Wharton Business School, Kellogg and India's leading business houses. It will have students from all over India and other countries coming to study there. The focus of the school's curriculum, to begin with, will be entrepreneurship and e-commerce. The board of governors is a veritable who's who of international and domestic business, and when they come to Hyderabad for board meetings every year they will see what we have to offer, and that could spawn later investment. They will judge us by the speed of our clearances, and by our adherence to commitments made. One project of this pedigree becomes a continuing opportunity to become credible in the international community of investors.

Future investors are also looking for political stability. Following the clear mandate from voters in the assembly elections of 1999 there has been a dramatic stepping up of interested foreign visitors to Hyderabad. The American Business Council is establishing a Hyderabad chapter. The American embassy is establishing a Foreign Commercial Services office here, as is the United Kingdom. The Germans have been coming to see what we have to offer.

They have begun to be reassured by three things: Our commitment to speed and transparency in government decision making, our track record in honouring decisions made, and the assurance that they will be dealing with the same chief minister for the next five years. The world outside has seen far too much political instability in India in recent years to want to risk constant policy changes.

Which is not to say that there is any room for complacency in Andhra Pradesh. Industrialists here have been at pains to point out to me that we must address the need for a revival in the manufacturing sector. Given the number of advantages the state has going for it—political stability, climate, port facilities, stable labour relations, a climate of entrepreneurship—it is still not sufficiently perceived as the preferred destination for all categories of investors. There are companies, they point out, which have exited this state, and other companies which went elsewhere. There is a substantial gap between MOUs being signed and the number that are actually implemented. The growth of small and medium enterprises is also lower in AP than expected.

We have to examine whether infrastructure is superior in other states, and whether return on investment is perceived to be higher elsewhere. And industry that is already in the state is at pains to point out that the government should not load its social responsibilities on one sector of the economy alone. Their perception is that industry is bearing all costs to subsidize the agriculture and service sectors. Our officials are constantly in dialogue with representatives of industry on these issues.

Meanwhile, in partnership with the Confederation of Indian Industry, we plan on setting up an institute for productivity and innovation that will improve the total factory productivity of the work force in the state and in the country. In terms of world competitiveness India's growth rates in labour productivity were 50 per cent less than those of Malaysia in agriculture. Our productivity in manufacturing, however, was slightly better than that of Malaysia's. Overall, between 1986 and 1995 India had an average growth rate in the labour productivity of the total economy of 3.35 per cent. The comparative rates for Malaysia and China were 5.78 per cent and 7.06 per cent.

Vision 2020 sets a growth rate of 11 per cent to be achieved by Andhra Pradesh by 2020. We would like to get there well before that date. Sector by sector we are looking at the facilitating policies that have to be put in place, including the regulatory changes required. More on these in the chapter on Vision 2020.

IV

TACKLING THE BASICS

10

HRD FOR THE FUTURE

- One out of two people in Andhra Pradesh cannot read or write.

- Less than 63 per cent of the students who enter primary school in India graduate from it.

- In some parts of Andhra Pradesh you have to travel between thirty and sixty kilometres to reach a primary health centre.

- There is one Indian doctor serving every 1325 Americans in the United States compared to one Indian doctor serving over 2400 Indians in India itself.

You cannot build a nation without human resources. But to provide one billion people with proper education and health care and then keep the brightest among them from leaving the country is a daunting task. The above statistics spell out a challenge which requires not just enormous resources but multiple, constantly changing strategies, and enormous optimism.

Today, out of every two children you enrol in school, one is likely to drop out, and in the case of scheduled caste and scheduled tribe children, the rate is even higher. The dropout rate in Andhra Pradesh was found to be 45 per cent, going up to 74 per cent in the case of scheduled tribe children, during a multi-donor review mission of the District Primary Education Programme conducted in November-December 1999.

As the population grows the challenge grows. The state cannot keep up with the demand a growing population makes of schools and teachers. That is partly why half a century of planned development has not been enough to bring every child in India into school. The country's pattern of habitation and sheer geographic spread has made the task even more difficult. We have a million habitations, many of them very small. To reach schools and medicare to all of these requires huge financial resources.

Andhra Pradesh constitutes 7.9 per cent of India's population. At the current rate of growth 18 million people are added to the population of India every year, of which my state's contribution is 1.2 million. Given finite natural resources and the costs of providing infrastructure and services, that is a daunting prospect. Apart from schooling, the state is expected to provide enough foodgrains per capita, housing, jobs and medicare to these huge numbers.

That is why fertility reduction is at the core of our human resource development efforts. In 1997 we prepared for the first time, both in the history of the state and, I believe, in the history of the country, a state-specific population policy. This was backed up with state government allocations, in addition to the Central government funds provided for population control.

The country has had an ongoing family planning programme for four decades, but as far as we are concerned, it has not·succeeded in lowering the fertility rate in Andhra Pradesh to the desired extent. In 1983 Parliament adopted a National Health Policy which set some goals for AD 2000. The total fertility rate target, according to this document, was

2.3, the desired couple protection rate 60 per cent, and it envisioned bringing down of the crude birth rate to 21 per thousand. (The total fertility rate signifies the average number of children born to a woman in the state during her reproductive cycle.)

In all three respects Andhra Pradesh has performed better than the all-India average, but we are not satisfied with that. We expect that we have met the above goals in our state by now. In 1996 our total fertility rate had already been brought down to 2.7, against the set target of 2.3 by AD 2000 and the national figure at that point of 3.5. Our couple protection rate was 48.8 per cent as compared to 45.4 per cent all-India, our crude birth rate was 22.7 compared to a national average of 27.4 per thousand.

By 2001 we will have brought down the total fertility rate to 2.1. But we are propelled by the example of other states in southern India which had already achieved, and indeed exceeded, the goals for 2000 by 1996, going by the Sample Registration Survey figures. We chose not to measure ourselves against the poorly performing states, but against Kerala.

The four southern states of Andhra Pradesh, Tamil Nadu, Kerala and Karnataka are ahead of the rest of the country in terms of achieving population stabilization goals. Andhra Pradesh is third, after Kerala and Tamil Nadu, and Karnataka fourth. Part of the reason why the south has fared so differently is because the coercion that was practised during Indira Gandhi's Emergency did not take place in the south. Therefore this part of the country was spared the backlash that saw the programme grind to a halt in the late 1970s in the states which needed it the most. Throughout this period and the 1980s the family planning programme retained its momentum in the southern states.

In my first term as chief minister in Andhra Pradesh we reviewed the achievement in family planning within the ambit of our development goals for the state and came to the conclusion that to be effectively implemented population control has to follow a state-specific programme. There are two reasons for this: family planning has always been a national programme, funded a 100 per cent by the Centre, and one consequence of this has been that the states have not really accepted ownership for the programme. In most of the other states nobody talks about population, though it is the most crucial problem confronting our nation.

Given the demographic and socio-cultural diversity prevailing in the country, an effective population stabilization programme simply has to be state-specific. The problems we face in Andhra Pradesh are totally different from UP's or Kerala's problems. If we are to implement a programme we must have our own interventions and strategies to tackle our particular problems. We have found from experience that decentralizing is very essential.

When the Government of India releases funds to the states no flexibility in utilization is allowed. Some of the schemes they provide are just not relevant to Andhra Pradesh, though they may be for UP. We could utilize those funds in a different way but we are not allowed to.

We discussed these issues and set our own demographic goals, which are separate from those of the Centre and are more ambitious than national goals. We have analysed what our specific problems are and then tailored our schemes and interventions to address them. The state government has to fund all these, because the Government of India only funds schemes specified by it.

There are many reasons why you cannot have a monolithic approach to delivering services in a country like this one. To take just one example, even patterns of population density affect strategies for providing health or education services. If you compare Kerala and Andhra Pradesh, the relatively compact population settlement patterns of the former make it far easier to provide coverage. The latter, however, has around 33,000 settlements with populations below 1000. In Kerala 90 per cent of all settlements have populations above 10,000. This has made it easier to make Kerala literate: one school can cover a greater section of the population. You can even provide a choice of schools to settlements of that size.

Similarly, the distance that people have to travel to obtain health care is less in Kerala. This makes providing health care easier. A PHC there could handle 200 deliveries in a year, whereas in AP, with far more scattered population, the comparable figure would be perhaps thirty deliveries. Different strategies are needed for the two states. The Central government stipulates that a PHC must cover a population of 30,000. In Andhra you have to travel between thirty and sixty kilometres to reach a PHC, and up to eight kilometres to reach a sub-centre. In Kerala you would have to travel no more than seven kilometres to reach a PHC and less than one kilometre to reach a sub-centre.

This makes Kerala's task much easier in reaching both literacy and population goals. And the age of marriage for women changes when people are literate. Andhra Pradesh's average age of marriage for girls is 15.5 years, one of the lowest in the country. In Kerala it is 19 years. Occupation and migration patterns are also different. The number of married women in the reproductive age group who live with their husbands is 60 per cent in Kerala, owing to the high rate of migration. In Andhra the figure is 93 per cent. That too has a bearing on the number of babies being born.

The fertility decline that has occurred in the southern states has happened for different reasons in different states. In Kerala it has been due mainly to female literacy, access to health and family welfare services, and a strong political and community commitment to the small family norm.

In Tamil Nadu the fall in birth rate is ascribed to sustained political commitment, improved access to maternal and child health services, as well as improvement in women's status through education and employment.

Andhra Pradesh is an example of a state where fertility reduction has been achieved despite low literacy levels among women. In no district in the state except Hyderabad, which is fully urbanized, has the female literacy rate crossed 50 per cent. In almost half the districts, it is even below 30 per cent. The Telengana region in particular has very low levels of female literacy: in two districts in this region it drops to below 20 per cent.

The infant mortality rate in the state is also high, and this poses a major challenge to improving the demography of the state. But it also adds to the mystery of what accounts for the fertility decline in Andhra Pradesh. We have a theory for this. It is because we have had, historically, a very focussed and committed implementation of the family welfare programme as a whole in the state.

Not just the family planning programme but also the mother and child health programme, basically related to antenatal care of pregnant women, deliveries, anganwadis, and post-natal care, and then immunization care of the child. It has been a really successful programme, with several independent surveys showing that Andhra has been one of the best performing states in the country where these services are concerned.

For instance, the latest national family health survey conducted in 1998-99 found that over 90 per cent of Andhra's women were covered by antenatal care, and immunization coverage was also good. The same person who delivers the mother and child programme also talks to the women about family planning. And because of the confidence they have in this system which is taking care of their overall health they are willing to listen to the other message.

So despite low literacy and a very low age of marriage, Andhra's family planning achievement is the third in the country after Kerala and Tamil Nadu. It is a programme that is not resisted in the state. The other interesting theory that officials administering the health programme have to offer (and on which there is no formal study) is that in some way the low age of marriage has actually worked to the advantage of the programme.

They have found that women undergo the operation at a very early age in Andhra Pradesh, at around twenty-five years, by which time they have already had two or three children. Since the sterilization programme has been implemented in Andhra Pradesh in a focussed, consistent manner since the early 1970s, the women who are today mothers-in-law have actually undergone the sterilization operation themselves, hence there is no resistance from them. Elsewhere in the country they are a strong force in resisting family planning.

Where the state has been far less successful is in lowering its infant mortality rate, which continues to be high. Over the years we have narrowed down the causes to infant diarrhoea and pneumonia and the wrong practices which prevail in tackling these. Also to malnutrition at birth. Much of infant mortality is neonatal mortality, death within a month of birth. We are putting a range of health schemes in place to encourage families in the rural areas to go in for more institutional deliveries. A great deal of education is required to tackle infant mortality, and literacy in the mothers and mothers-in-law would certainly help.

Fifty per cent of all deliveries take place at home in Andhra Pradesh, whereas we want this figure to be more like Kerala's, where over 90 per cent of births are in hospitals or primary health care centres. Both maternal and infant mortality can be tackled better if births take place in institutions. We have put in place two schemes, one to cover incidental costs including the food and travel of the attendant, if the family opts for an institutional delivery.

The other has been to find a way of letting rural families know what an institutional delivery will cost so that they are encouraged to opt for it. We have negotiated a package with the Indian Medical Association as well as private nursing home associations to announce a rate which covers antenatal visits, the actual delivery, as well as a post-natal package of check-ups for the mother and immunization of the children for three months after the birth.

This rate is being publicized. The idea is that even if a family does not want to go to a government hospital for the delivery and is staying away from private nursing homes in the rural areas for fear of what it will cost, they will now have the information on the basis of which to take a decision. The package will cost Rs 650 in the rural areas and Rs 950 in urban areas. It includes the cost of blood infusion that the mother may require. More and more nursing homes across the state are accepting these rates.

In the last five years, since 1994-95, there has been a doubling of the health budget in the state. This was sorely necessary to strengthen the health infrastructure. A more than fivefold increase in bed strength is being effected.

The drugs budget has been doubled, and despite terrific resistance we are trying out new systems of drug procurement and distribution. We are also shifting from bulk drugs, so common in government dispensaries, to strip-packed drugs, so that requirements for tendering are eliminated and there is more insurance of quality.

Critics ask, why are people still dying of epidemics in your state? Sixty-two per cent of all diseases in Andhra Pradesh are communicable diseases, therefore improving water supply and sanitation is urgently necessary. Also, huge problems still remain in terms of availability of drugs and doctors, and of timely access to medicare. Resources are limited. The plain truth is that after half a century of spending, government has still not delivered a well-maintained infrastructural network for health or education. For many years now, the system has had no money to spend on maintenance.

One result is that the common man all over the country opts increasingly for private health care, however exploitative it may be. The presence of these practitioners has to be taken into reckoning in planning the state's overall health strategy. Currently we are looking at health insurance options, both for government employees as well as for vulnerable sections of the populace.

Information technology too holds great promise to make health services more efficient and expand their reach to rural areas. When I visited the USA in September 1998 I saw how telemedicine was being used at the Massachusetts General Hospital. With the rapid expansion of connectivity services like telemedicine, citizens would be able to have access to expert medical advice. In future, community health workers could consult with specialist doctors and render better medical care. Even patients would be better informed about diseases and medication.

Efficiency in delivering of health services would ensue with IT. The inventory of drugs and medicine available at different locations in the state has been computerized and will soon become online. The referral system from lower level medical institutions to more specialized institutions will also become possible online. This will be a great convenience to patients who need not undergo repetitive tests and carry their medical records with them.

Along with health care, education, particularly primary education, remains a tough challenge. In November-December 1999, a joint supervisory mission of a vast multi-phase, multi-donor project was attempting to assess, armed with formidable statistical tools, how much closer Indian children had come to getting what could be called an education.

They used forty parameters, bristling with acronyms, to

measure whether more children were coming into the school system, were they staying in it and were they learning anything. The donors were the World Bank, Unicef, the European Commission and others, and they had evolved the practice of conducting joint supervision missions each year led by a different donor each time. The programme was the District Primary Education Programme, begun in 1994, running in fourteen states, yet another massive effort to reach the elusive goal of getting every Indian child into school.

DPEP has three major objectives: increasing enrolment, improving retention and learning abilities of children and developing institutional capacity in the state for providing school support. What works in one state does not work in another. And when a goal is reached it requires enormous strategizing and effort to retain the achievement.

Perhaps the single biggest stumbling block to equality of opportunity in India is the rural school, which is often just a classroom-less, teacher-less notion. Millions of our children have access to nothing better. The quality of schooling in the public sphere denies the majority of children the foundation they need to develop marketable skills.

Teachers in rural areas in many parts of the country are not available to teach. They may be posted at a rural school, but if they are ingenious, they will know how to draw their salary from the village school while manipulating an attachment to an urban school. When a schoolteacher's job is advertised in a district, a great many apply because they want government jobs. But thereafter they try their level best to stay in urban centres, or places closest to their homes. This is partly because of a lack of suitable amenities such as housing, as also a suitable school for one's own children. A teacher with children going to high school may not want to be posted in a village with only a primary or middle school.

It is not that successive governments have not addressed the problem: they have. Both Central and state government schemes for extending rural primary education abound. In our state alone the AP Primary Education Programme has run for a good ten years prior to DPEP. Countrywide, literacy has risen from 16 per cent at the time of Independence to 52 per cent at the time of the 1991 census. But other Asian countries have done much better. Thailand's rate of literacy stands at 91 per cent, Malaysia's at 84 per cent, China's at 81.5 per cent and Indonesia's at 75 per cent.

In Andhra Pradesh one out of two people is illiterate. Among the southern states our literacy level has been the most dismal. And countrywide, the state ranks 26th in terms of general literacy, 29th in terms of female illiteracy. There are also considerable disparities between the literacy levels of specific groups such as rural women, the scheduled castes and scheduled tribes, and backward classes in the state.

There are regional differences too—while Hyderabad district may have 72 per cent literacy, in Mahabubnagar, one of the poorest districts in the country, the figure is 30 per cent. The number of adults who are not literate is estimated to be one crore in the state, and the school drop-out population is around forty lakh.

In both the state and Central budgets, therefore, the allocation for primary education has to receive a major boost. Since resources are scarce, we turned to the World Bank for assistance in extending the District Primary Education Project. But money is only the first step. Primary education will deliver results only when the system through which it is delivered changes enough to make a difference.

Universalization of elementary education is a goal accomplished in three stages: access, enrolment, retention.

First there has to be a school for the child to go to. In a number of habitations in many states there isn't one. Madhya Pradesh conceived of its Education Guarantee Scheme as a strategy to provide access to education in many scattered habitations. If there were forty children of schoolgoing age in any habitation, the state government promised that it would open a school there, manned by a guruji. Consequently, well over a lakh habitations were covered by such schools.

We have a similar strategy to target small habitations without access to a school. These are called alternative schools or mabadi schools (Telugu for 'our school'), and are opened if there are a minimum of twenty-five children who require schooling in that habitation. These are already running and we plan to extend the number to 15,000 such schools under the aegis of the District Primary Education Programme. Primary schools for all school-less habitations with a population of 200 or more are now being opened.

The issue here is the quality of such on-demand schools and the teachers who are likely to be drawn from the local youth. Critics have said that what the Constitution guarantees in its fundamental right to education is a good formal school with a qualified teacher, not a stopgap arrangement. I would say the goal is to continually upgrade schools of this kind, but not hinder access of these children to schooling until the human and monetary resources permit the establishment of a full-fledged primary school. It is the same approach as in the health system, where we are engaged currently in upgrading all existing rural health facilities.

The next goal, that of enrolment, is only partly facilitated by expanding access. Persuasion is still the need of the hour. It is an ironic situation where the might of the state backed by well-intentioned foreign donors cannot convince a child and his or her parents that the child should go to school. That neither child nor parent perceives enough value in this transition is a comment on the quality of education we have offered so far.

Elaborate strategies have been drawn up to raise enrolment over the years, but now the community's role is increasingly being seen as central to both enrolment and retention. When money has been spent in the past it has not delivered results because nobody demanded accountability, either from the teacher or the contractor. In Andhra Pradesh we came around to the view that many of these problems could be resolved by using a valuable local resource, one that has a stake in the education of children: their parents.

From 1995 itself we had begun to examine the nature and dimensions of the problem, and decide what kinds of impetus the school education system needed. We came to the conclusion that a radical shift in the structure of supervision and accountability was called for if there was to be a meaningful improvement in the quality of primary education. We then began to draft legislation that would legally empower local communities to have a say in the functioning of government schools.

In April 1998 the Government of Andhra Pradesh enacted the School Education (Community Participation) Act 1998. It sought to mandate the participation of the local community through the empowerment of parents who had, after all, the most stake in ensuring the future of their children. It did this by legislating the creation of parent-teacher associations, school committees and panchayat education committees. Each school, however small, would have a parent-teacher association in which parents of all the children studying in the school and the teachers of the school would be members. This constituted the general body of the stakeholders.

This body in turn would elect the school committee consisting of four parent members and the headmaster as a member-convener. Above the school committee would be the Panchayat Education Committee at the level of the gram panchayat, with two representatives from each of the schools in its area, constituted under the chairmanship of the sarpanch. The school committees would be elected if there was a contest, or else chosen by consensus.

In July 1998 we began constituting committees for all the schools and eventually one and a half lakh were constituted,

90 per cent of them by consensus. Fifty per cent of the seats in these committees are for women; representation in all the committees for weaker sections is also provided for. The Act provided for a two-year term for these committees, and a significant provision was the power to recall. The parent-teacher association was vested with the power to recall any of the members of higher level committees in the case of non-performance or misconduct on the part of such members.

Since parents cannot assume financial and supervisory responsibilities overnight, a one-day training programme was organized for all members of school committees on their duties and responsibilities, in the last week of August 1998. We then organized regional conferences for school committee presidents which I addressed.

We envisioned the following responsibilities for the parents: first of all they would ensure enrolment and retention of children in school. They were expected to keep a tab on the overall performance of the school and the children, review and monitor the school health programmes, distribute textbooks—and rice—for the midday meal.

The Act conferred on the parent members significant financial responsibilities. They were to manage the school education fund for the development of the school. They could hire the services of local persons as teachers, instructors—or preraks—on a voluntary basis or on payment of fixed honorarium and meet the cost from the school education fund. And, most important, perhaps for the first time anywhere in the country, the state government disbursed funds to the parents to execute the construction of school buildings.

Now school building works under the District Primary Education Programme have been entrusted to the school committees. These have opened bank accounts to be operated jointly by the committee chairman and the headmaster of the school. Funds for school works are being released to the school committee accounts. In the initial phase 25,000 buildings were constructed under DPEP with an estimated cost of Rs 250 crore.

Engineering guidance for the planning and construction of school buildings comes from personnel drafted from the various district engineering departments. The committees engage site consultants who provide technical guidance. The latter were given a three-day training course on various aspects of the construction of school buildings. The relevant department brought out a construction manual in Telugu to help the school committee members in effective monitoring and supervision of civil works.

Thanks to the active involvement of the local communities and the use of low-cost local construction materials, the quality of our civil works has been commended by appraisal missions for being better and cheaper than that of schools in other states.

However, the whole aspect of community mobilization and community sensitization is a slow process where things do not happen overnight. The community relates more easily to physical assets, particularly when its own literacy is not so high. In the civil construction stage there has been a lot of involvement and enthusiasm. In one tribal block, the committee members collected a substantial amount of money from the community for the construction of the school.

A mid-term assessment of how the school education committees were functioning in fifty schools each of Vizianagaram, Nellore, Kurnool, Karimnagar and Warangal found that while their involvement in various physical aspects of the running of the schools was considerable, there was far less comprehension of the pedagogic aspects of the DPEP programme in the majority of the school committee members.

The twin challenges of enrolment and retention require both physical and pedagogical responses. In the last three or four years we focussed heavily on the first. On providing school buildings, compound walls, toilets, enough classrooms

and drinking water. There were allocations in the programme
for this essential infrastructure and this part was implemented
with both speed and care.

Six thousand schools have been sanctioned, 36,000 school
buildings constructed under DPEP, Janmabhoomi and other
schemes, 80,000 teachers have been recruited and 24,000
more posts of teachers have been notified for recruitment
during 1999-2000.

But the drive to strengthen infrastructure and recruit
teachers was the easy part. Achieving enrolment, and even
more than that retention, and supporting and encouraging
teachers to do their jobs better is going to require a lot of
commitment and supervision. The school education
committee chairpersons received one day of training initially,
and it is becoming clear that it was not enough. Training for
these new voluntary roles needs to be more frequent and
more intensive.

The joint review mission found that Andhra Pradesh had
been second only to Madhya Pradesh in terms of percentage
increase in enrolment. Village education committees which
exist at the village level have been taught to map habitations
to identify houses where the children do not go to school.
Many strategies are being deployed to reach children who
stay out of school on account of migration, or child labour, or
disabilities or other problems.

We run summer schools and back-to-school programmes
for drop-outs, we have possibly the strongest network of
residential schools in the country for children of the scheduled
castes and scheduled tribes, we run transitional schools to
bring child labourers into the educational mainstream and
residential bridge course camps for girls. Despite continuing
efforts there are still children who are difficult to reach in
most districts of Andhra. The school education committees
are not as yet equipped to reach these with the conventional
mobilization drives they do; other strategies have to be
worked out for them.

Retention is again another challenge guaranteed to keep educational planners and administrators on their toes.

The presence of teachers in the classroom has to be ensured and the quality of teacher-learner materials, teaching methods and textbooks improved. Teachers need support from outside; though an elaborate resource group system has been worked out, we are discovering that they may have been loaded with too many responsibilities to be able to perform effectively.

Our other major initiative of the last few years has been an attempt to tackle the problem of rampant absenteeism among schoolteachers, which makes a mockery of the existing schools. We are experimenting with a transfer policy that gives teachers a say in which place they are transferred to. Known as teacher transfer through counselling, it allows them to state their choice of posting and then uses a performance-linked system of awarding points to make the actual transfer decision fair and transparent. The system of transfer by counselling described elsewhere in the book for other departments was first tried out with teachers.

Each application, duly certified by the concerned headmaster, is given entitlement points based on certain parameters. For each year of service in an interior area applicants are given points based on the degree of and remoteness of location of the school. They are also given points for length of service, subject to a maximum of five points. Consideration is also given to working spouses.

Entitlement points are given on teaching performance, with this defined in terms of percentage of passes in the subject taught by the applicant in the final examinations of the previous academic year. Each applicant is eligible for a maximum of ten entitlement points. To avoid the problem of interior schools and schools located in interior mandals losing teachers in favour of roadside schools, the principle of equalization of vacancies is applied before affecting the transfers.

Following this process, transfer orders are issued on the spot, and the resultant vacancies added to the list of vacancies. This exercise has brought absolute transparency to the issue of teacher transfers and helped obviate unhealthy practices, delays and litigation. It has also meant a loss of clout for those who used to exercise discretion in the matter of teacher transfers. There is obviously unhappiness in those quarters, but the school system benefits if the teacher is happier with his or her posting.

The other solution resorted to in order to overcome both the human and monetary resource crunch in education is the induction of para-teachers into the system. Madhya Pradesh and Rajasthan call them shiksha karmis, we call them vidya volunteers. Local youths are picked up if they meet the basic qualification of having studied up to high school and are given short-term training and deployed in single-teacher schools to assist the teacher.

These youth are locally recruited—by the panchayats in Madhya Pradesh, by the school education committees in Andhra—and therefore accountable to the local community. At one level the experiment works well. But the review mission has voiced concern over whether the short-term training they receive is adequate for them to cope with the pedagogy after class two, particularly where teaching mathematics and science is concerned.

Why are we resorting to para-teachers? Because more than anything else they help to tackle the serious problem of teacher absenteeism, which is a major problem. Teachers are not local people, the community has no control over them. In certain cases there were no teachers at all because there is a huge shortage of teachers. So the para-teacher deployment amounts to making 'teacher power' available.

States that have got past the stage of ensuring access to school and enrolment have been able to focus on quality. In Kerala, for instance, they are now able to focus on the pedagogic aspects and transform the classroom atmosphere so that the teaching is more activity-based, involving children in thinking, problem solving and creativity.

We are slowly getting there. New textbooks are being introduced into the system, teachers are being trained in new methods, resource persons are being regularly deployed. We recognize that the challenge is to bring enough quality into the four walls of the newly built schools to keep children from dropping out.

I believe that the future orientation to education will have to change if India is to attain a position of leadership and excellence in the information age. We will have to inculcate values, attitudes and skills relevant to a networked society in a global village. Take the case of Malaysia. It is setting up Smart Schools where the focus is not merely on imparting computer skills but also on a new pedagogy that emphasises thinking skills, creativity, innovation and a capacity to work in teams. Indians are brilliant individually but we are not so adept at working together. The era of the standalone individual, just like that of the standalone computer, is over and gone. Unless we learn to collaborate and work efficiently in teams we will be out of sync with the imperatives of a networked world.

Information technology holds the prospect of a paradigm shift in education. With networks and satellite communications reaching out to the remotest of places, distance learning will bring the best of education within reach of every individual. Already virtual universities are springing up in different parts of the world. A good example is the Virtual University of Monterrey in Mexico. Such universities will ensure that the traditional brick and mortar universities will soon become extinct.

It is for this reason that I have been emphasizing the need to extend modern communications to every village, every habitation and every home.

11

RECHARGING THE ENVIRONMENT

In an environmentally ravaged India there are modest parameters for judging progress. In Mahabubnagar, which is one of the poorest districts in the country, a village called Chityala usually records the lowest rainfall in the entire mandal. It had one functioning borewell for irrigation and none for drinking water. Several other borewells had been dug here, but they too had failed. The water from the bore was good for irrigating only a couple of hectares. In addition there were 225 open wells in the whole village which were going dry.

But in the last two years 120 of the open wells have recharged. Hussainayya, a farmer of the village, has stopped migrating to Karnataka for work, and Tirupathirao, who had given up on cultivating paddy and shifted to horticulture, has resumed cultivating paddy on two acres despite the scanty rainfall. Progress is when environmentally induced hardship recedes somewhat. Before watershed development was taken up here in 1995, 127 families were migrating in search of work because they could not cultivate enough to feed themselves. In 1998 the number dropped to thirty-two. Acreage under cultivation in this village has increased, not dramatically but modestly. The average tree cover per hectare has gone up from 265 to 324, again not spectacular but certainly an improvement.

What is new in Chityala between 1995 and 2000 is some 200 hectares of contour bunding, six percolation tanks that were not there before, a check dam and some eighty-five small gully control works. All measures to prevent runoff of the meagre rainfall the area gets. The local people tell you that because of the gullies they have dug across the sloping village lands, 'running water has been made to walk'. The face of this village has not been dramatically transformed; it is not strikingly green yet. But its ecology is definitely on the mend.

In Anantpur, which is Andhra Pradesh's most drought-prone district, there are close to a hundred villages where people have to walk several kilometres in search of potable water. The annual rainfall here is second only to Jaisalmer, which receives the lowest rainfall in India. In 1995, 247 watersheds in this district were taken up for treatment at the cost of Rs 20 lakh each. Some of them have regenerated enough to support the cultivation of two crops a year.

Can we deal with economic deprivation without dealing with ecological poverty? As forests disappear, water tables fall and the poor migrate in larger numbers to urban slums, it is becoming clear that the answer is no. Sustainability is going to be a key issue for India in this millennium.

In the last two or three years we have been making some progress on three critical fronts: developing watersheds, restoring forest cover, and monitoring air and groundwater pollution. In all three areas local people are being brought back into the execution and the monitoring.

Why? Environmentalist Anil Agarwal makes some simple but eloquent points about why the country is faced with such a deep water crisis. His analysis holds true for other environmental resources as well, such as forest and land.

As long as people were involved in the management of critical natural resources such as water a point of scarcity was not reached, he says. Rainwater is much greater in quantity than either river or groundwater, and it was on this resource that communities used to focus. Since rainwater management is decentralized, as long as it was the primary source of water, water management remained in the hands of local communities.

When governments took over water management over the last 150 years they began to focus on river and groundwater, because it was a centralized system looking for centralized sources. With dams and tubewells, technology came into the picture. Because communities were no longer involved, nobody was interested in conserving rainwater and rainwater harvesting practices in many parts of the country died out.

When the government began providing water it also did so at very low rates for politically opportune reasons, and over-exploitation quickly became the norm with both industries and households. The result is the current crisis where though 80 per cent of India's drinking water needs are met by groundwater, this resource is becoming increasingly scarce and frighteningly contaminated.

In April 2000 the spectre of drought once again began to loom large over some parts of the country. The AP government began to examine measures to make water harvesting mandatory all over the state. Simultaneously we began looking at the possibility of putting a ban on tubewells in areas where the groundwater had dropped below a specified level.

We are discovering in the state that to restore the degraded environment we will have to make some radical departures from conventional 'government' ways of managing environmental programmes. Environmental regeneration does not happen by decree. If Anna Hazare has been able to regenerate, single-handedly, 2000 acres of degraded land, it is because he is able to motivate people.

We have had decades of work put in by both governments and panchayats, with crores of rupees being pumped into water management programmes. Does the state of our tree cover reflect this? No. Less than 17 per cent of the so-called forest land in Andhra Pradesh is under tree cover. So it is time for a change in approach. The Central government recognizes this. More and more Central schemes are now stipulating that local committees be involved in implementing government schemes.

The Drought Prone Area Development scheme seeks to restore watersheds so that groundwater everywhere in the country can regenerate. There may have been a time not so long ago when watershed development was not a phrase that was part of a politician's vocabulary. Increasingly, however, politicians are having to recognize the havoc ecological poverty is causing in their constituencies.

In December 1997 we launched a ten-year action plan for the development of 100 lakh hectares of degraded lands in the state. In the first phase construction of 4500 watersheds covering an area of 22.50 lakh ha have been taken up. Each of them is governed by an association whose primary members are the farmers who have land there. They conduct meetings and decide what works to take up. The government pays for the earth work and wages.

Farmers from Chityala, mentioned earlier, went to Anna Hazare's village Ralegaon Shinde to see for themselves the kind of change watershed development can bring about. They have now banned goat grazing in their own village.

In Hyderabad every twenty days or so remote sensing data arrives at the planning department to help us track the status of watersheds in the state. When Rajiv Gandhi was prime minister he had asked whether remote sensing could help alleviate drought. So the Department of Space picked twenty-one districts all over the country, including Anantpur in AP, to experiment with mapping natural resources at the village level.

On a 1:250,000 scale the Andhra Pradesh Remote Sensing Centre maps watersheds and prioritizes them in different colours so that the most degraded ones can be taken up first. These maps also help to convince politicians as to why one area should be taken up before another.

Encouraging the participation of the local people in the management of resources that were once protected from them has begun to mean that such protection is no longer necessary. All over the state the forest department has begun to implement a Ministry of Environment and Forests scheme called van sanrakshan samitis (joint forest management groups) with varying degrees of success. Some of these groups are visibly more enthusiastic than others—a reflection on how much the forest rangers can motivate them.

Once the people living around these forests have begun to get wage labour through conservation works on degraded forest land, they have stopped stealing wood from the forests themselves. 'We now get wages through the year so we do not destroy the forests any more,' they tell visitors. Their labour is used to build check dams which prevent rainwater run-off and help recharge the borewells in the area. Both the watershed committees and the joint forest management committees quickly become multidimensional because they are linked up with the other self-help groups in the village. School enrolment, family planning and thrift group activities all begin to coalesce around these local environment protection efforts. They ensure a multiplicity of benefits that keep the village folk from losing interest in the core activity.

People's participation is a catchphrase that is sliding glibly into government and donor vocabulary. Currently, however, it is participation lubricated with government funds, which pay people for the conservation works they undertake to restore their own environment. The day has to come when people are willing to contribute their labour to protect the environment without expecting to be paid for it. Nevertheless, regeneration cannot be postponed until then.

Combating degradation by industry is a daunting challenge in a scenario where we as a state are desperate for more industries to come in and create employment.

An analysis by the member secretary of our Pollution Control Board shows why concern over industrial pollution at the Centre or state headquarters was not translating adequately into improvements on the ground. He lists who the actors are in the area of environment management and at which level they have an impact.

There are eight principal actors:

a) Government/environmental regulatory agencies,

b) polluters or generators of waste,

c) victims of pollution,

d) decision makers in the productive sectors of the economy,

e) data on environment quality, and remedial technology,

f) the market for environmental services,

g) voluntary organizations, and

h) the judiciary.

Their actions carry weight at four different levels: the local level where the impact of damage or remedial action is the greatest, the district level, and the state and national level. Not all actors are equally active at every level. When you add weightages for where each of these has greatest impact you discover that all the players who have influence are at the state or national level: the government, the decision makers in industry, and the environmental services market. The last concentrates its influence where the money is, at the state and national levels. NGOs too have the greatest impact when they operate close to the seat of power.

The polluters and victims, on the other hand, are the most active at the local level. The judiciary is environmentally active top down. Public interest litigation schemes only operate at the Supreme Court and high court levels.

The result is that environmental information, decision making and criticism are all centralized, with little changing on the ground. Victims of environmental degradation and their local level NGO partners are low on both knowledge and resources that will enable them to fight effective battles through either the media or the judiciary.

The kind of environmental strategy that we now want to put into place recognizes the limitations of what has been happening so far. We want to remove the limitations that local actors operated within by putting them directly into decision-making mechanisms which will operate at the local and district levels, rather than at the state or Centre.

Vision 2020 outlines the new strategies. Future industrialization will be forced to locate in zoned areas with access to safe, water disposal systems, and new technologies with zero discharge levels will be encouraged. We will have to create market-based enforcement mechanisms, with incentives for those who shift to the zoned areas and switch to new technologies.

We want to create local standards from each zone based on carrying capacity. This will be determined on the basis of sub-basins and tributary action plans, including lakes and their catchment, rather than just river action plans.

All primary stakeholders have to be involved in setting these standards, including the industries, the local people, local NGOs, and local university departments. It has to be a consultative process.

If carrying capacity is the criteria the parameters according to which standards are going to be fixed will not be according to concentration of discharge, but according to the assimilative capacity of the area where it will be discharged. We are empowering local communities to monitor compliance with these standards, and training them to do so effectively.

This approach has already been put into action. The local input into planning will now come through a very simple system called a committee system which we have begun introducing in Andhra Pradesh. There will be stakeholder committees at each micro watershed point of action. We are training local people for these and empowering them under section nine and eleven of two Acts, the water and air Acts. Technical consultants from local universities are to be associated with these committees, as are sarpanches and NGOs. The size of these decision-making committees is confined to six people.

This is a big step forward in decentralizing decision making with regard to the local environment. These committees will take decisions on the siting of industries. From 10 April 1997, in any case of siting of an industry clearance from the stakeholder committee is a local requirement. There is a public hearing as part of the clearance process.

There are those who feel local committees can be bought over by vested interests. Of course, anything can be distorted, anything can be corrupted. Even the committee system can be corrupted. They can take money, but since they are local people, if they are corrupt, if they take money and then take a decision accordingly, they will be answerable to their community. Right now we are seated some 700 kilometres away from the impact zone and taking decisions on siting industries. The corruption level of discretion in the present system is very high. The new system, we think, is more likely to check corruption.

Perhaps the most vital role the local committees will play is monitoring of the environmental conduct of local industries. Currently the Andhra Pradesh Pollution Control Board attempts, with a staff of one hundred personnel, to investigate more than 150,000 polluting industries in the state. Regional offices at Visakhapatnam and Vijaywada have two or three skilled employees each where they require a minimum of forty engineers and analysts to effectively monitor pollution.

With the local committee system not only will the monitoring system become more decentralized and, therefore, one hopes, more effective, it will also improve the interface at the local level between the polluters and the affected parties. Our pollution control board is also looking at the manner in which it needs to decentralize. Its major work is granting permissions and monitoring. Both functions were earlier done through officials. Now they will gradually convert to doing them through committees.

These have to be trained to conduct inspections, indeed trained continuously. We may require two separate committees, one before the industry comes up and one after. Already the board has attached university departments to its zonal offices. Nagarjuna university is attached to Kurnool zonal office, the Environmental Protection Training and Research Institute is attached to the Hyderabad zonal office, Vijaywada and Visakhapatnam also have local university departments attached to them.

The standards evolved by these committees would differ according to location because they would be based on the perceived threat to the environment of the region. The rules are, however, the same for all polluting units. Similar local agencies exist in other countries: the State Environmental Protection Commission in China has a network of 2400 environmental protection boards as part of local governments and municipalities to monitor compliance with laws

Unlike other environmental regulatory bodies, from the year 1998 the Andhra Pradesh Pollution Board has an annual action plan that is being adhered to. It is broken down into monthly goals which are monitored. The overall rationale for this action plan derives from the sectoral goals outlined in

Vision 2020, for a clean and green Andhra Pradesh. These describe the public and private sector initiatives required to achieve sustainability by the year 2020.

Four broad goals translate into thirty-one aspects for implementation and monitoring. The goals are to achieve improvement in water quality in critically contaminated water bodies and waterways, improvement in air quality in critically threatened airsheds, elimination of hazardous wastes and reduction in the use of hazardous materials progressively, and the setting up of administrative and community support systems to help these initiatives succeed.

How does the board's monthly monitoring exercise work? At the end of each month a report has to be prepared which lists progress made on each of the thirty-one aspects, while listing the target and the agency whose responsibility that particular target is. Included in the range of tasks to be accomplished month by month, year by year is steps taken towards drafting and enacting legislation.

For instance, specific legislation is needed to set up ward committees in Hyderabad, Vizag and Vijaywada and to empower the committees to target and collect user charges for waste management. The action plan tasks also include monitoring specific polluted locations according to the directions of the Supreme Court and reporting the status to the court.

Other tasks include establishing check centres and mobile night patrols to check effluent tanker movements, conducting water and air sampling and analysis from affected areas, keeping a tab on whether specified industries have prepared their on-site and off-site industry plans, and so on.

The action plan-based activities have begun to make an impact and help sharpen the performance of the Pollution Control Board. The board gives each employee tasks and targets and a clear time frame within which these have to be achieved.

Some categories of industries are responding better than others. The bulk-drug industry has gone from the stage of primary treatment to secondary treatment, and further on to evaporation and solid waste management, and from there to looking at prevention, which is the classical western pattern of development. Thanks to constant chivvying from the courts and the government, industry is slowly developing a long-term outlook. There are now groups of industries in Andhra Pradesh who are at all three stages: treatment for end of pipe, evaporation and solid waste management, and prevention.

Our most notoriously polluted areas, of course, are Bolaram and Patencheru in Medak district. Groundwater from villages around the Patencheru Industrial Area have recorded levels of mercury that are 115 times the permissible limit, arsenic at 70 times the permissible limit, and similarly unacceptable levels of manganese and nickel concentrations. Most of the 400 industrial units here dump pollutants into drains and soil. The strategy has to be to reduce the quantity of effluent because the quality of the effluent cannot change—the effluents are of a kind that cannot be treated.

That is something we should have known twenty years ago when these industries came up. They discharge effluents which do not respond to biological treatment—basically inorganics, metals and salt. The strategy therefore has to be to reduce them through evaporation, but as soon as you do that you are increasing solid waste. We were constructing a landfill in Hyderabad, a treatment, storage and disposal facility where solidified wastes from these industries can be stored safely. But a court stay order has held up its completion.

The other strategy we are attempting in Patencheru and elsewhere is to give the industries incentives to change their raw material, so that a particular waste stream is eliminated. They will have to go in for changes of boilers and processes and the recovery of salts and materials which they can recycle or re-use. It is very expensive to do this—only the large and the medium industries are currently doing it out of 400 units.

With the carrying capacity approach industries will be given standards for release of effluents, and we will monitor their releases with a water flow meter to see how much load of that particular parameter they are discharging. Monitoring a few industries like that will not be a problem. For the future we will think in terms of a facility for deep-sea dumping of high-salt effluents, after treatment to conform to marine standards. This would mean that the effluents would have to be transported 600 kilometres after treatment.

What are the policy implications of working towards sustainability? There are several. At one level we have to set prices to gradually reflect the full economic cost of providing resources such as water, coal, fuel and electricity in a way that will encourage conservation. It is because of politically opportune pricing of water and power for decades that these have been overexploited.

We also have to reform municipalities to make them financially stronger and able to tackle problems like urban pollution. We have to improve urban infrastructure to cope efficiently with migration and enhance our returns from the public facilities we provide. We have to develop mass transit systems to reduce vehicular pollution. The extent of non-point pollution from agriculture is large. In Andhra Pradesh we will have to apply standards to agriculture too.

Ultimately we have to make environmental conservation integral to development planning. However, the integration of thirteen different action plans of Vision 2020 on an environment platform has still not taken place. Stakeholder departments of government are slow to respond, they require a lot of pushing to prioritize environment in their scheme of things. Thanks to the availability of a monthly monitoring format, however, pressure can be kept up on them.

12

CATCHING UP ON POWER

Contrary to what my friends in the opposition parties would like to project, the primary purpose of economic reforms is not to make workers insecure or to marginalize the poor. It is to make the future viable. Of no sector is this more true than the power sector. If it is not reformed, darkness looms ahead. Because in every state, the system that provides the power has been stretched to the point of collapse.

Everybody needs power: students, farmers, industry. Nobody is willing to pay for what it actually costs. In agriculture, unlike industry, the risk is high, and it can be argued that farmers have to be protected till the element of risk is reduced. Nevertheless, the fact remains that demand for power is only rising, with no resources available to either expand the system or maintain it as it needs to be maintained. No wonder that in parts of the country, output from some power plants is no more than 10 per cent of installed capacity.

In the last five years a handful of states have picked up courage to attempt reform of the state electricity boards. Others have followed suit. The public face of this attempt has been angry farmers, workers on strike in several parts of the country to resist bifurcation or trifurcation of the electricity boards, and irate consumers being asked to pay more for power that is frequently unavailable.

Populism in power pricing, which all parties have indulged in in the past, turning a blind eye to power thefts, besides the neglect of maintenance of generators and transmission lines, has meant a deterioration of the system over the past half-century. Today installed capacity in the whole country is 92,000 MW, which is far in excess of demand. Total demand at peak time never exceeds 65,000 MW. But what is generated is not more than 60,000 MW at the best of times.

Though the shortage really is of no more than 5000 to 6000 MW countrywide, the fact that it exists despite several times that figure in excess installed capacity speaks a great deal about the performance of the power sector. The national average output or plant load factor (PLF) is 64 to 65 per cent, which includes a PLF of 80 per cent for the National Thermal Power Corporation's super thermal plants and one of 10 per cent for some plants in Bihar.

Throughout India we are neither able to generate as much power as we have capacity for or transmit it to where it is needed. Generation is below par because there is no money for inputs such as coal, oil and gas, and transmission is poor because the resources to maintain the transmission system are unavailable. We have not invested enough in transmission lines or modernized the system. Lines and transformers have a life, after which they have to be replaced. These physical deficiences get compounded by commercial factors. We don't charge optimal prices, or tackle theft effectively enough.

Nor are we augmenting the distribution system the way we should be. There are those who would say that the organizational structure of the power sector has also contributed to this. State electricity boards are monolithic, monopolistic, government-owned and organized. They have no competition and are not properly regulated. If there was competition there would be incentives to beef up performance.

So, is the system crying out for reform? Indeed it is. Is it politically prudent to attempt it? The answer used to be no. If you wanted to be re-elected, raising the cost of providing electricity would have been considered suicidal. But today people in the countryside can see from the shortages they face that we need to urgently augment power production. Demand is increasing, supply is not keeping up. Why? Because there are no resources in the system. They are now forced to understand that in order to get power continuously, they have to be willing to pay for it.

Free power is bringing diminishing electoral returns. The Akalis in Punjab discovered this when they faced defeat in the 1999 parliamentary elections despite implementing an electoral promise of free power. The Congress party in Andhra Pradesh promised free power if it was elected in the assembly elections in the same year. My party did not. I repeatedly told people in the villages that they would have to choose between getting continuous power supply or getting it free. The message went home.

When the losses of state electricity boards mount to a point where the state budget faces a huge deficit as a result, shying away from the issue is no longer an option.

In the last four years in Andhra Pradesh we have tried to map for ourselves and others in the country a politically acceptable route to reform. But major problems still remain and reforms have only just begun. And at the end of the day the question arises as to what is the route that a country like ours should follow on power. Can it meet its future needs through monolithical, state-run enterprises? Are huge privately owned power plants the only option to huge publicly owned ones? Or are there other options that a country of a billion people should explore?

Because power amounts to infrastructure that is basic to

progress, power management has become a challenge basic to governance. What options does a government have in a democracy whose needs run the gamut from basic power for everybody, to enough power to fuel a higher level of economic growth? What are the political implications of attempting hard-nosed reforms? And how should a political party handle these?

When the crunch came in Andhra Pradesh we opted for transparency as a strategy. When we decided to follow the cause of publishing white papers on different aspects of the state's economy in 1996 we also produced such a paper on the Andhra Pradesh State Electricity Board.

It showed clearly where the problem lay. Not in generation, where the performance had in the two preceding years been among the highest in the country in terms of plant load factor. It lay in financial performance. The deterioration in finances began from 1985, when agricultural loads started to grow significantly. The state began to consistently energize one lakh pumpsets per annum, which was much higher than the Planning Commission's target of 50,000 pumpsets for Andhra Pradesh.

Over the next ten years the entire pattern of power consumption in the state changed. Agriculture went from being around 23 per cent of total power consumption in 1985 to almost 51 per cent in 1995. Industrial consumption went down from being 50 per cent of the total to 26 per cent over the same period. Since the latter used to cross-subsidize agriculture, in financial terms this was bad news for the state electricity board.

If you take the current prices of providing power to the two sectors you can see why the problem became so acute. Today we charge 17 paise per unit as tariff from farmers, and Rs 4.30 per unit from industry. It costs us in Andhra Pradesh Rs 2200 crore a year to supply farmers with power, and what we recover is no more than Rs 100–120 crore a year. And we give more power to agriculture than any of our neighbouring states.

As the 1996 white paper showed, in terms of percentage share of agriculture to total sales, AP was considerably ahead of Karnataka, Maharastra, Madhya Pradesh, Orissa and Tamil Nadu. In terms of percentage share of industry to total sales, it was well behind these states.

It is very difficult to precisely quantify commercial losses because metering is absent for the 1.8 or 1.9 million pumpsets that farmers have in the state. The APSEB did some sample metering. Ten pumpsets were fixed with meters in each mandal. We have 1125 mandals. About 11,000 meters were fixed and based on this sample metering the extent of commercial losses we were incurring was gauged.

We are not alone in our inability to levy realistic tariffs from the agricultural sector. Today most states charge between 10 paise and 50 paise per unit; some state governments still give power free to farmers. But given that the agriculture sector in Andhra Pradesh is one which consumes the most power, the burden becomes unbearable.

The low, unmetered flat rate encourages profligate consumption, necessitating substantial power cuts on HT consumers, whose tariffs are well above the cost of supply. Efforts to meter agricultural consumption have been met by angry resistance from farmers. So, apart from mounting losses, the result is that power shortages are experienced in terms of energy and peak demand year after year.

One result of this is that we are losing our industrial customers, who have been increasingly turning to captive generation for their needs. The latter is now of the order of 1600 MW in our state. The state electricity board is, therefore, steadily losing those customers who do bring in revenue.

From 1989 debt began to show up in the finances of the board. Section 59 of the Electricty Supply Act stipulates that electricity boards will ensure a rate of return on net fixed assets of 3 per cent. This became increasingly difficult. In 1990-91 and 1991-92 this was achieved by way of subsidies from the state government. The following two years it was achieved by making book adjustments. Finally, when all methods of adjustment were exhausted, the 3 per cent rate of return was achieved in 1994-95 by writing off equity to the tune of Rs 944 crore, an unprecedented financial accounting practice, resorted to in sheer desperation. The year in which we published the white paper we were heading for a revenue deficit of Rs 1533 crore, the mounting losses aggravated by the failure of monsoons which affected hydel generation.

Though APSEB's financial record has been pretty disastrous, its physical performance has been good. The thermal stations are noted for their high plant load factors year after year. Individual power plants in the state have even won gold medals. The average PLF during 1999-2000 was 82.33 per cent, which was the highest in the country. Its addition of 1791 MW of new generation capacity in the Eighth Plan was also the highest among all the states in the country.

During the period 1991-92 to 1996-97 the network of APSEB has been augmented by 26.4 per cent, thereby achieving the highest network expansion among SEBs in the country. The distribution system was expanded vastly to cater to the load growth and to improve quality and reliability of supply. Despite all this, however, the system is unable to keep up with the demand.

There are other reasons for this. Currently 32 per cent of the total power produced and supplied disappears as commercial losses. Its components are theft and inaccuracies in meters including slow, stuck and burnt meters. This is an ingenious example of how even an aberration can spawn regular employment in government. There are Detection of Pilferage divisions in every district, known as DP divisions. that have their work cut out. In 1997-98 a total of 27,779 cases were detected, of which 12,400 were finalized. The value of the amount realized from these offenders was Rs 5.65 crore.

Once transmission and distribution are separated as functions, pinning down where the losses occur might be easier.

As the physical performance of our plants was good we hesitated initially to go in for reforms. But this performance has been offset by the mounting costs of subsidized power to agriculture and huge commercial losses caused by power theft. Persisting cash flow problems resulted in outstanding liabilities of over Rs 2500 crore by the end of March 1999 from its generation, transmission and distribution operations. The revenue deficit is of the order of Rs 230 crore every month.

With these sorts of liabilities how do you mobilize the resources needed to bring in capacity additions in generation, transmission and distribution to meet the ever-increasing growth in demand? Ours was one of the first states to get private power plants going on-stream. The first two fast track plants in the country, the 216 MW Jerugupadu power plant of GVK industries and the 208 MW unit of Spectrum Power Plant, Kakinada, had come up in the state.

But though we were committed to buying the power produced by these independent power producers, we were completely strapped for cash ourselves. The poor creditworthiness of APSEB, which was the sole buyer of IPP (independent power producers), has been making it difficult for the power sector to attract private investments.

Given these daunting problems faced by the power sector, the government of Andhra Pradesh appointed a high-level committee as early as 1995 to review the government's approach towards private participation in the power sector. The committee would suggest guidelines in the matters of restructuring and privatization of the power sector and on tariff policy. The committee was headed by a former member of the Planning Commission, Hiten Bhayya.

This committee suggested a radical restructuring of the power sector on functional lines through unbundling of generation, transmission and distribution functions into different corporate entities. It also advised setting up of a new regulatory environment that would fix rational tariffs and facilitate private investment in generation and distribution. Following this, the government of Andhra Pradesh formulated its policy in February 1997 in regard to reforms of the power sector.

In practical terms the reform process amounts to doing all of the above. Besides, it ensured that while the government may continue to direct and determine the overall policy framework for the power sector as a whole, it would withdraw from the regulatory function.

This general policy statement was followed up by a detailed policy statement issued in October 1998. The general public was taken into confidence about the alarming status of the power sector in the state and the need for and the objectives behind the proposed reform of the power supply industry.

Radical changes in the government sector are bound to be greeted with immense alarm. The APSEB's 74,000 employees were instantly up in arms. They set up a joint council of action in 1996-97 that expressed its stiff opposition to reforms. We held detailed discussions with them to reassure them that their interests would be safeguarded in the reform process and that there would be no retrenchment. Though one union resisted till the very end, gradually the opposition has been defused. A tripartite agreement between the workers, the unions and the government was signed.

Meanwhile, the state government enacted the AP Electricity Reform Act 1998 and made it effective from February 1999. The main components of the Act were the creation of an independent regulatory commission to be called AP Electricity Regulatory Commission and the facilitation of the reorganization of the electricity supply industry on a functional basis through the creation of separate corporations for transmission and generation under the Indian Companies Act 1956.

Subsequently two corporations, AP Genco and AP Transco, have come into existence. The first focusses on generation, the latter on transmission and distribution. The distribution wing has been hived off into a number of smaller companies. In time they could be privatized. But AP Transco will remain a part of the government.

How does unbundling of generation and transmission help? It makes for better focus, leading to growth and efficiency. The state electricity board was a very large undertaking with more than one crore consumers. Another five lakh new connections are pending. It supplied 7000 to 8000 MW of which it generated 5600 MW. To handle this order of generation you require a large transmission system and larger projects: hydel, thermal and gas. If the board of directors has to focus on these major activities it can do so more effectively if the functions are separated.

The Central government also held two chief ministers' conferences where this was discussed and decided that for better functioning of the power sector it would be necessary to follow the reform process and unbundle the state electricity boards.

Now that the process has been initiated the order of investment called for to rehabilitate and expand the power transmission and distribution system, to renovate and modernize the existing generation facilities of APSEB and to undertake capacity building in new power sector entities is enormous. We estimate that the investment required will be of the order of $3750 million. The World Bank has agreed to support the state government through financing a part of this requirement, to the tune of US$1000 million, through a series of loans.

Following the onset of reforms financial institutions have also become considerably more forthcoming. They are coming forward to assist in financing of various transmission, distribution and generation schemes, something they were reluctant to do earlier because of the revenue deficit. Now they have the assurance that there is a regulator in place who will be looking into the tariff aspects and the rationalization of these.

There is a view that we should take reforms further than just unbundling and appointing a regulator, that at the end of the day, the units should not be totally government-owned. That, to change the style of management, you should bring in the private sector. Either by divesting government-owned generation units, or by getting private management into the generation. Since the assets in Andhra Pradesh have a good physical performance, the private sector will want to come in. No scenario should be rejected outright, but it will be wiser to make haste gradually. I believe reforms will succeed in a country like this only if people are constantly consulted, persuaded, and kept informed of the choices the government has before it.

In January 2000 we decided to issue a white paper on the power position every month, with weekly bulletins at the local level setting out complete details. Tariff revisions will inevitably come; they will be accepted more easily if people are prepared, and convinced that the government has also done its best to control pilferage and transmission losses. Then I will place before the people that this is the tariff we are levying, this is the loss I am incurring, what are my options for recouping them.

Today 20 per cent of the current consumption of power in the state is in the domestic sector, 33-34 per cent is consumed by industry, and 39-40 per cent by the agricultural sector. If the government chooses to continue to supply power cheaper to agricultural consumers it will have to provide for such a subsidy in the budget and place it in the assembly. The rate of tariff for agriculture should not be allowed to affect the balance sheet of the utility.

As I said earlier, we have to protect this sector till the element of risk in agriculture is substantially reduced. Crop insurance will have to be introduced. We are trying to mobilize every drop of water to irrigate every inch of land, thereby spending huge amounts on the Watershed Development Programme, particularly in upland areas like Rayalseema. A lot of irrigation projects have to come up on the Krishna river. If we provide water, there will be agricultural activity throughout the year, and farmers will be more willing to pay for the power they consume.

The huge cost today of providing power over a huge distance, and the enormity of the total loss in transmission and theft—32 per cent of the power produced—underscores the fact that it is time to rethink our approach to power.

In a country with scattered habitations, distance, terrain and high costs militate against meeting the needs of a billion people through mega power projects alone. Why install transmission lines and carry power for hundreds of miles? Why not have small generation taking place locally, to meet local needs? The technologies exist elsewhere in the world.

Over the last five years our approach to governance in Andhra Pradesh has been to draw lessons from the best practices being implemented anywhere in the world. Even as we work doggedly at implementing the reform process, where power is concerned, we have begun to seriously look for small, decentralized solutions. For the future, we would like to completely rethink the approach to providing power.

13

PEOPLE VS POVERTY

In the first week of January 2000 a newspaper reported from Gundranipalle village in Nalgonda District that a fairly tumultuous gram sabha meeting had been held. A ruling party sarpanch and her contractor husband were being grilled by the people of the village for not doing anything about a borewell that had failed and there had been no drinking water in that village for the past one week. They were shouting at the top of their voices, citing the example of a neighbouring village where when a pump failed a substitute had been rented.

After shouting back, the sarpanch walked off.

When the gram sabha resumed and the visiting nodal officer began reviewing the state of completion of the number of works taken up in the village, there were further questions.

Why, for instance, were grants being disbursed for only twenty individual latrines when seventy had been sanctioned?

This is not an isolated example. After three years of a programme called Janmabhoomi there is increasing evidence that one of its central messages is going home to people in the villages: that the nodal officers in charge of overseeing Janmabhoomi are accountable to them. The programme provides for development works to be taken up in villages in consultation with the people of the village through gram sabhas.

Janmabhoomi was an effort to draw upon all existing funds for rural schemes to take up projects prioritized by the local people. The common allegation by the opposition is that ruling party contractors have cornered the funds under this scheme. If that is the case people will not tolerate it, as the instances quoted show. Because, slowly but surely, we are creating a demand for accountability through the same programme.

All key government functionaries and elected representatives at the mandal level are supposed to visit each and every habitation at least once before the next round of Janmabhoomi and report to the gram sabha about action taken on issues raised in the previous round. There is a fresh round every three months.

Though there are complaints that gram sabhas are not sufficiently representative, and that mandal officers don't give sufficient notice before holding these, there is growing evidence that village folk are picking up courage to do something they have never done before in their lives: question government officers who are supposed to deliver development schemes.

The earlier stance used to be one of supplication: please, sir, give us a borewell in our village. Today, there is a significant shift. They treat a borewell or a school building as their due. The precursor to Janmabhoomi, Prajala Vaddaku Palana, was a programme to take the government to the doorsteps of the people. To implement it the same village functionaries who were never available even during working hours, had to work till eight o'clock at night. As they see an unseen government hand enforcing accountability among government servants, people are emboldened enough to demand service from these officials.

In doing so they are overcoming their awe of officialdom in a country where only 2.8 per cent of the people are employed in the organized sector, and less than 2 per cent in government. It is the first step towards resisting corruption and neglect of duty by the government machinery.

A mandal officer who might not have visited more than ten villages in his mandal before now has to conduct gram sabhas in thirty to forty villages in one week when the Janmabhoomi rounds take place. He schedules five in a day, in some cases not announcing them sufficiently in advance. But when he arrives and word spreads people pin him down and ask him about the status of the works undertaken in the last round.

Many thousand crores of government funds have gone into development schemes over forty years of planned development. The assets created under these schemes have not transformed the face of rural India. Sewage still overflows from open drains, handpumps don't work, the roads disappear under slush and water in the rains. Taps leak. Street lights don't function. Schools are ill-equipped. Community halls are in poor condition.

When I travel from district to district for every round of Janmabhoomi I tell them that they have to use the mechanism of the gram sabhas to demand accountability. The mandal officers are accountable, the MLAs, sarpanches and village-level party workers who are supposed to attend these meetings are also accountable.

Before we began our campaign for transparency in the implementation of rural development schemes nobody knew what government work had been sanctioned for that village. Today if you walk into a village in Andhra Pradesh you are likely to see painted on the walls of a school or community building details of what works have been sanctioned in that village, for how much money, and who the contractor is. If nothing has come up, the villages know whom to question.

Critics of Janmabhoomi say that when there is local self-government through panchayati raj, when there are elected representatives of the people right down to every village and nagar palika, why does Andhra Pradesh need to nurture self-help groups or associations of those who are stakeholders in the development process? Why create a parallel structure?

That is a little like saying there should be no citizens' action groups in civil society because we already have elected members of Parliament and members of legislative assemblies. We are not in favour of bypassing panchayati raj, but people's participation is different from representative democracy. Local self-government is still government. What we are talking about is organizing people, enabling them to participate in the development process, increasing their access to the institutions of government and the services they provide.

Organizing people into self-help groups involves creating a participatory structure at the community level, providing opportunities for people to take part in debates and discussions. But the radical departure is in disbursing government funds through such groups, as we have done.

Once again, the question arises, why are funds not given through panchayats to spend as other state governments have done? First, let me clarify that panchayat representatives are not excluded from the self-help groups or from the Janmabhoomi process—they are an integral part of it. The habitation-level committees to which departmental employees are responsible are headed by the sarpanch.

When government functionaries go to a habitation as part of Janmabhoomi they take the sarpanch along with them. They also take the mandal president and the ward member with them. Thus all the elected representatives at the district level, mandal level, and gram panchayat level accompany the government functionaries to the people. One of the objectives of Janmabhoomi is also to make local self-government more effective. We want the gram panchayats also to preside over

the gram sabha. We have said categorically that no gram
sabha should be held without the sarpanch presiding over it.

The panchayati raj institutions till recently said, you
hand over Janmabhoomi to the zilla parishad, you hand it
over to the mandal parishad, and you transfer, true to the
spirit of the 73rd amendment, certain subjects and functions
to the local bodies. We are doing that. Under the
Constitution's 73rd amendment I have transferred to the
panchayats certain subjects such as agriculture, animal
husbandry, health, education, water supply, and poverty
alleviation. Also, under the 74th amendment, we are giving
certain subjects for urban areas to the local city government.

However, even if you transfer a subject to the local
bodies, they also come under the category of government.
Local self-government is not outside the state. It is part of
the state mechanism even if it is not a centralized state
mechanism. You will have the same bureaucracy, the same
functionaries who have been working in the government
department. Now they are being transferred to the concerned
government, that is all. You have a district agricultural officer
who was earlier working under the state government and
heading the department, now he or she will be working
under the zilla parishad. Therefore, local self-government is
ultimately also government.

To view panchayat raj as the panacea for all that is not
happening in terms of grassroots development is naïve. It is
yet another Indian mindset: that if you route money for
development schemes directly to local bodies, local
government, development will happen. It will not happen.
In Maharashtra they have done this—there also, there are
vested interests. In other countries they have laid stress not
just on delegation of powers but also on accountability. From
top to bottom, everybody should be accountable. That is the
system I want to establish now. Local bodies should also be
accountable to the people.

Even if you hand over all funding from all sources to the panchayats, is it ultimately going to reach the people? How do you ensure that the money reaches the habitation-level committees? The panchayati raj people will say, you hand over the money, we will ensure that it goes to the people. However, we have found that in decades of their functioning they still do not have any kind of participatory structure. You have institutional arrangements such as the zilla parishad and the mandal parishad, but if you look at the democratic roots, you have nothing.

So the self-help groups are ultimately going to be the roots of democracy at the local level. The gram panchayat today is as far down as the panchayati raj system goes. You are supposed to have one gram panchayat per village, but you even have one for two. Whereas in a habitation there could be as many as 100 to 200 self-help groups of ten to fifteen members each. When you bring them into the decision making, you are truly devolving power to the people.

Finally, it is also true that party affiliations have percolated down to the panchayat level. These loyalties could vitiate the redistribution of funds and schemes that they are supposed to undertake. The opposition often claims that panchayat leaders owing allegiance to the ruling party are cornering all the benefits of government schemes. They should not then complain if we route some of these benefits directly to self-help groups.

This chapter is about some of the participatory approaches to governance that we are attempting in Andhra Pradesh. Janmabhoomi was launched on 1 January 1997. It evolved out of the experience gained in implementing earlier schemes: Prajala Vaddaku Palana (taking administration to the doorstep of the people), Sramadanam (contributing free labour for development) and micro-level planning from November 1995 to December 1996 in the state.

At the core of a programme like Janmabhoomi is the

concept of decentralized planning. Government funds have been coming into the villages since the inception of the planning process in this country, new Central government schemes are constantly being launched, and old ones modified. But poverty and inequity persist.

We felt that a major reason for the failure to make a dent despite all the inputs is that excessive centralization in planning and decision making have dampened the initiative of the people. It has also made them passive recipients of the development process. The process that we have devised in Janmabhoomi is an attempt to reverse that. It is a collective process of needs identification that the government undertakes with the people. It addresses in addition to community needs, individual needs as well as family needs.

It is not yet another new scheme, it is a new approach which draws upon all the existing government schemes as a resource. There are no separate funds for Janmabhoomi. It draws resources from forty or more schemes, either Central or state, that are already in operation.

At the heart of the process is the gram sabha, or village meeting. There is an operational definition for the term in the Andhra Pradesh Panchayat Raj Act of 1994: it should consist of all persons whose names are included in the electoral rolls for the gram panchayat. For Janmabhoomi gram sabhas are convened every quarter, and we have been trying to have these in every habitation.

In these village meetings people discuss and identify all their felt needs. Based on the feedback we receive, we try to establish a micro-plan for the village. The government departments concerned and institutions at mandal level prepare a plan. On the basis of this the gram sabha prioritizes the works it wants taken up in the village.

The choice made by it will be the basis on which the gram panchayat, the mandal parishad and the zilla parishad will sanction the works. We go for each round with some core

activity. For the majority of people education is a priority, so
are health, drinking water and environment protection,
including planting of trees.

There is one elementary reason for involving local people
in decision making: they know about local conditions better
than those who sit in secretariats and design schemes. They
know the soil, which local trees are the hardiest, and the local
breeds of cattle. Because of our failure to incorporate this
local wisdom we have been rewarded with several instances
of inaccurately located check dams, wrong alignment of
canals, and inappropriate introduction of exotic breeds of
cattle.

Participatory planning enables people to highlight their
particular concerns. There are priorities that are identified in
the interaction with villagers which our government schemes
are not addressing. For instance, during one round of
Janmabhoomi we took up animal health because we had
feedback from our nodal officers in the field to show that this
was an area of concern. In some districts people wanted
deworming of milch cattle, others wanted vaccination of
animals against foot-and-mouth disease, or help with the
blue tongue disease which was widespread in some districts.
These are the kind of problems which in the normal system
of governance might not get prompt attention from local-
level agencies.

So decentralized planning is one objective of
Janmabhoomi that we are trying to implement to make rural
and urban works more relevant to felt needs. There are other
important drawbacks in the current development process that
need to be addressed. One is the notion that the government
is a provider of schemes and services and citizens are
beneficiaries. This is a paternalistic approach which has led
to a good deal of passivity on the part of people who should
be active partners in the development process. It may explain
why they do not maintain community assets built by the
government.

We are trying to change the focus from beneficiary to partner by making people contribute something in terms of ideas, money, material and labour. The experience of the Sramadanam programme in the state has shown that people's direct contributions go a long way in giving them a sense of ownership over community assets. In the past couple of years it is possible to see in the countryside school buildings that have got a fresh coat of paint, compound walls for schools, re-excavated irrigation channels, and new roads built with contributed labour.

We have attempted to systematize their involvement in works taken up under Janmabhoomi by specifying the contribution that must be made for different categories of works. In the creation of new assets as well as in irrigation maintenance, people are expected to contribute 50 per cent of the earthwork. In building concrete roads in waterlogged areas, people are expected to contribute 25 per cent of the labour in slum areas, and 50 per cent of the labour in other areas.

In listing the kind of requests from the community that will be considered as part of Janmabhoomi we decided we would consider nothing either too big or too small. A community can request a major irrigation project, a bus service, a hospital, or a degree college at one end of the spectrum. It can also request a gamut of non-financial needs: government land required for community purposes, provision of agricultural extension services, tackling of polluted water sources, provision of teachers in the local school, issues relating to the sanction of individual pensions, or even a request for providing wage employment during the lean season. There are more than 200 categories of community and individual needs that we have tried to cover under Janmabhoomi.

The kitty has not gone up. What has happened is, you have three works to execute, and you are doing them through tender contract. Today we may do one through a tender contract, and two through self-help groups. For instance, a DWCRA group or a mothers' committee will take on the contract for an Anganwadi building and get the work done, putting in the labour contribution themselves.

We have also identified a category of works which will receive no government funding at all: minor repairs which cost less than Rs 5000, community halls and youth club buildings, works in religious institutions, the building of statues, the construction of sports facilities, the digging of borewells, jungle clearance, desilting of tanks other than drinking water tanks, and all works that are not on government land. All these have to be done by people themselves by mobilizing resources and voluntary labour.

The need for transparency and accountability are also being addressed. Leakage in the implementation of government schemes is assumed to be very high. By bringing transparency into the process one can check some of that leakage. Individual benefits such as old-age pensions are now distributed in gram sabhas, before all the people in the village.

Further, a visitor to any village in the state will find that the walls of centrally located buildings such as schools or community halls are used to declare what works have been taken up in that village, at what cost, and whom the contract has been entrusted to. If the work is not happening, everybody gets to know and can raise questions in the next gram sabha.

When a collective round of needs identification takes place we expect the government to be accountable to the people. How do we ensure that government functionaries are accountable to the village community? We do it in two ways. We make departmental staff working at mandal level present to the community an 'action taken' report. It highlights what are the needs collectively identified during the last round of Janmabhoomi, what action has been taken by the government department concerned, and what action could not be taken, and for what reason.

Another way of making them accountable and responsible is by using the self-help groups in the village which monitor progress on works. There are forest protection committees, water users' associations, the group of youth assisted under the chief minister's programme for empowerment of youth— CMEY, the DWCRA groups, and the school education committees. The presence of six self-help groups in every habitation ensures accountability.

Now, we have organized a community-level participatory structure called the people's council. It is a habitation-level committee which consists of group leaders of all the six self-help groups, together with the sarpanch of the panchayat as chairman. If there are non-governmental organizations working in that habitation, they too are represented in that committee.

We have also created a channel of institutionalized feedback which starts in the village and reaches back up to the state capital, indeed, all the way up to the chief minister. After each round, the nodal officers for each mandal have feedback sessions with chairpersons of habitation level committees. There are 1125 mandals in twenty-three districts. They also interact with chief engineers who are responsible for the works.

These nodal officers then come to Hyderabad and we have a feedback session which stretches over four to five days. I attend these sessions, address them and listen to them. The feedback we get in this way is on what is wrong with the Janmabhoomi process. The suggestions go to the cabinet, the cabinet also discusses them. We have been changing our guidelines and our policies according to this feedback.

■

The concept of involving self-help groups in governance

derives in some cases from Central government schemes. When they have worked exceptionally well in our state, we have put in additional funds from the state budget. The best example of this is a scheme called DWCRA (Development of Women and Children in Rural Areas) which has caught the imagination of our rural women. Through it we are beginning to transform an invaluable human resource: women.

Every day I talk of human resource development. Women form 50 per cent of the human resources of this country and I don't see how we can build a nation if we do not use them. Where brain work is concerned they are as good or better than men. They bring more concentration and more devotion to their work. In the board exams in the state, girls do better than boys. Given any opportunity they will do equally well, and sometimes better than boys, that is my conviction.

I want to carry women along and give them equal economic and social opportunity. Despite low levels of literacy, they are gifted with common sense. If the decision is in their hands they will go for family planning; not only that, they will also persuade their husbands to do so. And given the opportunity, women would take even better care of their children.

The purpose of DWCRA has never been to only promote savings and credit. As the name of the scheme—Development of Women and Children in Rural Areas—suggests, it is about enhancing the economic and social status of women and children. In each district, it is implemented by the District Rural Development Agency. Soon after women enter this movement, they are exposed to continuous rounds of training that are constantly being given to thrift group members. Capacity building training is mainly on group dynamics, self-help concepts, literacy, immunization, sanitation and skill development.

At the World Micro Credit Summit held in Washington in 1997, it was recognized that the women's self-help movement was one of the most important catalysts in reducing socio-economic poverty. It declared, 'The time has come to recognize micro-credit as a powerful tool in the struggle to end poverty and economic dependence.' It announced that it was launching a global movement to reach a hundred million of the world's poorest families with credit for self-employment and other financial and business services by the year 2005.

Going by current trends, four million of these are going to be in Andhra Pradesh. Today 40 per cent of all the self-help groups in India are in our state. In every single district covered, DWCRA has exceeded its achievement targets, even doubled or tripled them.

The argument that the self-help movement undermines panchayati raj is an ignorant one that does not fully appreciate the dynamics that this thrift group movement unleashes. It is not reflected in the statistics, only in the personal stories of lakhs of poor women in my state. Take Ellamma, who belongs to the Budagajangam caste of traditional beggars in Amangal in Mahabubnagar district. Like others in her caste, she used to beg. When she heard about the thrift groups that were coming into existence in her area, the idea of saving appealed to her, and she joined one that was formed by women of her caste.

'It opened a new world for me,' she told us. 'I entered an economic activity for the first time. Being in the group taught me to be clean. I used to beg, my children used to be dirty.

'Earlier people would never have allowed me to sit in a public meeting. But after joining the group people would come and talk to us, and I learnt about hygiene. I had money for the first time to buy soap and oil. I learnt to bathe daily, to bathe my children, then later to put them in school. I even got myself sterilized. People like me are now called to meetings in government offices.'

In Duggumarri, in Anantpur district, a group of scheduled caste women found the local schoolteacher refusing to admit their children to the village school on the pretext that there was no space. So they took out an amount of Rs 10,000 from their thrift kitty and constructed a shed with a thatched roof. It was spacious, well-ventilated, and had a slab floor. Then they invited the teacher to come and teach there.

DWCRA is for women who have no access to institutional credit because they have no security to offer. It is not just a question of facilitating income generation. It is a question of empowering very poor people in tangible ways. In Mahabubnagar, the literacy rate for women is 15 per cent, and the practice of enslaving women as jogins is prevalent in some pockets.

The district mobilized women thrift groups here in a big way from October 1995, using thrift as an entry point to reach women. Today there are 18.4 lakh women who are assiduously saving in the villages of this district, and the thrift amount with these groups is of the order of Rs 11 crore.

They often begin with buying and selling for marginal profit, with the loans they take. They take a bus to Hyderabad with others from their village, buy saris or utensils, and come back and sell them for a profit in their village. Others have taken loans for vegetable and fruit vending. And when the slow augmentation of their family income permits the luxury, they take a consumption loan from their thrift group and buy a TV set.

Often the motivation and enthusiasm triggers such rapid group formation that all of them cannot receive revolving fund assistance from DWCRA in one year. Assistance is then given on the basis of how they score on certain parameters. They are graded on how regular and continuous their rate of saving is, how much this thrift is rotated among members, the rate of recovery of the loans that members take, and the number of group members who stand to benefit. The groups are then provided with DWCRA assistance based on their ranking in these scores.

The significance of ten to fifteen women saving Re 1 a day and pooling it into a savings kitty is that it grows at the end of just two or three years into something as sizeable as a small bank. These are called MACS or Mutually Aided Cooperative Societies. An Act passed in 1995, the AP Mutually Aided Cooperative Societies Act, spells out the cooperative principles on which such banks must be run.

Here is how it happened in Moosapet, in Mahabubnager. When a savings group wanted to expand its loaning potential, it merged with some ten others in the same village to form a bigger savings group of 150 members. In the mandal there were 250 such groups representing thirty-three villages which contributed Rs 3000 each to form a capital investment of Rs 7.5 lakh. With a matching grant of Rs 6.5 lakh from a bank, this group went into business.

Where the original savings group would lend amounts no bigger than a few thousand, this one grants a group or individual loans of up to Rs 25,000 for starting a shop or a poultry farm or some other enterprise. Three women have taken Rs 20,000 to start a tent house business. The conditions are that a loan of Rs 5000 has to be repaid in twelve months, of Rs 10,000 in two years. There is a fine for defaulters but no one has defaulted so far.

This bank is called Adarshya Mahila Sahakara Samakhya Ltd. It has more than 30,000 members, and each of the 250 that came together to set it up are shareholders of the bank. Its directors, all local village women, meet twice a month. They hire the services of a local bookkeeper. The constituent groups of this bank maintain five books each: one for minutes of meetings, a cash book, an individual ledger, a loan ledger and a repayment book.

Their new solvency has given the women shareholders of this bank a social conscience. They give pensions of Rs 75 a month to fifty women in their villages, they run a small creche for the village children, and their activism has resulted in the local school being whitewashed, the nullah cleaned, and tree plantation, some of this under Janmabhoomi.

Further, the collective financial empowerment of women through the whole savings movement is expressed in what the DWCRA members said in Maheswaram mandal in Ranga Reddy district: 'Earlier our men took our money without asking. Now they cannot do it any more. Our money is not with us, it is in our group's account. Husbands approach the group for loans for buying seed, fertilizer, and pesticides for the fields. They repay the loan with interest.'

For every scheme that works well in one place it is possible to find examples of failure. Ultimately, it is the human element that makes the difference between success and failure. There have been cases where groups have failed even after getting matching grants. But the most vulnerable groups under DWCRA are those which have to wait for a long time to get a one-time grant that enables them to move from saving purely for small consumption purposes to saving for an income-generating activity.

This is precisely why we have begun supporting DWCRA from state government funds. In 1998-99 we allocated Rs 44 crore for it so that six lakh additional women could make the transition from saving to earning. And even more important than the money is the hand-holding our extension staff do, particularly in the early stages of group formation.

■

There is a time for the government to step in, and a time for it to step back. That sums up why we began involving stakeholders in irrigation reform. This segment is the story of the self-help groups known as the water users' associations.

With four major rivers running through the state and over 70 per cent of its people dependent on agriculture for their livelihood, successive governments in Andhra Pradesh concentrated on creating irrigation potential in the state. Harnessing the Godavari, Krishna, Vamsadhara and Pennar helped increase the net irrigated area from 1.5 lakh hectares in the Second Plan to 59 lakh hectares today. Plan outlays on irrigation over this period increased from Rs 62 crore in the Second Plan to Rs 3186 crore in the Eighth Plan. It became a critical input: over the years yields of foodgrains and other crops have almost trebled under irrigated conditions.

However, the other side of the story is that until a couple of years ago there was a gap of 41 per cent between the potential created and actual irrigation taking place. If you were to go to villages in the Godavari or Krishna delta in coastal Andhra's prosperous belt, you would find yourself in an irrigated heartland which until recently suffered from an unlikely problem. They did not have enough water for their crops! There was plenty of water, but it did not reach their fields. There was obviously something amiss in irrigation management.

In government parlance this was termed 'low utilization of water in irrigation commands'. In spite of increasing maintenance and operation expenses, the area irrigated under some of the major and medium projects was shrinking. A cess is supposed to be collected from farmers for irrigation use and this money ploughed back into the maintenance of the entire canal system. But the gap between revenues collected and cost of operations and maintenance had become enormous.

The irrigation department is huge, and as much as 25 per cent of the total plan allocations for Andhra Pradesh go into this sector. It employs thousands of people and awards works worth hundreds of crores to contractors. How well these are utilized is, of course, another issue. Despite the huge staffing and expenditure, over the years thousands of irrigation canals have fallen into disrepair to the point of becoming unrecognizable. Some of the pictures in this book will illustrate that.

This technological problem was a result of other problems, financial and managerial. From 1951 to 1957 there was self-sustaining revenue flowing from the irrigated areas in the state. The water cess being collected was enough to maintain the channels. Documents of the Government of India and the Planning Commission show that in 1957 there was a revenue surplus on water usage collection. Until 1962 collections were sufficient to balance expenditure.

Thereafter the problems began to set in. Water rates were not revised for political reasons. Just as it has not been considered politically wise to charge farmers the full cost of supplying them power, so also they were not charged adequately for the water their fields consumed. Maintenance of the systems could not be kept up because water charges remained low. The system has to get the money from somewhere: either from the government, or from the user. When the arrangement began, the user was paying. But forty-five to fifty years down the line the user was paying nowhere near what operation and maintenance was costing.

Politics was not the only reason for this state of affairs: corruption had also taken its toll of the irrigation systems in the state. Historically the irrigation service was provided by the irrigation department, and the revenue department would collect the money. It was the job of the patwari, the village revenue official, to assess how much water was being used by the farmer and collect charges accordingly.

What was happening, though, was that the patwari would under-report the water drawn by the farmer and both he and the farmer would benefit at the expense of the exchequer. With not enough revenue coming in it became increasingly difficult to put money into maintenance. In fact some of the shrinkage of the irrigated area mentioned above was probably due to under-reporting.

Restoring the network was essential if crop production in the state was to increase. Water would have to reach the tail ends of the canals, something that had stopped happening in many areas. In 1996 we felt the time had come to stop apportioning the blame and start correcting the system.

As I said earlier in this chapter, there is a time for the government to step in, and a time for it to step back.

I had noticed for many years that farmers are not able to make best use of the existing irrigation system. It was becoming clear that radical reform was needed. When I was a student, farmers used to dig their canals themselves. Now everybody thinks the government has to do the job. I wanted to revive the old thinking. I wanted to hand the management of irrigation back to farmers.

Canals feed water to their fields, if they are not interested in repairing these, who will do it for them? How can engineers or panchayats have the same sense of involvement? Since farmers had the most stake in efficient irrigation, participatory irrigation management seemed to be the route that we needed to explore.

When we started looking at the problem in 1996 my brief to my officials was that farmers have to be brought into irrigation management, and we have to find the best way to do this. We did not have a road map. But there was already a pilot scheme in operation where this was being attempted since 1994, at the Shri Ram Sagar Project. The command area taken up under the experiment was about 16,000 acres and thirty-five water users' associations, consisting of farmers who utilize the irrigation water, had been constituted. Our efforts to reform the administration of the irrigation system began with going to this area to see what the experience had been until then.

The official appointed to this task—of involving farmers in the management of irrigation—spent seven days in the field listening to the woes of farmers. They had many complaints about the engineers demanding money from them to re-excavate canals in their area. But even from their mixed experiences an interesting fact emerged. Though this project had been located in the worst possible area, it had yielded surprising results.

The area where it was located was an extremist-infested place, where the administration was not able to function normally because of Naxalite activity. Even so we found a 30 per cent increase in irrigation in that area. This had been achieved through very marginal interventions, such as removing silt in the canals, which helped take water to the tail end. Also by giving farmers a platform to negotiate, which was the water users' associations. When we saw the difference made by these elementary changes, we realized that this was the way to go for the rest of the state.

We began by appointing consultants for each of the major commands. Every big command area in the state is under an irrigation project. At Nagarjunasagar we have 35 lakh acres. At Sriramsagar 10 lakh acres. At each command we appointed an officer to conduct participatory sessions with farmers, to ask them, what do they expect from the irrigation system? After three to four rounds of discussions in various projects, the aspirations of farmers, the expectations of the irrigation department, the expectations of the government and politicians were all broadly consolidated.

We then had to decide whether to create a platform for collaboration with the farmers on an informal basis, or with a legal basis. In irrigation you are dealing with rights—water rights, land and title to land, you are also dealing with irrigation disputes. These things cannot be resolved in an informal fashion. Banks and courts will not accept that. So it became clear that an Act was needed to provide a legal framework to the joint management system between farmers and engineers that was evolving.

An Act was then drafted which is the first of its kind in India. It was called the AP Farmers' Management of Irrigation Systems Act. It was the expression of a consultative process.

It talked of the basis on which farmers should be organized, how water users' associations should be constituted, the rules by which these should function. We provided for a process of recall whereby members or presidents of the association could be recalled by a third of the total voting body if there was dissatisfaction with their performance.

The role provided for engineers in the Act entailed a paradigm shift for the engineering department as the competent authority. They would be working under the farmers' organizations. In the new system everybody's role had to change: that of farmer, engineer, and the administration. The government would no longer maintain, it would regulate. Further, the revenue department would no longer collect water charges, the farmers would.

Once it was drafted we had a wide debate on the Act. Intellectuals, political parties, universities, collectors, engineers—every relevant section's point of view was taken. In March 1997 it was passed, and in November that year we had the first statewide elections to more than 10,000 water users' associations, covering all the major, medium and minor irrigation schemes in the state. Fifty-five per cent of these elected their office-bearers unanimously, in 45 per cent of the cases the elections were contested. The Act was applicable to all irrigation schemes, except those under panchayati raj institutions, and all minor bodies in the scheduled areas of the state.

What was the Act supposed to achieve? The main objectives were the following: to restore the existing network and make it fully operational, to ensure equitable and reliable supplies of water to farmers, to bring about social audit and water audit in irrigation, and to enable the department to withdraw from maintenance and operations and concentrate on reservoir management and development of new systems.

To operationalize this approach water users' associations were created as an institutional structure. These presided over small areas of an irrigation command which were delineated on a hydraulic basis. There were supposed to be administratively and functionally viable. The WUA was the primary organizational unit of irrigation water users; each irrigation scheme could have one or more.

The farmers in that command area were to manage the system, maintain it, and do water management. Earlier everything was done by the irrigation department, which had kilometre-wide jurisdictions. It had its own workers who maintained the canals. Now the farmers are to maintain these canals themselves, with the help of the department's engineers. Each water users' association is divided into four to ten territorial segments, so that each area of the command is represented.

Each segment elects a member of the managing committee of the WUA, and directly elects its president. A group of WUAs under a distributary comprise a distributary committee, whose members are made up of the presidents of all the WUAs. They select a managing committee and president for themselves, and take decisions on all distributary related matters.

Above the distributary committees is a project committee, which is the apex body concerned with the management and distribution of water in the command of major and medium projects. The way it operates is that the project committee looks after the headworks, the barrage and the main canal, the distributary committee looks after the branch canal and medium drains, and the water users' associations maintain the remaining canals and minor drains.

Membership of the WUAs is based on ownership or tenancy of land in the authorized command of the WUA and not on the extent of land owned. It also means, however, that control over the water use is in the hands of local users of irrigation water, and there is no control with non- irrigation users who have membership rights in the WUAs but no voting rights.

Once these associations were constituted and began to assess on their own how much needed to be done in their ayacuts, we realized some sort of financial assistance would be needed to take up long-neglected works on a large scale. At that time the state was undergoing a financial crisis. We approached the World Bank and said we needed money to strengthen the working of the associations.

The World Bank became interested because it is their policy to support states that are attempting comprehensive reform in sectors such as irrigation and power. They were interested in new approaches to managing the irrigation system. They gave us $145 million for the irrigation reform we were attempting.

To begin with, minimum rehabilitation of the canal system was taken up. This was a bit like putting a vehicle which had been fully dysfunctional to work. It meant attempting maintenance work neglected over the years and bringing the water channels to a level of functionality from where the WUAs could take over the maintenance for the future, from their own revenues. Minor repairs of the canal system and bunds was undertaken. But the dynamics of how such work is done has now changed.

Earlier the department's engineers identified the works and executed them. Today this is done by the farmers. They identify and prioritize the work after a walk through the entire area. They make a list of works to be done and then look at the money available. Though it may seem that millions of dollars are now available, in practice what the money boils down to is Rs 100 per acre for each water users' association, and another Rs 100 for each distributary committee.

If this kind of money were to be given under the old system it would only go to contractors. Under the WUAs it goes a long way. They have a managing committee which meets once a month. In the first year after the WUAs were constituted 24,123 works were taken up, at a cost of Rs 107 crore. With it they managed to bridge a gap of 5.12 lakh hectares which were not getting water. It was basically earthwork: desilting of canals, and removing weeds, shrubs and jungles.

The farmers did a number of things that they found themselves in a position to do. If we had given the same amount of money to the irrigation department to spend, it might have gone to ten or fifteen places. Now it is in 24,000 places. The nexus between contractors, the irrigation departments and politicians has now really come under tremendous pressure.

Farmers are able to access machinery—they simply pay money and book excavators for their area. We send the money to the bank accounts of their associations. They maintain accounts. Once a year at least they have general body meetings. These works have to be prioritized at that meeting. The farmers have a vested interest in ensuring that the work gets done in their area at the earliest.

Those members of the managing committee who do not discharge their responsibility can be recalled under a provision under the Act. Already in the first two years of functioning eight or nine recalls have taken place across the state. Farmers are far from passive about their associations. On one occasion a WUA used the state government website to e-mail complaints to me about their association president.

Training programmes are being organized for the farmers and we have district-wise conventions where we use a computerized feedback survey to get their opinion on how their associations are functioning. At the same time we hold seminars and workshops for engineers on how to restore excavated canals which have fallen into such disuse that they have lost their configuration.

The farmers have become so empowered that they now articulate with considerable expertise on irrigation matters.

They point out faults in designs of irrigation systems and suggest that things would have been better if they had been consulted. Two years after the new system of management began they can see tangible gains in their own fields. In the villages of West Godavari they will tell you that they got water ten days earlier in the sowing season, and got an additional ten bags of rice per acre.

In some areas transplantation of paddy has been advanced by a month. And thanks to repair of minor drains, there has been less damage from heavy rain. On a statewide level, we are witnessing record levels of rice production in the last two years. If the emphasis in the first year was on restoring the canal network, in the second year it has shifted to fixing of sluice shutters at various offtake points to enable water regulation.

Alongside this whole process of institutionalizing participatory irrigation management, a restructuring of functioning of the irrigation engineers has also been undertaken. We have enhanced sanctioning powers down the line, in order to decentralize and speed up execution of the works. The executive engineer who could sanction up to Rs 1 lakh, can now sanction works up to Rs 5 lakh. The deputy executive engineers' sanctioning powers have been enhanced to Rs 1 lakh, and that of superintending engineers who are above executive engineers in the hierarchy up to Rs 20 lakh.

The test of the long-term viability of the WUAs will lie in whether they are able to become self-sustaining when the World Bank funding is out of the picture. Will they be able to recover enough from the water cess to do the operations and maintenance work on their own with the help and technical advice of the engineering department? Will they be able to resolve conflicts amicably?

Collecting water charges is going to take some getting used to, because these farmers have never had to recover money before from fellow farmers. The Act provides for them to both fix and collect these charges, 70 per cent of which will go to the WUAs, and 30 per cent to the government. By March 2000 a need-based sharing arrangement was to be worked out. The WUAs will need to fix viable rates for the user charges.

Disputes related to auctioning of fishing rights in the canals are already arising. There is also usufruct from the grassy banks of the canals which has to be auctioned by the WUAs. There is a potential conflict of interest situation here with the local panchayats who were earlier receiving an income from such usufruct. The associations will have to hone their own political management skills.

The plus point is that after the formation of these farmers' bodies reporting of water use has improved, so that collections are likely to reflect actual use much more than has been the case in the past few decades. They have to do these things effectively and transparently. We had training for office-bearers of WUAs in the beginning; this will have to be a constant process.

In the long term a major challenge for the WUAs will be how equitably they are able to distribute the water among those users who are at the head of the system, and those lower down. If water is left to flow freely, its availability will be in inverse proportion to the distance of the user from the head. The nearer the user, the more the water. Greater control over releases and distribution will come only when the WUAs are ready to exercise such control, using sluice shutters or gates.

But ultimately it will not be merely a question of sluice gates. This is a potentially contentious issue, involving conflict of economic interest. Will the farmers' organizations be able to persuade those among them who have long had more access to water to give this up in favour of tail-enders? This is a challenge they will have to come to grips with.

Successful water management initiatives in other parts of the country, such as Ralegaon Sidhi and the Pani Panchayats in Maharashtra, have derived their success from social regulation of water use. In the case of the self-help groups involved in watershed development we have been facilitating our farmers visiting other parts of the country to study examples worth emulating. We have to do the same for WUAs.

The challenge for our irrigation reform initiative is that the reforms will have to be carried into the realm of water use, whereby choice of low water consumption crops and adoption of better agricultural practices become part of the process of enhancing water productivity for all users.

14

RESTORING PEACE AND SECURITY

Without law and order neither citizens nor government can go about their daily business. But maintaining the peace presents its own challenge. In Andhra Pradesh the frequency of general crime is less than it is in many other states: we are ranked 19th in the country in this respect. But this relative peace is unfortunately marred by other threats to security which have posed major problems for us over the last two or three decades. Perhaps the most daunting of these is left wing extremism, which is also becoming increasingly entrenched in the states surrounding Andhra Pradesh. The other two kinds of violence that we have to deal with are faction fighting, which is endemic to the Rayalseema region, and communal disturbances which fortunately are on the decline.

The problem of left wing extremism gains sustenance on account of the misguided youth who are drawn into the fold of such movements. We are attempting to follow the twin approach of containing the elements perpetuating extremism, in collaboration with the Central government and other affected states, while negotiating with both the affected population, and those extremist cadres who are willing to consider surrender. We are also attempting to accelerate the development process in the areas where extremism thrives.

But first the background. For three long decades Andhra Pradesh has lived under the shadow of left wing extremism. The violent movement which began in Naxalbari in West Bengal in 1967, spread to Srikakulam district of Andhra Pradesh in 1969 and later spread to the Telengana region. In the mid-seventies it was brought under control by strong police action as well as administrative response enabled by the several splits that occurred in the ML parties. The post-Emergency movement witnessed a resurgence of the extremist movement and this time it resurfaced mainly in Andhra Pradesh and gained momentum with the formation of the CPI-ML People's War Group in April 1980 by Kondapalli Sitharamaiah. By the mid-eighties it had indoctrinated a number of youth, making it the dominant group in terms of its manpower, weaponry, striking power, finances, party network and its sheer spread. Through the nineties it used this base in Andhra Pradesh to develop both its network as well as politico-organizational structure in the surrounding states of Madhya Pradesh, Maharashtra, Karnataka, Tamil Nadu, Orissa and beyond these to West Bengal.

Left wing extremism is guided by the Maost dictum that power flows from the barrel of a gun. Elsewhere in the world this ideology has been overtaken by contemporary developments and that inclues China itself, as well as similar movements in Germany, Italy and Belgium. Here, however, the PWG is reinforcing its strength by developing fraternal relationships with other extremist groups in the country, including those operating in Bihar, Jammu and Kashmir, the North East, and in August 1998 it merged with Party Unity of Bihar to form a single party known as the CPI-ML People's War. Its basic strategy is to oppose parliamentary democracy and capture political power by overthrowing the lawfully established government through protracted armed struggle and area-wise seizure of power. It has been building up bases in rural and remote areas with a view to transforming them into guerrilla zones and later into liberated areas which ultimately extend, surround and encircle urban centres of power. It has three military platoons and more than seventy-one armed dalams.

Terrorism thrives on the media. The strikes of this extremist group draw national attention every now and then because it picks high-profile targets. The Andhra Pradesh minister for Panchayati Raj, Madhava Reddy, was killed in a landmine blast near Ghatkeshar in Rangareddy district in March 2000. In late 1999 a Madhya Pradesh minister sleeping unarmed inside his house was brutally murdered. A former speaker of the state assembly, an MLA, and a senior police officer were among those killed in Andhra Pradesh in 1999. But these hits mask the fact that most of the people killed by the PWG are from the scheduled classes, scheduled tribes and backward classes. The poor suffer the most.

The continuing violence is a deterrent to development and extracts a heavy price in loss of lives and damage to public and private property. At the end of 1999 we estimated that over the preceding ten years the group had killed 1551 people, damaged property worth Rs 111 crores, committed over 11,000 offences and killed 344 police officers. In December 1999 in a period of two weeks twenty-eight state road transport buses, thirty-three private buildings, seven telephone exchanges, two railway stations, two railway tracks, three culverts and ten private vehicles were damaged. When public facilities are destroyed, it is people who are affected.

It is becoming difficult to distinguish between the committed cadres of the PWG and the lumpen elements who are increasingly entering its ranks. The violence and extortion indulged in has encouraged the proliferation of splinter groups. At the end of 1999 these were fifteen in number. If they are the champions of the downtrodden, the question to ask is how the latter are affected by their activities.

Anything the government does is anathema to the PWG. It opposes land distribution by the government and does not allow people to cultivate assigned land. It opposes roads being laid for the benefit of people living in interior villages. It opposes developmental schemes such as Janmabhoomi, Prajala Vaddaku Palana (Taking government to the doorsteps of the people) and the Van Samraksha Samiti scheme (Joint Forest Management) which sets up forest protection committees drawn from the local villagers. Meanwhile the pattern of violence and extortion has been holding up industrialization of the Telengana areas for decades.

The TDP government's response has of necessity been multi-pronged. We have to resist the violence, which we have done by banning the CPI-ML PWG and its front organizations and stepping up the training of our police force. We have created a special cell for collecting information about the extremists, as well as an elite force called 'Grey Hounds' for anti-extremist operations in the forest and interior areas. At the same time I must stress that our commitment is to go strictly by the law in handling this problem. We have been collaborating with the Central government and other state governments to chalk out a common strategy against extremism. The Centre has agreed to share 50 per cent of the expenditure of the anti-extremist operations undertaken by the states since April 1996.

Alongside, our response has been to step up both the opening up of the interior areas where they operate, though they resist such an opening up, as well as to step up the development schemes operational in these areas. There is no alternative to attempting to wean away the poor from the extremists through development work in these areas. The state government prepared an action plan of Rs 1299 crores for all-round development of these areas which is currently pending with the Planning Commission.

The government is examining a proposal to purchase land which is presently lying fallow and uncultivated on account of the extremist threat so that it can then be distributed to the landless poor for cultivation. We are improving the road network in affected areas, improving irrigation so that agriculture can receive a boost, and encouraging the formation of water users' associations in these areas as well.

Persuasion has to be a consistent aspect of any strategy to tackle such an entrenched and violent movement. We regularly convene meetings in the affected areas so as to educate people about the development programmes available, as well as to educate them about the futility of the approach advocated by the extremists. The electronic and print media, as well as culture troupes, are roped in to spread the message. The state also organizes counselling of the parents and relatives of those who are underground so that the youth can be persuaded to leave the extremist fold.

The TDP government has also been doggedly pursuing a surrender and rehabilitation policy to draw out cadres, who we think are essentially misguided youth. A cadre member who surrenders is given a reward and rehabilitation package which could extend up to Rs 4 lakh for starting a business or taking up cultivation or pursuing studies. The man or woman is given a house site. During the last five years more than 1100 extremists and their sympathizers have surrendered. In a Dial your CM programme held on Doordarshan in December 1999 we attempted to lay before the people of the state the challenges posed by the continuing violence and our strategy for meeting these.

Every time the PWG makes a successful strike and claims a high-profile victim, the impression gains ground that they have the upper edge in the battle they are waging against the state. But there are other indications to show that their influence is waning rather than increasing. Despite their calls for a poll boycott, whenever elections of any kind are held, people still turn out to vote in the rural areas. Since 1994 the PWG has campaigned for a poll boycott. Before the assembly elections held in September 1999 wall posters sprang up in the Telengana areas where the PWG is active, threatening to cut off the fingers of those who voted. Yet the voter turnout in these areas was between 58 and 60 per cent.

People are beginning to resent the intimidation and threats the extremists subject them to. The lumpenization of the movement has meant that they use their dalams to settle personal scores. People also resent the fact that industries which could give local people jobs are staying away from these districts because of the prevailing climate of terror and extortion. Extremism thrives in a climate of neglect by the state. In a situation where the state is constantly taking initiatives on the development front, the climate of terror created by extremists will be viewed by people as counter to development.

In Peddamallapuram village of East Godavari district, women put up a stiff resistance to the dalams of the PWG operating in their area. In Nizamabad, villagers tried to resist the militants, who hurled a hand grenade on them which fortunately did not explode. Meanwhile villagers apprehended the militants and beat them with sticks due to which two militants died on the spot.

As elsewhere in the state, the districts of the Telengana region which are affected by extremism have seen the slow but sure inroads of progress made through schemes like Janmabhoomi. Public works identified by local people have been taken up in these villages. Self-help groups of women have been able to increase the savings of households. We are consciously reaching out to the youth in this region with employment schemes so that they can see productive alternatives to the armed revolution preached by the cadres of the PWG. All this is resulting in a steady erosion of support to the extremists.

To keep up the morale of both the people and the police forces who become victims of extremism we have also stepped up compensation for victims, including where possible house sites and jobs. Compensation is also given for the property damaged and destroyed by the extremists. It is a costly battle that we have to wage until the range of solutions yield results.

■

The other major challenge to law and order which is endemic and peculiar to the Rayalseema region of Andhra Pradesh is factionalism. The region is ridden with feuds which originate from village rivalries dating back a hundred years or more. An Imperial gazette published in 1908 records Koilakuntla in Kurnool district as the birthplace of factions in the Rayalseema region, the causes being personal rivalry and land disputes. The rivalries and constant resort to revenge are deeply ingrained in the daily conduct of people who live here. The area is arid but rich in mineral wealth. However the latter cannot be exploited fully because people are reluctant to invest in these areas. Rayalseema's development is effectively hampered by the law and order problems created by the feuds.

The factors are entwined with the region's politics, and rival groups have assumed party alignments. Leaders of both major parties in the region are involved in police cases. Traditionally crude bombs and axes have been used as weapons by the factions of Rayalseema to settle scores. Murders used to be common in this region and even when court cases were instituted it was not uncommon for rival sides to use court appearances by arrested persons as occasions to settle scores.

Tackling factionalism embroiled with politics is a difficult task. Here again the approach has to be multi-pronged. At the political level it has been my attempt during the assembly elections as well as the recently conducted municipal elections to select candidates for the TDP who are not involved in these factions.

We have had to form faction control squads in Rayalseema districts, conduct intensified raids for vehicle checking and provide special arrangements during court attendance of accused persons to prevent harm from coming to them. We tried to improve standards of investigation to ensure convictions. The three law and order initiatives which have been most important have been the stress on the strict impartiality and neutrality of the police force, increased accessibility of the police to the public to contain the role of factional violence in the day-to-day lives of villagers, as well as regular cordon and search operations to unearth illicit firearms, explosives, and illicit liquor.

Persuasion and education are also approaches being attempted. Peace committees in the region have had some success, but we need to institutionalize these. The police themselves have been using street plays and cultural performances to educate the local people on the harm done to the development of the region on account of the factionalism.

A major challenge for the administration has been resisting interference from political leaders who are embroiled in the faction fighting themselves. Senior police officers were constantly shifted from their postings because of political pressure. This was having a deleterious effect on their ability to be effective. We have been trying to address this problem.

The third category of violence that the state used to be prone to was communal violence. Our approach is that the government will not identify with any group. However, there has been a decline in the incidence of this. We are firmly committed to maintaining our secular credentials and this is demonstrated by a steady decline in the number of communal

incidents in the state. From 1028 incidents in 1990-94 the
number has come down to 694 in 1995-2000. Over the same
period the number of killings has declined from 289 to 18.
We keep a constant watch on the activities of communal
fundamentalist organizations. We have also set up a special
counter-intelligence cell at the state level equipped with
vehicles and modern gadgets to monitor the movements of
communal elements and check the involvement of agencies
such as the Pakistani Inter-Service Intelligence (ISI).

At the end of the day, a successful law and order policy
has to incorporate new skills and approaches. In a civil
society there is no place for police brutality. We are waging
a steady battle against police excesses and custodial deaths.
The number of deaths in police custody was up from 37 in
1997 to 41 in 1998 and came down to 25 during 1999.
However, even a single case of death in police custody is a
matter of grave concern and therefore we need to humanize
the police through constant effort. Our police should deal
with the weaker sections and women with sympathy and
sensitivity.

Changing the image of the police in the public eye will
require sustained training and sensitization of the police on
the one hand, and greater public awareness of the constraints
under which the police works, on the other. Training is also
required to handle the new types of white-collar crime that
are on the rise. Training has not only to address attitudinal
issues but also equip policemen with specialized skills in
crime prevention, detection and investigation. For example,
the rapid expansion of global networks will require a totally
new set of skills in handling cybercrimes.

The police force will increasingly have to use modern
technology in dealing with crime. I have found that use of a
simple technology like videographing events during communal
disturbances can prove immensely useful in identifying
troublemakers and also providing valuable evidence to bring

them to book. Computerization of fingerprint data, which we have done, has cut down the time taken to zero in on suspects.

I recall an interesting episode while judging the performance of the police in handling crime. I was reviewing the monthly crime data in a meeting with superintendents of police at Hyderabad when a number of officers told me that it was extremely difficult, if not impossible, to assess police performance by looking at crime data. If the police were judged by, say, the reduction in murder cases, it was possible to book cases of murder as cases of suspicious death, thus achieving an immediate improvement in performance. I pointed out to them that ideally the performance of the police should be judged by how secure the ordinary citizen felt, rather than by crime statistics alone. Ever since we have been conducting regular surveys to judge public perception of how secure people feel. We are not only gauging public opinion in regard to the police but also coopting citizens under a 'maitri' programme for maintaining law and order.

The approach is to have voluntary committees at the village and mohalla levels which will inform the police quickly about a likely disturbance or breach of peace. Such committees can also help by volunteering for patrolling, for assisting in traffic management and in protecting local women from harassment. Our plan is to have these voluntary committees attached to police stations with the station house officer (SHO) functioning as the team leader.

The volunteer committees can have fifty to hundred members. Interested members of the community will be asked to apply, and those with a clean record and reputation selected. They will be issued identity cards. Members who do not participate in community activities can be removed from the committee. We launched this scheme on Ugadi Day, in the year 2000.

15

A ROAD MAP FOR VISION 2020

> Our vision of Andhra Pradesh is a state where poverty is totally eradicated. Where every man, woman and child has access to not just the basic minimum needs, but to all the opportunities to lead a happy and fulfilling life. A knowledge and learning society built on the values of hard work, honesty, discipline and a collective sense of purpose.
>
> —*Vision 2020*

On Republic Day 1999 we released a document entitled Vision 2020 that had been in the making for more than a year. I am aware that it represents such a quantum leap in government thinking that the cynical will call it a pipe dream. But my logic is simple. If Indians are second to none in the world in achievement—as hundreds of non-resident Indians from Andhra Pradesh and elsewhere have proved—we should facilitate that level of achievement here.

We have to create conditions for rapid growth. We have to set ourselves goals for development that make up for the time lost. Just because the last fifty years have not been as well utilized as they could have been is no reason to scale down our ambitions for the next twenty. We can continue thinking of ourselves as a poor country or we can shed that fatalism and seek radical departures from the past.

Vision 2020 is an exercise that we began in 1997 by constituting fourteen task forces. It was inspired not just by Malaysia's vision document but by my own experience and belief that five years is too short a period for planning—it does not help you establish a direction for the future. For a vision, a reasonable time-span is twenty years. Twenty-twenty means perfect vision. But our vision document is intended to be hard-headed rather than grandiose. It is as much about removing poverty and promoting sustainable development, as it is about creating a superb infrastructure and plugging into the global economy.

Some of the basic questions that arise when you are planning for the future are, what should be the role of the government? How do we reduce the quantity of governance and enhance its quality? How should the government re-invent itself in the Indian context? Our answer to that is that the government will have a critical role to play in implementing the growth agenda but do fewer things itself. In line with global trends the government in this state too should become more sharply focussed, acting primarily as an enabler and facilitator of growth.

That will mean refocussing both priorities and spending. As Vision 2020 has underscored, today the state government plays a pervasive role in the economy. It runs a number of public enterprises including transport; until recently it even used to manufacture refrigerators! It operates key sectors like mining in addition to playing an extensive role in agriculture. It dominates the social sector: particularly health and education. Its role as a regulator is both broad and deep: it keeps tabs on virtually every sector of economic and welfare activity, and micro-manages price control and policy making for the private sector.

What it really needs to focus on is basic education,

primary health care, poverty alleviation and rural infrastructure. But its resources and manpower are so stretched that it is unable to do that. Social sector spending in Andhra Pradesh has been decreasing steadily. Today it spends 2.5 per cent of its gross state domestic product on education and 1.2 per cent on health as compared to 3.2 per cent and 1.7 in 1980-81. Resources for creating trunk and rural infrastructure have also shrunk. These areas now receive only 2.2 per cent of GSDP as compared to 3.2 per cent in other states.

Instead, money that can be put to better use is going into subsidizing the losses of pubic enterprises and into establishment costs which need to be drastically pruned.

A reversal of spending priorities is therefore spelt out in Vision 2020: reduce administrative and other non-developmental expenditure such as support to public sector undertakings from 40 per cent of the budget to 20-25 per cent by 2010. Raise expenditure on basic health and education, food security and rural development from 17 per cent to 30-35 per cent of the budget. And increase investment in infrastructure from 6 per cent of the budget today to 15-20 per cent.

Infrastructure is critical for future growth of industry as well as for development of education and health services. Three types will have to be created: trunk, arterial and specialized infrastructure. Trunk, the first of these, will constitute the infrastructure backbone of the state and will include power, major highways, telecommunication links, ports, airports and industrial estates. Arterial infrastructure comprises power distribution networks, local telecommunication loops and smaller highways and roads which connect villages and cities to the infrastructure backbone. The third category is infrastructure required to develop specific sectors such as information technology, horticulture and dairy.

Impressive targets have been set for 2020 with regard to

power, ports, roads, airports, and telecommunications. This includes installed capacity of 36000 MW of power, a doubling of total road length in the state, many more ports and airports, a telephone density ten to fifteen times higher than what it is today and a high bandwidth telecommunication network in the growth corridors as well as value-added services at all major nodes.

All this will require a mix of public and private investment and considerable reform in this sector. Today infrastructure in the state is largely controlled and operated by government monopoly institutions. Since the government's role as provider for all groups, particularly the underprivileged, has overridden economic priorities, the prices of many infrastructure services are subsidized and often do not reflect the cost of providing them. This has disrupted the economics of the sector. Investment does not generate returns, cutting off a source of profit for the government and making it difficult to attract private investment in the area.

Being public sector units, the capability and efficiency of government infrastructure agencies has also remained low. Therefore, to make the provision of infrastructure economically sustainable price reform is critical. Services have to be priced to reflect the cost of providing them. Subsidies have to be focussed and structured in a way that makes them transparent transfers from the state budget to a given utility. In addition, budget allocations for this sector have to reflect the entire revenue earning potential of this sector.

Restructuring government infrastructure agencies is also critical. A continuum of options has been envisaged. To move from low-impact interventions to high-impact ones you could merely improve operational performance, or go a step further and corporatize major public sector utilities, setting them up as separate autonomous bodies. You could go even further and deregulate, and introduce competition.

For even greater impact you could securitize viable projects or sell PSU equity stake. There would be low implementation risk at the lower end of this continuum and higher implementation risk with greater degrees of privatization. At one end of the continuum which is confined to improving operational performance the degree of government ownership will be high. At the other end where you sell PSU stake, the degree of government ownership will be low.

The financial requirement of this sector is enormous. The state will need to invest Rs 16 lakh crore by 2020. Even if it increases budgetary support for infrastructure to 25 per cent of the budget—which is substantial—it will not be able to fund all the infrastructural requirements of the growth agenda. The private sector has to, therefore, be invited to participate in infrastructure creation.

While the process of creating infrastructure will generate large-scale employment, its development will influence how much investment comes into Andhra Pradesh. The quantity and quality of power, roads, airports, ports and telecommunications available in a location will influence the decision of industrial and other players.

The construction industry will be a major beneficiary of the infrastructure building thrust, with business and employment opportunities being generated in building roads, power plants, industrial parks, ports and irrigation systems. China has adopted this approach of viewing infrastructure as a driver of growth. It plans to attract investment of up to $100 billion in this sector over the next few years.

To achieve Vision 2020 the state will have to practically double the current growth rate, which has now reached the all-India average of 5.2 per cent. A tall order, admittedly, but not impossible. Only with a growth rate of 9-10 per cent can the quantum leap that we envision in the quality of life of people in the entire state be achieved.

To achieve this, a very focussed emphasis on specific

sectors that offer high growth opportunities has to be accomplished. The task forces that prepared our vision document studied both the state's strengths as well as opportunities created by global trends, before identifying those growth engines which will, in the long term, have maximum economic impact.

Only when an exercise of this kind has been undertaken can facilitating policies be put in place. Increasingly, such initiatives in anticipating and capturing opportunities have to become part of the challenge of governance because good administration by itself cannot create job opportunities or boost the state's economy.

All countries started with agriculture but then sought growth in other areas. There is no other way. Agriculture cannot provide total employment and create wealth. Service and industry helps create more wealth and also increased growth. I was born in an agricultural family. Everybody thinks that those born in an agricultural family have to confine themselves to agriculture. But today those who are born in agriculture have shifted to industry, services and politics. That is the sign of a developed country. I want to take advantage of these trends. Previously, what was happening was that one had to run the course of transformation from agriculture to industry to services. Today information technology makes it possible to go straight from agriculture to services.

The way to build opportunities created by global trends has been shown by countries like Singapore, the Netherlands, and the US which built major trade and logistics centres in their countries. Andhra Pradesh is in a position to create India's primary logistics centre by taking advantage of both its own geographical position as well as the country's increased participation in global trade.

Some of the basic requirements for such an ambitious proposal already exist. The state has good rail linkages to other parts of the country, it has a long coastline with one major port, two intermediate ports and ten minor ports which can be used to link India with international markets, once upgraded. We also have several airports, though currently these have limited facilities.

Despite its historical economic backwardness and low human development indices, Andhra has many strengths to build on which were taken into account while planning for growth engines as part of Vision 2020. It has plenty of cultivable land, ranking among the top five Indian states in this respect. Its water resources are fairly abundant, if only its irrigation potential can be fully utilized. Two major rivers, the Krishna and Godavari, flow through it. Sixty per cent of the state has ample rainfall. And it has the second largest mineral reserves in India, notably massive deposits of coal, limestone and bauxite.

Assets such as location have to be leveraged. AP has the second longest coastline in the country, providing several gateways for international trade. Its ports provide quick access to countries such as Singapore and Malaysia. And within the country it is within easy reach of Delhi, Mumbai, Kolkata, Bangalore and Chennai. As the two fastest growing cities in the country, Hyderabad and Visakhapatnam are emerging centres of national importance.

The state has a great deal of agricultural wealth, it leads all other states in the production of poultry and is among India's top producers of fruit and rice. If to these strengths you add speedy reform and capability building the state will have the edge. Most Indian states and many other countries are in the race to capture global investment. What will separate the winners from the losers will be the ability to move fast, reform the government, create infrastructure and develop human resources.

The first step has been to identify which should be the growth engines of our economy, which will contribute a sizeable part of the state's gross state domestic product and employment. Nineteen primary growth engines have been identified, six in agriculture, six in industry, and seven in services. These are rice, dairy, poultry, horticulture, fisheries, agro-industries, in the first instance. As for industry, the growth engines that will create the highest economic impact in the short term are infrastructure and construction.

The other areas of industry which have been identified as growth engines are mining-based industries, labour-intensive export-oriented industries such as garments and leather, pharmaceuticals, and small-scale industry. As for services, we have identified basic information technology services, knowledge-based services, logistics, tourism, small-scale services, health care and education. However, the process of identifying and developing growth engines is a dynamic one.

The state will need to re-prioritize its thrust areas as its competitive strengths change over time. As Andhra Pradesh moves up the ladder of economic development, it may need to de-emphasize some areas and identify others. It is not the only state or country pursuing high growth sectors with attractive opportunities. For instance, at least six Indian states have the stated goal of becoming forces in the IT industry. Many South East Asian countries with higher currency values will be aggressive in labour-intensive sectors such as garments and leather products.

The growth engines have been chosen to maximize the potential of different regions in the state. For instance Telengana has coal, so we will develop mining-based activities in this region. It has a strong maize production base which will enable development of poultry and agro-processing. It grows grapes, which has further potential for agro-processing. Nagarjunasagar lake and the Nizam's historical legacy give it tourist potential. Finally, Hyderabad's educated, IT-literate labour force will facilitate the establishment of a knowledge corridor in that city.

Similarly, in the coastal Andhra region rice will be a growth engine, as will dairy because of the availability of fodder. Mango produce from here travels to many parts of the country, and can become the basis of an agro-processing industry. The long coastline will sustain fisheries as well as lend itself to the creation of a logistics hub. Rayalseema has minerals, a horticulture base as well as a major tourism revenue-puller such as the Tirupathi Devasthanam. All three regions have competitive labour costs which can facilitate the setting up of labour intensive, export-oriented industries.

Identifying potential is only the first stage in this ambitious attempt to stimulate growth. It is the easy part. Enabling this potential to take off calls for enormous will and resolve on the part of the state government because it has to be the catalyst. It has a critical role in developing growth-engine specific infrastructure, and equally vitally, in making regulatory changes required for the development of these growth engines.

To allow market-based growth and to prudently regulate this growth the state must create favourable regulation and simplify procedures for investors. Some laws and policies will have to be scrapped or substantially modified, many will have to be strengthened, supplemented and have their enforcement procedures spelt out. In some areas new laws and policies will have to be formulated.

For instance, if rice has to become a major earner the ban on exports will have to be scrapped, restrictions on transport and storage lifted, and procurement levies scrapped or rationalized. Similarly the development of horticulture calls for a reduction of duties on cold chain systems, and the formulation of a contract farming mechanism which we do not have as yet. The development of pharmaceuticals as a significant industry calls for the modification of price controls as well as the patent law.

Development of an IT/knowledge corridor calls for

increased privatization of the telecom sector and formulation of cyber laws and enlightened policies on intellectual property rights.

Apart from making the regulatory changes required to push investment into growth areas the state has a crucial role in developing growth-engine specific infrastructure. This is currently missing in many areas. The absence of adequate post-harvesting facilities in horticulture, for instance, causes around 25-30 per cent of the fruits, vegetables and flowers produced every year to rot. This includes facilities such as cold storage, cleaning, grading and packing facilities and refrigerated transport.

To develop infrastructure for economic growth based on agro-industries horticulture, poultry, dairy, rice and fisheries we will need market yard infrastructure, horticulture parks, irrigation infrastructure, efficient rural transport systems, and storage/warehousing and cargo-handling facilities at ports, airports and railway stations. We will also require fully developed export-processing zones near key ports.

Entirely new infrastructure will have to be built to drive growth in areas where Andhra Pradesh has little or no base. To build a world-class logistics hub a blueprint will have to be developed for the triangular zone connecting Visakhapatnam, Vijaywada and Kakinada. You need large container terminals at Visakhapatnam and Kakinada as well as distribution and customs clearance centres. You need to create a separate rail terminal at Visakhaptanam and/or Kakinada, as well as an inland container depot. You also need to configure the road network differently.

To develop mining you need a granite processing park at Nellore/Prakasam district. You also need dedicated rail lines between mines and consumption areas. To make Hyderabad an IT mega-hub, a broadband digital highway is a basic requirement. This entails a manifold increase in bandwidth in the state.

With a vision document at hand the next requirement is a road map. We are currently in the process of preparing this. Every department has been asked to break up the long-term target for 2020 into a series of achievable milestones. Annual targets also have to be set. Where will the resources come from to achieve Vision 2020? That is something that can be worked out best by examining the long-term picture in terms of achievable projects.

Industry has helped us identify some mega projects for private investment. One is a set of six toll expressways, the longest of which will be between Chennai and Visakhapatnam. Another is joint-venture partnerships for quality infrastructure. These include industrial estates in Visakhapatnam, Ranga Reddy and Anantpur districts.

There are others as well.

To prepare a road map the next stage is going to be to define the present scenario and identify the way forward, sector by sector. The Confederation of Indian Industries has done an initial, limited exercise for us for each of the core industries. We have to build on that.

Let me give you two examples here. In agri-business, for instance, we have the following strengths: the highest growth rate in the country in the use of tractors, pumpsets and fertilizers, the leading producer of poultry in the country, and second only to Karnataka in cocoon production. Brackish water prawn culture and pisciculture have taken off in a big way in the state.

But there are drawbacks as well. The gross irrigated area in the state has come down by 1.5 per cent in the last few years. Farmers are moving to irrigated areas resulting in an increase in fallow land. Without financial assistance many of them are unable to cultivate land. Irrigation facilities need to be expanded. Further, developing the irrigation infrastructure is a major priority with this government. It has allocated almost Rs 6000 crore to irrigation in the Ninth Plan to complete existing major projects and start viable new ones. At present 33 per cent of the agricultural land is irrigated. We could take it up to 60 per cent.

The way ahead would require accelerated action simultaneously on the following fronts: investment in providing irrigation facilities, faster disbursal of subsidies, investment in warehouse and cold storage, self-certification by seeds and chemical producers, education of farmers, and improvement in transport facilities.

Another area where Andhra Pradesh has potential is pharmaceuticals. It accounts for one-third of the bulk drug units in the country. It has availability of a huge pool of skilled people in the pharma sector. But its research and development facilities are inadequate, there has been a significant erosion of profits, and the growth rate of pharma is declining vis-á-vis the national average.

The way to develop in this sector calls for building dedicated industrial estates for bulk drug manufacturing, strengthening R&D efforts to encourage basic research, assistance to existing units to expand, providing fiscal incentives, as well as facilitating the establishment of test laboratories of international standard.

To provide capital and fund infrastructure development, in order to achieve the goals enunciated in Vision 2020, is going to require enormous investment in all sectors of the economy. We estimate that the total investment required will be of the order of Rs 30 lakh crore, more than 50 per cent of which will be spent on creating infrastructure.

Where is the money going to come from? At least 70 to 80 per cent will have to be met through private resources. Therefore a public-private partnership will be at the core of the government's policies and procedures. Though Andhra Pradesh has garnered foreign direct investment of Rs 2000 crore since 1991, that is only 2 per cent of the total foreign direct investment in India since 1991. We are working steadily at removing infrastructure bottlenecks to growth, at reforming policies and simplifying procedures, and at improving the productivity of our labour force.

Restoring the state to financial health is as important and urgently necessary as seeking investment. We are already pursuing a fiscal adjustment programme aimed at restructuring expenditure, improving expenditure management, augmenting revenue, and framing growth enhancing policies. These initiatives have been discussed elsewhere in the book.

We are trying very hard to change the composition of the state government's expenditure in favour of development spending. We are increasing the operation and maintenance budget allocation so that maintenance of assets such as the canal irrigation network can be improved. As mentioned earlier, we are increasing substantially the allocations for education and health. And we recognize that we will have to raise the state's capital budget substantially because the share of capital expenditure to total expenditure had declined substantially over the last ten years.

The basis on which Andhra Pradesh's development should be judged in 2020 is: how effective we have been in alleviating poverty. Our poverty eradication strategy has to shift from subsidies and welfare programmes to creating more jobs, improving basic services such as education and health and focussing anti-poverty programmes far more sharply to target the genuinely needy.

CONCLUSION

One can accomplish nothing without a vision. As James Broughton said, 'The only limits are, as always, those of vision.' Once there is a vision, the rest falls in place. My dream is to see my state as a Swarna Andhra—a golden state. To implement it, resources need to be harnessed. Technology is one resource, but the most important are human resources. Once the people share this vision and start working towards it, a new spirit will be created, a different way of doing things. It is all the more important for us as we have such a long way to go.

This was evident too when at the start of the new millennium the president of the United States of America stood at a podium at Hi-Tec City in Hyderabad and reminded his listeners of the divide between those who have access to the Internet and those who do not even have access to clean water. Every Indian politician is acutely aware of this divide. If visitors choose to remind us of it, is because the contrasts that our country presents strike them more forcefully.

In the summer of 2000, as this book goes to the press, the number one priority for my state is water. Water for irrigation to prevent rural migration and water for the cities whose urban populations are swelling. Each year in summer Hyderabad reels under a water crisis. Some of the other cities in Andhra Pradesh are also beginning to suffer the same fate. One solution which is being pursued is an exorbitant scheme to bring the water of the Krishna river by pipeline to the cities.

However, it is becoming increasingly clear that the real solution is a return to the water harvesting practices that used to be prevalent in many parts of the country. Not only have these gone out of use, but also unregulated sinking of tubewells has become the norm. We in the state government are moving towards making water harvesting mandatory. We are also getting ready to link the freedom to sink tubewells to the prevailing groundwater level in a given town or village. If we do not push the citizenry towards more responsible water use, the crisis will only grow.

Water, power, food, jobs: these remain the government's priorities even as we are seeking to make Hyderabad the foremost information technology destination in the country. I see no contradiction in this: the poor are the government's priority, but creating an environment conducive to wealth creation is also the responsibility of the government. The government has therefore to facilitate the efforts of those, such as professionals in various fields, who can generate wealth. This would mean more money for the government by way of taxes, and more resources for programmes that assist the poor. The main aim is to help improve the living standards of the citizens in the shortest but also the most sustainable way. Clarity of objectives leads to clarity in implementation.

Mr Clinton talked of the digital divide, a term that the developed world has been using a great deal. The term can be used both literally and figuratively. The physical divide actually is easier to bridge than it seems. Laying optic fibre cable down to the village level is something private players will do if the government assists their entry. It is very much easier, really, than providing water to every village. The availability of water is scarce, when it is available it is brackish and needs treatment. Providing water is something private players will not do, at least not at a cost that the poor will be able to bear. That is the figurative digital divide that we have to address ourselves to.

As economic reforms accelerate there will be a period when the divide between those who benefit directly from them and those who will only see the benefits at a later stage, will widen. The role of the government will be to insulate the poor from the harsh effects of the reforms and hold the prices of their basic necessities. There is no contradiction in pushing both for reforms and subsidies. The latter will protect the poorest, but they have to be far better targeted if they are not to burden the exchequer. The reason we simultaneously need reforms is because in the long run they will help the economy to grow. Without more employment opportunity we cannot remove poverty.

To provide the basics that have eluded the very poor, state governments will need resources. Summoning these in adequate measure will be every chief minister's biggest headache in the short term. Providing access to schooling and potable water for every one of 67,505 habitations in the state remains a challenging task. During my stewardship of Andhra Pradesh over the last five years I have looked East more than West, because in the East Asian miracle I see where India can be in the future. But I do not see that happening until we put every child in school and give him or her an education that can be put to use.

Meanwhile there is no reason to hold up bridging the physical digital divide, because there is now enough evidence in India and abroad to show that connectivity is also becoming a felt need for the poor. In April 2000 I received an e-mail from Siddhapur village in Nizamabad district to announce that the village had just inaugurated its rural-Internet facility. The funds for the computer purchase had been mobilized by the villagers: every house had contributed towards its cost.

In Madhya Pradesh, in Dhar district, a village computer network went on-stream on New Year's Day 2000 with local youth trained to work as operators. From the computer centres that this network services, farmers can access daily market rates and decide in which wholesale market to sell their produce. We are setting up the same kind of system for our ryotu bazaars, where farmers bring their produce directly, eliminating the middlemen.

Today the gap between the first world and the third world is essentially one of opportunity. The US has more computers than the rest of the world combined. Bulgaria has more Internet hosts than the whole of sub-Saharan Africa. South Asia with 23 per cent of the world's people has less than one per cent of the world's Internet users. Even a doubling and tripling of users will not bridge the gap.

The cost of access is a deterrent for the poor. To buy a computer in the US costs a month's wages. In Bangladesh it costs the equivalent of eight years of wages. So the first step Andhra Pradesh has taken in bridging the digital divide is to provide connectivity. Several private players have stepped in and we anticipate that rural connectivity will become possible over the next two years. By the end of 2000 all 1125 mandals in the state will become connected by fibre optic networks. In the total connectivity scenario we also expect hybrid coaxial networks to play a part since cable television is increasingly reaching villages. Many people living in Indian villages have relatives abroad, and feel the need for e-mail connectivity.

When there is connectivity there will be a felt need for computers. Both Tamil Nadu and Andhra Pradesh are facilitating private sector initiatives in setting up a network of rural Internet kiosks to meet this and other needs. Ultimately, greater rural connectivity will enable us to provide more jobs in the hinterland.

If we have lagged behind in providing the basics to the entire population, we have to make good that gap. But for that reason we need not hold up the provision of other services which will become equally basic in the near future. Both the physical and virtual divide between the haves and have-nots must be bridged. That is the challenge of the millennium.

REFERENCES

INTRODUCTION

1. K. Srinivasulu, Prakash Sarangi, 'Political realignments in NTR's Andhra Pradesh,' *Economic and Political Weekly*, 21-28 August 1999.
2. Ambrose Pinto, 'Andhra Pradesh, Politics of Opportunism,' *Economic and Political Weekly*, 4 September 1999.
3. Interviews with: N. Chandrababu Naidu, Uma Reddy Venkateshwarulu, P. Lakshmanna, R. Ramchandriah, R. Radhakrishna, D. Venkateshwar Rao, S.V. Prasad.

THE POLITICS OF GOVERNANCE

1. GOING FORWARD

1. P. Sainath, 'Dregs of Destiny,' *Outlook*, 19 October, 1998.

2. REINVENTING POLITICS

1. William D. Eggers, 'Reinventing Government: The Wonder Down Under,' www.governmentexecutive.com/features/0397s4.htm.

3. CHANGING EQUATIONS

1. Yogendra Yadav, 'Electoral Politics in the Time of Change, India's Third Electoral System 1989-99,' *Economic and Political Weekly*, 21-28 August, 1999.
2. Intervention by P. Ashok Gajapati Raju, Finance Minister of Andhra Pradesh representing N. Chandrababu Naidu, Chief

Minister, Andhra Pradesh, fifth meeting of the Inter-State Council, 22 January 1999.

3. Mahesh Rangarajan, 'One, Two, Many Indias?' *Seminar No. 480*, 'Cruel Choices'.

4. Draft Resolution on Constitutional Reforms, Telugu Desam Party, Mahanadu 1999.

5. Letter from M. Karunanidhi, Chief Minister, Tamil Nadu to N. Chandrababu Naidu, Chief Minister, Andhra Pradesh, 18 June, 1997.

6. State Government's Representation at Inter-State Council Meeting, New Delhi, 15 October 1996.

7. Mahesh Rangarajan, 'Election 99: Winning Was The Easy Part', *Economic Times*, October 1999.

THE INNOVATIVE GOVERNMENT

4. SIMPLIFYING GOVERNMENT

1. White Paper on Establishment levels and costs in Andhra Pradesh, June 1996.

2. Recommendations of the Committee of Secretaries on the Reorganization of the Secretariat.

3. Government of Andhra Pradesh, Fourth Census of State Public Sector Employees, 1994.

4. Report of the study team of the Government of India on Administrative Reforms, September 1997, Government of India, Ministry of Public Grievances and Pensions, Department of Administrative Reform and Public Grievances.

5. Status Note on State Level Public Enterprises and Select Cooperative Institutions, GA (Public Enterprises) Department, June 1996.

5. INNOVATING WITH THE BUREAUCRACY

1. Report of Workshop on Tender Reforms in Andhra Pradesh, Hyderabad, 10 November 1998, Government of Andhra Pradesh, Irrigation and CAD Department.

2. Citizen's Charter, Municipal Corporation.

3. Citizen's Charter, Hyderabad Metropolitan Water Supply and Sewerage Board.

6. INFORMATION TECHNOLOGY IN GOVERNANCE

1. Draft Resolution on Information Technology, Telugu Desam Party, Mahanadu 1999.
2. Note on Use of Information Technology in the Government of Andhra Pradesh, Chief Minister's Office, March 1997.
3. Vision 2020.

FINDING THE MONEY

7. STATE FINANCES: GETTING GRIMMER

1. N.J. Kurien, 'State Government Finances: A Survey of Recent Trends,' *Economic and Political Weekly*, 8 May 1999.
2. Nirupam Bajaj and Jeffrey Sachs, 'Reform in the States,' parts I, II, III, the *Hindu*, January 24, 25 and 26 2000.
3. 'The End of Free Meals?' *BusinessWorld*, 22 November, 1999.

8. FENDING OFF BANKRUPTCY: THE ANDHRA PRADESH EXPERIENCE

1. Status Note on Revenues of the State, Revenue Department, June 1996.
2. Status Note on State Level Enterprises and Select Cooperative Institutions, June 1996.
3. Pattern of Expenditure on Welfare Sector, June 1996.
4. State Finances—the Factual Position, June 1996.
5. State Finances, the Factual Position—Revisited after Two Years, Finance and Planning Department, Government of Andhra Pradesh, May 1988.
   Resolution on Financial Position, Telugu Desam Party, 1999.

9. ATTRACTING INVESTORS

1. Incentives for the Information Technology Industry, Information Technology and Communication Department, Government of Andhra Pradesh.
2. Document: CII-Government of Andhra Pradesh Joint Task Force Meeting, 28 October 1999.
3. Document: CII-Government of Andhra Pradesh Joint Task Force Meeting, 28 October 1999.
4. Tourism Policy, Government of Andhra Pradesh, 1998.
5. Vision 2020

TACKLING THE BASICS

10. HRD FOR THE FUTURE

1. Andhra Pradesh Population Policy: A Statement and Strategy, Department of Family Welfare, Government of Andhra Pradesh, 1997.
2. P.N. Mari Bhat, Francis Xavier, 'Findings of National Family Health Survey: A Regional Analysis,' *Economic and Political Weekly*, 16-23 October 1999.
3. K.S. James, 'Fertility Decline: Andhra Pradesh, a Search for Alternative Hypotheses,' *Economic and Political Weekly*, 20 February 1999.
4. DPEP Final Aide Memoire, Tenth DPEP Joint Review Mission and Second In-Depth Review Mission, November-December 1999.
5. Andhra Pradesh School Education (Community Participation) Act, 1998.
6. Study on the Awareness of DPEP Activities and the Contribution of School Committees to School Improvement, Dr K. Seshidhara Rao, Chief Coordinator, Mid-term Assessment Survey, AP DPEP, Hyderabad.
7. Rashmi Sharma, 'What Manner of Teacher. Some Lessons from Madhya Pradesh,' *Economic and Political Weekly*, 19 June 1999.
8. Human Development Reports, The Human Development Centre, Islamabad, 1997.
9. Draft Resolution on Health for All in Andhra Pradesh, Telugu Desam Party, Mahanadu, 1999.

11. RECHARGING THE ENVIRONMENT

1. Action Plan 1999-2000, Andhra Pradesh Pollution Control Board, Hyderabad.
2. 'What Goes Down, Must Come Up,' *Down to Earth*, 31 August 1999.
3. 'Changing Colours,' *Down to Earth*, 15 June 1999.
4. 'Defining our Todays, Confining Tomorrow, Making the System Work Better for the Environment.' Paper by Tishya Chatterjee, Member-Secretary, State Pollution Control Board.

5. 'India's Environment: A Look at the Future,' *Down to Earth*, 31 March 1999.

12. CATCHING UP ON POWER

1. Finances of APSEB, Andhra Pradesh State Electricity Board, June 1996.
2. Power Sector Reforms, A.P. Government Website, www.andhrapradesh.com.
3. 'Andhra Speeds UP Move to Privatise Distribution,' *Business Standard*, 2 February 2000.

13. PEOPLE VS POVERTY

1. Jasveen Jairath, 'Participatory Irrigation Management, Experiments in Andhra Pradesh,' *Economic and Political Weekly*, 2 October 1999.
2. The Andhra Pradesh Farmers' Management of Irrigation Systems Act, 1997.
3. 'DWCRA and Women's Empowerment,' Panchayati Raj and Rural Development Department, Government of Andhra Pradesh.
4. Resolution on Self-Help Groups, Telugu Desam Party, Mahanadu, 1999.
5. Janmabhoomi, Operational Guidelines.

14. RESTORING PEACE AND SECURITY

Briefing Paper, Dial Your CM, 20-12-99.
Public Partnership in Police Work. Project on Community Policing. Andhra Pradesh Police.
Note on Left Wing Extremism, Andhra Pradesh Police.
Note on Faction in Rayalseema Region, Andhra Pradesh Police.

15. A ROAD MAP FOR VISION 2020

Vision 2020

INDEX